The English Country Cottage

The English Country Cottage

by

R. J. BROWN

ROBERT HALE · LONDON

© *R. J. Brown* 1979
First published in Great Britain 1979
Reprinted 1980 (*twice*)
Reprinted 1981
Reprinted 1982
Reprinted 1983

ISBN 0 7091 7381 4

Robert Hale Limited
Clerkenwell House
Clerkenwell Green
London, EC1

Printed in Great Britain by
Redwood Burn Limited, Trowbridge, Wiltshire
and bound by Western Book Company

Contents

Acknowledgements

From the Notes and Bibliography it will be evident that I am greatly indebted to the help of a number of writers going back to the turn of the century. Among them I would particularly mention John Woodforde and G. E. Fussell whose respective books, *The Truth about Cottages* (first published in 1969) and *The English Rural Labourer*, have been invaluable in the preparation of Part One, "The Cottager – His Life and Housing". I would also like to extend my gratitude to R. W. Brunskill, whose book *Illustrated Handbook of Vernacular Architecture* is now a standard work on vernacular architecture, to Alex Clifton-Taylor's book *The Pattern of English Building Materials* for its help on building materials, and also to the books of Gillian Darley, M. W. Barley, C. F. Innocent, Eric Mercer, and G. E. Mingay.

Also I would like to express my appreciation for the help and co-operation I have received from numerous public bodies, in particular the staff of the following Public Libraries: Birmingham, Brighton, Cambridge, Colchester, Hull, Ipswich, Lincoln, Manchester, Norwich and Taunton; and also to the staff of the library of the Royal Institute of British Architects, and the British Museum Reading Room and Newspaper Library.

R. J. B.

Glossary

Barge-Board: A timber board, sometimes carved, fixed at the gable end and following the slope of the roof to mask the ends of the horizontal roof timbers.

Batten: A small strip of wood used horizontally to hang or attach tiles, slates, etc.

Bond: The regular arrangement of bricks or stones in order to avoid a continuous vertical joint and so increasing the strength of the wall.

Brace: A diagonal timber, either straight or curved, to strengthen framework.

Cames: Grooved bars of lead for joining small pieces of glass into a larger sheet.

Casement: A window, either of metal or wood, which is hinged on one side, so opening inwards or outwards.

Catslide Roof: A roof having the main slope extending uninterruptedly over an extension.

Cladding: A material covering the external face of the building but which is not structural.

Closer: A small brick – a half header – used to complete the bonding pattern at the return of the wall or at a jamb.

Collar, Collar Beam: A horizontal timber placed above wall-plate level spanning between and tying together a pair of rafters.

Damp-Proof Course: A horizontal layer of impervious material inserted in a wall to prevent rising damp.

Diaper: An all-over pattern of diamond, square or

lozenge shapes generally used in brickwork and formed with bricks of two colours.

Dormer: A window projecting vertically from a sloping roof and having a roof of its own.

Dripstone: A projecting moulding over the top of a door or window to throw off rain.

Eaves: The horizontal overhang of a roof projecting beyond the face of a wall.

Gable: The vertical triangular wall at the end of the roof.

Galleting: The use of pebbles or chips of stone inserted into the mortar courses generally for decoration but sometimes, when the mortar joints are large, for strength.

Gauge: The part of a roofing slate or tile which is exposed to view.

Header: A brick or stone so laid that only its end appears on the wall-face.

Herring-Bone: Stones, bricks or tiles laid diagonally and sloping in opposite directions to form a zigzag pattern.

Hip: The sloping external intersection of two inclined roof surfaces.

Inglenook: The area under a large chimney or firehood.

Jamb: The vertical side of an opening for a door or window in a wall.

Jetty: The projection of an upper floor beyond the storey below on a timber-framed house.

Joist: One of several horizontal parallel timbers laid between walls or beams to carry flooring.

Lath: A thin, narrow strip of wood used to provide a backing for plaster.

Light:	The vertical opening of a window framed by mullions.
Lintel:	A horizontal timber, stone or concrete beam spanning an opening.
Mortar:	The material used in bedding, jointing and pointing brick or stone with another.
Mortice:	A socket cut in a piece of wood to receive a tenon.
Mullion:	A vertical structural member sub-dividing a window.
Newel Stair:	A spiral stair with steps framed into a central vertical post.
Outshut:	An extension of a building under a lean-to roof.
Plinth:	The projecting base of a wall often with a splayed top.
Pointing:	The exposed face of the joint of brickwork or stonework which is smoothed with the point of a trowel.
Purlin:	In timber-framed construction, a longitudinal horizontal timber supporting the common rafters and in post-and-truss structure framed into the trusses.
Quoin:	Dressed stones or distinctive brickwork at the external angle of a wall.
Rafter:	One of several timbers supporting the roof covering.
Random:	Not laid in courses.
Rendering:	Cement or lime-plaster covering to external face of a wall.
Reveal:	The side-wall of an opening or recess which is at right angles to the face of the main wall.

Ridge:	The apex of a roof.
Rubble:	Unsquared and undressed stone.
Sash:	A glazed wooden window which slides up and down by means of a pulley.
Shutters:	Timber boards between which semi-liquid material can be poured for building a wall.
Soffit:	The underside of a lintel, beam or arch.
Straight Joint:	A vertical joint in brickwork or masonry exactly over a vertical joint in the course below.
Stretcher:	A brick or stone so laid that only its long side appears on the wall-face.
Strut:	In roof construction, a vertical or diagonal timber which does not support a longitudinal member.
Swag:	An ornamental festoon of foliage, etc., which is fastened up at both ends and hangs down in the centre.
Tenon:	The end of a piece of wood reduced in width in order to fit into a mortice of another piece of wood thus making a joint.
Tie-Beam:	The main horizontal timber of a truss joining together the feet of the principal rafter at the wall-plate.
Torching:	The filling in with lime and hair mortar of the uneven space between the underside of tiles or slates on an unboarded or unfelted roof.
Transom:	A horizontal structural member sub-dividing a window.
Truss:	A rigid framework spanning the building used to support the ridge, purlins, etc., that carries the common rafters.

Underbuilt: A wall added beneath a jetty.

Valley: The sloping internal junction of two inclined roof-surfaces.

Yoke: A short horizontal timber joining the rafters together near the apex of the roof often supporting a ridge.

Illustrations

13

PART ONE

The Cottager – His Life and Housing

The Medieval Cot

Throughout history there has always been a landless class of person whose only distinction has been they had a cottage in which to live and little else. In Anglo-Saxon times he was known as a 'kotsetla', slightly better off than the later cottager for he occupied at least five acres. In the Domesday Book they are called 'cottars' or 'borders' – one an English word meaning a person who lives in a cot and the other a French one derived from the Frankish *borda* meaning a wooden hut. Over 80,000 in number, they represented almost a third of the total population of the country.

In the social scale of feudal England the cottars or borders were, of course, near the bottom. At the top was the lord of the manor and beneath him the franklins, men not of noble birth but free, not tied to the manor, and paying rent for their land in cash or kind. Below these came the villeins, who were bonded – tied to the manor and unable to leave the lord's estate – but who had a house and land which they cultivated for themselves, paying rent to the lord either in the form of labour services on the lord's demesne or with goods. Below the villeins came the rural craftsmen, who were provided with some land but not dependent on it. It was after these that the cottars or borders came, renting particular cottages within tofts or garden curtilages, which often carried with them from two to five acres of arable land together with common rights. Besides their obligatory manual services on the lord's demesne they were probably employed as hired labour, either on the demesne, on a franklin's holding, or possibly on the land of a wealthy villein, in order to make sufficient to survive. At the end of the social scale came the serfs, who had by law no rights but who might, in practice, occupy some land.

The medieval village was very different from the village of today. It was smaller, rarely containing more than 100 people, with the only substantial buildings being the manor house, church and, perhaps, the mill. The remainder of the village would be a cluster of flimsy buildings, either spaced out around a village green or strung out along the rough track leading to the manor house. Each house or cottage would stand within its own toft, which on clay or wet sites would be raised and surrounded by a ditch; or in well-drained sites surrounded by substantial walls or hedged and fenced banks. Within these tofts were grown the few vegetables and herbs essential for the well-being of the population. All but the freemen were tied to the spot and each village was practically self-supporting with only necessities, such as iron and salt, being imported from other districts. Also, with communications so poor, little of the produce of the village flowed into the areas of high population.

The land around the village was generally divided into five main portions: the demesne, which generally surrounded the manor house, and was reserved for the lord's personal use; the free land occupied by the franklins; the unfree land occupied by the villeins, some cottagers or other class of bondsmen; the common land on which the tenants of the manor and certain cottagers could feed their stock; and finally, the waste land which provided fern and heather for bedding or thatching, furze and turves for fuel, and timber for hurdles, fencing and building. Over much of the country the cultivated land was worked in the open-field system, divided into fields – two, three, or occasionally four – each being separated by turve baulks. In the two-field system one field would lie fallow while the other was cultivated, while in the three-field system one would lie fallow while the other two were under tillage. Each field was then divided into strips, divided by unploughed baulks to separate each individual holding. Each freeman or bondsman entitled to land would work two, three, or more strips, depending on their status, in different parts of each field. The open-field system of farming in strips was not universal in England and the manor varied in many parts of the country. The open-field system was particularly strong in the Midlands but elsewhere, in East Anglia, Cheshire, Kent and Northumberland, many of the manors did not conform to this standard pattern.

It was in these circumstances that the cottagers worked. The lucky ones, by virtue of their holdings, had some land and the common right to pasture, but many had none and were forced to work as hired labour. Most of a man's day, from sunrise to sunset, was spent in the open-fields either working his own strip or on that of another person. Whatever their status, life was a continual routine of ploughing, sowing, weeding, harvesting and tending animals; a constant struggle against the ever-encroaching waste lands. His cot was, therefore, no more than a shelter – a place to eat and sleep and a place to shelter from the extremes of the weather.

The excavation of deserted medieval settlements has produced some evidence as to the construction of these cots. Generally they were of one room, although some of the larger ones had two rooms, varying in width from between 10 feet to 18 feet – the limit a roof could be spanned without a central post or aisle – and in length from about 15 feet to 40 feet. However, the single-roomed cot, which was the most common, was about 16 feet by 12 feet and the larger two-roomed cot some 30 feet by 14 feet. Many cots also had some form of outbuilding, usually about 6 feet square, which was probably used as a store.[1] It seems that these dwellings had low walls with a low roof and were without chimneys and sometimes even a window, and were generally filled with smoke from a central open-hearth fire.

Clearly, in most cases the construction of these dwellings was undertaken by their occupiers, for, from the quality of workmanship and material found in excavated buildings, little, if any, skilled labour was required. The buildings were always constructed either of thin timbers, of earth, of turf, of chalk, or of stone, all of which were close at hand, costing the cottager nothing. Timber gathered from the wastes was most commonly used, the light unsquared poles lashed together and filled in with wattle and daub. The irregular alignment of the uprights obviously made the use of wall-plates impracticable, and their irregular spacing made them incapable of supporting any kind of framed roof. Mud walls without timber supports were also used extensively at this time, as was turf, particularly in the South-west where no other suitable material was available. Stone, picked from the surface of the ground either in the toft or in the open-fields, was also used from the end of the twelfth century onwards in almost all the stone-producing areas. Roofs were obviously unsquared poles lashed together and thatched with whatever suitable material came to hand. Like so many medieval buildings, including churches and castles, these cots were often whitewashed. The cost of building these cottages on a Northamptonshire estate was, in about 1300, between twelve and twenty-five shillings each.[2]

All these medieval dwellings were of frail construction and archaeologists have shown that this necessitated their repair or rebuilding at least once a generation, often on completely new foundations and to a new alignment. This frailty has often been documented. The medieval village of Conisborough, Yorkshire, is said to have been entirely blown away in a gale,[3] while during the reign of Henry VI the inhabitants of the village of Morpeth, Northumberland, are recorded as trembling for the safety of their fragile cottages in a strong wind.[4] Even in London, in the year 1212, ordinary houses were so unsubstantial that the aldermen of the city were provided with crooks to pull them down when they either caught fire or did not comply with the regulations.[5] In the church of St Benet's, Cambridge, there is a thirteenth-century crook said to have been used by a single man to pull down cottages which had caught fire.

Within these small, cramped uncomfortable cots lived the family, sleeping on straw-filled pallets placed around the central hearth. Frequently poultry and a few head of livestock not slaughtered for food, wintered with the human inhabitants, sharing with them the warmth from the open fire. The poor widow in Chaucer's *Nun's Priest's Tale* lived in such a two-roomed "narwe cotage" standing in a yard "enclosed al aboute with stikkes, and a drye dych withoute" and the "chauntecleer amoung his wyves sat on his perche, that was in the halle".

1. Timber-framed cottage, West Hagbourne, Oxfordshire.

2. Seventeenth-century cottage at Salford Priors, Warwickshire.

Some insight into the household effects of this period can be ascertained from the tax assessment made in 1296 and 1301 for the town of Colchester and the surrounding villages. Taxation was, at this time, based on personal property and levied at a rate of one-fifteenth. Assessors went round from house to house compiling lists of goods and chattels and from these returns it is clear that many of the dwellings were no more than hovels and almost half had no household goods at all, with the inhabitants possessing only a bed and a few cooking implements, and sometimes only the clothes they wore. The lists also indicate that the majority of people lived in dwellings of one room.

In the middle of the fourteenth century the structure of medieval English society changed. At the end of 1348 the Black Death reached England and in the following year destroyed more than one third of the population; further visitations in 1361 and 1369 depleted it still further. Entire villages were wiped out and in many counties the population was reduced by a half. The immediate result, due to the heavy mortality, was an acute shortage of labour to work the land. The cottager suddenly realized his worth and demanded wages. Because of the demand many left their own manors to hire their services to other landowners for money. Almost immediately Parliament acted, and in 1351 the celebrated Statute of Labourers was passed, which not only restricted people to their own manor but also prohibited wages being offered or accepted in excess of the amount provided before 1348. Those breaking the Statute were put in the stocks. The Statute seems to have had little impact, for nine years later another Act was passed stating that the fugitive labourer should, if re-captured, be branded on the forehead and returned to his village. Other Acts followed, but in the later ones power was given to the Justices of the Peace to fix wages in their own districts according to prices. The shortage of labour, coupled with the decrease in demand for food due to the depopulation, enforced many landowners to change from arable to sheep-farming. No longer requiring the services of the villeins and other bondsmen to work on his estate, the landowner demanded money rents rather than payment with service or goods.

The Black Death unwittingly laid the foundation of the future wealth and prosperity of the country. The wool trade flourished and the wealth of the sheep-farmers, weavers and merchants increased. For the first time small farmers became independent of the manor and the era of hired workers on the land began. For many, however, life changed little. William Langland gives a description of the poor towards the end of the fourteenth century in *The Vision of Piers Plowman*:

> The needy are our neighbours, if we note rightly;
> As prisoners in cells, or poor folk in hovels,
> Charged with children and overcharged by landlords,

What they may spare in spinning they spend on rental,
On mild or on meal to make porridge
To still the sobbing children at meal time,
Also they themselves suffer much hunger,
They have woe in wintertime and wake at mid-night
To rise and rock the cradle at the bedside,
To card and to comb, to darn clouts and wash them
To rub and to reel and put rushes on the paving.
The woe of these women who dwell in hovels
Is too sad to speak of or to say in rhyme.

During the fifteenth century wealth spread rapidly and many found themselves free men for the first time. Also for the first time more substantial houses, which bore some comparison with that of the lord of the manor, appeared in the villages and countryside, built by a new class of person, ranking in status between the wealthy noblemen and the lowly cottager. For the cottager these improvements had to wait for another century or more, but he became increasingly aware of his own position and his ability to sell his services to the highest bidder in a society still short of labour. This new-found freedom also had its drawbacks: the responsibilities of the new landowners differed from those of the old manor; and old age, sickness and unemployment reduced large numbers of the population to pauperism.

Birth of the English Cottage

The manorial system had been breaking-up before the Black Death but this, the Peasants' Revolt and finally the War of the Roses hastened its decline, and with it the structure of rural society changed. The old medieval terms, 'franklins' and 'villeins', were no longer used, being replaced in the sixteenth century by 'yeomen' and 'husbandmen'. Below the husbandmen came the village craftsmen and others not dependent on the land but engaged in some form of rural industry and, like before, they often had some stake in the land. Below these came the labourers – no one in Tudor England called himself a cottager.

The wealth of the nation was no longer derived from the exportation of raw wool but instead wool for the expanding cloth industry. Attracted by the high prices, many landowners turned to sheep, grazing them on land which had formerly been arable. To gain greater control over the quality of the sheep much land was enclosed and these enclosures imposed great hardship in some areas. Whole villages were abandoned because of these enclosures and even churches were used as sheep-pens. Much legislation was introduced in an attempt to check these enclosures and in 1534 Henry VIII laid down that no one was to keep more than 2000 sheep, but the situation continued to deteriorate. More and more people went in for sheep-rearing for these animals needed little attention given enough land on which to graze. In 1563 another Act of Parliament was required, not only to control the number of enclosures but also to provide additional arable land for the increased population, but although this Act checked the number it did not stop the process. In 1593 the Act was repealed, but a series of poor harvests from 1594 onwards caused renewed panic and in 1597 Parliament resorted to fresh anti-enclosure measures.

The result of these enclosures was that hundreds of people were unemployed and forced to leave their homes and became vagrants or settled as squatters on the wastes. Many complained that sheep were ruining the land and that the enclosure of wastes and commons took away an important part of the livelihood from the villages. Sir Thomas More was one who protested, and in his *Utopia*, published in 1516, he described the fate of the small farmer:

> The husbandmen be thrust oute of their owne, or els either by coveyne and fraude, or by violent oppression they be put besydes it, or by wronges and injuries thei be so weried that they be compelled to sell all by one means

25

3. Timber-framed cottage, Hanley Castle, Hereford and Worcester.

therfore or by other, either by hooke or crooke they must needes depart awaye, poore, selye, wretched soules.

In 1517 a Commission was appointed to enquire into the problem, and in addition to listing the day, month and number of people evicted, the report sometimes described the fate of the evicted. Most of the villagers "left weeping" for a life of "idleness and misery" or were "compelled to leave and go wandering" and to die "in poverty".[1] This enquiry showed that the main areas of trouble and discontent were in the Midland counties.

Protests against the social distress caused by enclosures were inseparably associated with attacks on the sheepmasters, and later, towards the end of the sixteenth century, on the cattle-graziers as well. Although these enclosures caused concern there were many others, often devised by mutual consent between two or more farmers, which encouraged better use of what arable land remained. The increase in the population forced up the price of foodstuffs and the price of corn rose considerably more than most other commodities, encouraging the larger farmers to buy out many of the smaller owners. While the fortunate had an opportunity to buy or lease more land, the unfortunate were reduced to a landless class, moving either into the towns in hope of employment or building themselves cottages on the waste. In the years 1540 to 1570 many yeomen began to build up large estates, and with the dissolution of the lesser monasteries in 1536 and the suppression of the greater abbeys in 1539 more land changed hands during this period than any time since the Norman Conquest.

Apart from enclosures, two Acts in the seventeenth century affected the poor and the labouring classes. First was the Poor Law of 1601 which entrusted each parish to look after its own poor and to levy a poor rate to provide, if necessary, cottages on the waste or common for the aged; to find apprenticeships for poor children; and to see that the able poor were set "in work". The Poor Law was amended again and again in an effort to find a remedy for the distress of the poor. In 1662 the Law of Settlement and Removal finally confirmed the idea that local poverty should be taken care of locally. The preamble to the Act stated

> that by reason of some defect in the law, poor people are not restrained from going from one parish to another, and do therefore endeavour to settle themselves in those parishes where there is the best stock, the largest commons or wastes to build cottages and the most woods for them to burn and destroy; and when they have consumed it, then to another parish and at last become rogues and vagabonds.

To remedy this defect the Act provided that any person coming into a parish, who neither rented a house of the annual value of £10 nor was able to give security against becoming a burden on the poor rates at any further time, could, on application to the overseers, be moved back to his or her place of settlement. Each parish, therefore, tried to rid itself of its impotent poor, as they were called, so they would be chargeable elsewhere, which resulted in the large number of vagrants and rogues at this time. The effect on the labouring poor was that they were tied to their own parish without any freedom to move to other villages, where perhaps employment was better, if they wished to qualify for poor relief at some future time when misfortune might overtake them.

By the middle of Queen Elizabeth's reign there was much new building. All over the South-east the gentry were building new country houses and this trend spread northwards and westwards. Yet it was not only the gentry who were rebuilding, for the farmers with their newly-acquired wealth moved out of the villages and built new houses, as is evident from the number of Elizabethan timber-framed farmhouses to be seen today in the South-east, East Anglia, the Midlands and along the Welsh border, as well as the large number of dated stone farmhouses to be found along the limestone belt in Gloucestershire, Oxfordshire, Northamptonshire,

Leicestershire and Lincolnshire and in North Yorkshire and Lancashire. For the lower classes, however, this new building surge was more out of necessity than any great increase in their wealth, for the population was increasing rapidly. At the beginning of the fifteenth century the population was estimated as $2\frac{1}{2}$ million, this rose to an estimated $4\frac{1}{2}$ million by 1600 and at the end of the seventeenth century had risen to approximately $5\frac{1}{2}$ million. In 1688 Gregory King calculated that more than half of the population were "decreasing the wealth of the nation," that their expenses exceeded their earnings and that the deficiency had to be made up from poor relief, charity or plunder. Out of an estimated population of 5,500,000 the total number of cottagers and paupers, together with their families, was 1,300,000; labouring people and outservants and their families represented some 1,275,000 persons. In addition to these there were some 150,000 small farmers who, with their families, were often worse off than many of the labourers. Clearly with such a large population of landless people there was a need for many cottages.

It was not only the increase in the population that caused this demand for new cottages. Another was the continuing break-up of the manorial system, the great households with their large number of retainers were forced to seek employment elsewhere. Similarly, with the dissolution of the monasteries there were many thrown upon their own resources. Many undoubtedly drifted into the towns, others probably became vagrants, but most, it seems likely, were slowly absorbed into farming, spending their lives as squatters on the edges of the wastes and commons.

Small encroachments of the wastes had been going on continually throughout the country with or without the authority of the manorial courts. Each one of these encroachments was made by someone in need of some kind of dwelling, who had no land on which to put it. So numerous were these encroachments that it became necessary in 1549 to pass an Act to regularize their position and make the land attached to these houses – as long as they did not exceed about two acres and "doth no hurt" – free from any retribution by the owner of the waste.

The period 1550 to 1660 has been described as the golden age of cottage-building, for beside the new timber-framed farmhouses rose new cottages to replace the decayed, chimneyless hovels of the medieval village; although many of these, particularly in Cumbria, Northumberland and County Durham, lingered on far into the eighteenth century. Records indicate that this rebuilding reached its peak between 1580 and 1640, though this varied from area to area, occurring later the further northwards one went. In the manor of Epworth, Humberside, it was stated in 1630 that no fewer than 100 new cottages had been erected in the past forty years. Similarly, at Misterton it was said in 1596 that thirty new cottages had been erected in the preceding forty years. At Brigstock, Northamptonshire, about forty houses were built between

1600 and 1637, besides others which had been enlarged or modernized. On the Pelham estate, Sussex, between 1581 and 1616, there were numerous appeals from widows and aged labourers to build for themselves cottages on the lord's waste.[2]

So great was the number of cottages being built that in 1589 Parliament intervened when an Act against the Erecting and Maintaining of Cottages was passed. The preamble to this Act refers to "the erecting and building of great numbers and multitudes of cottages, which are daily more and more increased in many parts of this realm". The Act directed that no new cottage should be built unless at least four acres of land was assigned to it and that no cottage was to be occupied by more than one family. The Act did not apply to towns or to housing for quarry and mine workers, and others not engaged in agriculture, such as craftsmen, tradesmen and seafaring folk. The excellent measures contained in the Act were, however, impossible to enforce and in practice there were many exceptions allowed by the parish authorities. Nevertheless, the Act remained in force until it was finally repealed in 1775.

Not only new cottages were built at this time; such was the pressure on housing that many larger houses were sub-divided and many barns and other farm buildings were converted for the labourers' use. The manor house at Wylye, Wiltshire, was divided into eight tenements in 1631, each family having two or three rooms. In some of the villages of Rockingham Forest, due to the influx of many landless people from other areas, the need for housing was so great at this time that a considerable number of barns, stables and malthouses were converted into dwellings. All woodland areas attracted people from outside for there was both work and a ready supply of building materials.

What were the cottages like in the sixteenth and seventeenth centuries? The thousands of oak-framed Tudor cottages which survive today were not mere cottages to their first inhabitants, but residences of men of means – farmers, merchants or tradesmen – which have been degraded over the centuries to cottages, either by the engrossing of land or by the original owners moving to better houses elsewhere and abandoning their old dwellings. It is doubtful whether any houses that originally ranked as cottages have survived from a date earlier than about 1700, although many houses dating from before this had by this time become cottages. The distinction between primitive structures and permanent houses is one between those built by their occupants and those constructed by craftsmen. Certainly all the houses that survive from the sixteenth and seventeenth centuries are the work of craftsmen, but records fail to show how often, if at all, craftsmen were used to construct cottages. In 1577 William Harrison, an Essex parson who contributed to Holinshed's *Chronicle*, wrote:

4. Cottage at Alrewas, Staffordshire.

5. Cottage at Aldbury, Hertfordshire.

Never so much oke hath been spent in a hundred years before as in ten years of our time for everyman almost is a builder, and he that hath bought any small parcel of ground, be it ever so little, will not be quiet till he have pulled downe the old house, if anie were there standing, and set up a new after his own device.

Whether this referred to cottages is unknown.

   Clearly there were many who had to be content with a one-roomed hovel of sticks and mud. Descriptions of their houses can be found in the writings of a few contemporary travellers and topographers. Richard Carew[3] describes the older cottages in Cornwall as being built with "walles of earth, low thatched roofes, few partitions, no planchings or glasse windows, and scarcely any chimneys, other than a hole in the wall to let out the smoke". The description actually refers to husbandmen's cottages in "times not past the remembrance of some living", but by his own day these had improved and probably the description is more applicable to the houses of labourers in about 1600. Some hundred years later Celia Fiennes[4] found that the houses at Land's End

are but poor cottages like barns to look on, much like those in Scotland – but to doe my own Country its right the inside of their little cottages are clean and plaister'd, and such as you might comfortably eate and drink there.

In Suffolk, according to Robert Reyce,[5]

the mean person and the poor cottager thinks he doth very well if he can compass in his manner of building to raise his frame low, cover it with thatch, and to fill his wide panels (after they are well splinted and bound) with clay or culm enough well tempered, over which it may be some of more ability, both for warmth, continuance, and comeliness, do bestow a cast of hair, lime, and sand made into mortar and laid thereon, rough or smooth as the owner pleaseth.

At Wensleydale, North Yorkshire, the tenants had "for the most part small houses, no better than their cowhouses built without mortar or loam". Similar houses were to be found elsewhere. In the Lake District Lieutenant Hammond[6] in 1634 noticed "poore cottages . . . I thinke the sun had never shone on them . . . sicke they were as we never saw before, nor likely ever shall see againe". Little had changed there by 1698 when Celia Fiennes[7] saw villages

of sad, little hutts made up of drye walls, only stones piled together and the roofs of same slatt; there seemed to be little or noe tunnells for their chimneys and have no morter or plaister within or without; for the most part I tooke them at first sight for a sort of houses or barns to fodder cattle in, not thinking them to be dwelling houses, they being scattering houses here one there another, in some places there may be 20 or 30 together.

Near Carlisle she passed by "the little hutts and hovels the poor live in like barns some have them daub'd with mud-walls others drye walls". The rebuilding, which had taken place further south, did not arrive here until the eighteenth century and so it is possible that similar cottages to those described by Hammond and Fiennes were to be found in the stone areas further south a hundred years or so before.

The fact that few, if any, labourers' cottages of the sixteenth and seventeenth centuries are known to survive provides further evidence of their inadequate and flimsy construction. Bishop Hall,[8] about 1610, found the condition of most cottages little better than those in Chaucer's time:

> Of one baye's breadth, God wot! a silly cote,
> Whose thatched sparres are furr'd with sluttish soot,
> A whole inch thick, shining like black-moor's brows,
> Through smok that down the headlesse barrel blows:
> At his bed's-feete feeden his stalled teme;
> His swine beneath, his pullen ore the beame;
> A starved tenement, such as I gesse
> Stands straggling in the wasts of Holdernesse;
> Or such as shiver on a Peake-hill side,
> When March's lungs beate on their turfe-clad hide . . .

Not every Tudor and Stuart labourer was condemned to live in a miserable one-roomed hovel. Clearly, from the evidence of probate inventories, many were better off and at least some, particularly in the seventeenth century, lived in reasonable cottages, probably those built in the previous century and discarded by farmers and tradesmen. In the South-east, particularly in Kent, by the middle of the fifteenth century the one-roomed cottage began to be replaced with one of two rooms and this trend spread slowly northwards; although in the North the one-roomed cottage remained in use for some farm labourers well into the nineteenth century.[9] By 1600 only a small proportion of the population in the South-east lived in a two-roomed cottage – which had a hall and either a parlour or chamber – the majority had more and nearly all houses, except those in the poor coastal areas, were of two storeys. Further north, in Lincolnshire and Nottinghamshire, the single-roomed house, which had been prevalent in 1550, had by about 1600 begun to be abandoned for a house with structural divisions into house and parlour. So, as the seventeenth century progressed, many labourers and other poor members of the community were able to take advantage of the favourable economic climate which prevailed between 1580 and 1640 to improve their domestic conditions. This was not only accomplished by building a new cottage but often by adopting and extending an existing one. The single-roomed cottage could have a structural division between the living and sleeping half, perhaps incorporating a chimney stack, or it could be chambered over to provide bedrooms upstairs, or it could have an outshut at the rear to form a kitchen, buttery, drinkhouse or milk chamber. Seldom was a separate kitchen provided in a labourer's cottage, the cooking still being done in the hall or 'house'. It is obvious that some single-roomed cottages in 1550 had become two-roomed cottages by 1600, and by 1640 had become three- or four-roomed cottages.

As the wealth of the nation increased during the seventeenth century so too did the housing and living standards of its people and although it was more beneficial to the yeomen and husbandmen, there is much evidence that labourers also benefited considerably. William Harrison tells us that towards the end of the sixteenth century unemployment had practically disappeared and that specialist craftsmen and tradesmen were more numerous. In some areas it was possible for a farmworker to combine agriculture with some peasant industry and his wife and children to undertake one of the cottage industries, like spinning and weaving.

In Hertfordshire, where labourers were often engaged in two or three employments at once, they were better off than in almost any other county and this was reflected in their housing. It was in those regions where rural industries were divorced from agriculture – as the wool villages of Suffolk and some of the mining villages of Derbyshire; or where they were absent altogether, as in Herefordshire – that the agricultural labourer was very poor. The income from these rural industries and the domestic system may not have been great, but it was sufficient to improve the domestic life of the family. It was a sad day for the farmworker when these crafts left the villages and returned to the towns.

The sixteenth and seventeenth centuries were a period of transition between the old feudal system of medieval England and the agrarian revolution of the eighteenth century. New industries developed – nailmaking in the Midlands, chair-turning in the Chilterns, knitting in Gloucestershire, lace-making in Devon and Somerset, weaving in the Cotswolds and Suffolk – and in these areas where trade flourished so did the living standards and housing of their people, as is evident from houses which survive today in the Cotswolds and the weaving villages around Lavenham and Kersey in Suffolk. From this period some of the earliest and best cottages to be seen in England today were built.

The Agrarian Revolution

The eighteenth century was a period of great change and the industrial and agricultural revolution that took place during the century, particularly in the second half, brought to some immense wealth. Those who benefited from this prosperity loved to build. The English aristocracy and wealthy middle classes employed architects to design the many mansions, often in the Palladian style, which sprung up on the large estates throughout the country. The smaller landowners built gracious country houses, the professional businessmen the small Georgian town houses of red brick or stone, seen in so many of our towns and villages today. The farmers moved out of their old houses in the villages to new brick or stone farmhouses on their new holdings. From the numerous pattern books which were produced the local builder could construct the symmetrical houses, so characteristic of the Georgian period, which their clients wanted. Yet, for the majority this wealth and increase in living standards passed them by and as the century progressed the conditions of the poor became intolerable. While the houses of the rich became increasingly luxurious with their delicate plasterwork and elegant furniture, the houses of the poor made little progress and, in fact, generally deteriorated. Not for them a small red brick Georgian-style cottage, but a timber-framed or mud hovel with only one or two rooms and little furniture. Furze or dung was burnt on the fire, not only to provide warmth but in many cases the light necessary to undertake the many evening jobs required for the family's survival. For some this was certainly the age of elegance but for the majority it brought nothing but poverty and degradation.

The beginning of the eighteenth century, when towns were growing and absorbing the products of the countryside, was a period of growing prosperity for the cottager. Real wages were higher than at any time since the reign of Henry VI and living standards slowly improved. Foreign visitors expressed their surprise at the variety of the diet, at the neat clean cottages of the farm-workers and the dress of their women-folk.[1] Compared with the peasants of other countries the English labourer lived tolerably well. Fresh meat began to be eaten by all classes and wheaten bread ceased to be a luxury of the wealthy and, by the accession of George III, had become the staple diet for half of the population. William Cobbett, looking back, described the period as the golden age of rural England.

This situation was not to last. Great changes in English agriculture took place as the eighteenth century advanced and the new techniques

34

introduced by Jethro Tull, Lord Townshend, Robert Bakewell and Thomas Coke meant a new era for English agriculture. The success of their methods and profitability depended on large farms and the investment of large amounts of capital in the land. This could only be achieved by the displacement of the strips in the open fields by large consolidated farms, which could only be brought about by enclosing the remaining commons and wastes and buying out the smaller farmers.

Enclosures, either by the reclamation of the wastes, or the break-up of the open-field farms, or the appropriation of the commons, had continued spasmodically since medieval times, but as the century passed the process gained impetus. The social upheaval caused in the previous period of enclosures during Tudor times, when less than one per cent of the total arable land had been affected, was nothing compared with that during the period 1760 to 1810. Between the years 1700 and 1710 there was only one enclosure, but slowly the number increased until between 1750 and 1760 there were 156; between 1760 and 1770, 424; between 1770 and 1780, 642; before reaching its climax between 1800 and 1810 when there were no fewer than 906. Each enclosure required an Act of Parliament and Commissioners were appointed to investigate the various claims, each man receiving in a single block roughly the same area as the total area of his strips in the open-fields. The cottager, having survived the scrutiny of the Commissioners, discovered that he not only had to pay his share of the legal costs of the enclosure procedure but also had to put up a fence around his land to confirm its enclosure. The cost of this was beyond many cottagers and this, coupled with the fact that they either lacked the means to work their new land economically or that the land allocated to them was unsuitable for the crops they needed and grew in the open fields, resulted in many selling their holding to the wealthier holders. Also many of the squatters, who had in previous years cultivated some land on the outskirts of the village, were evicted, having no kind of legal right. Thousands were subsequently reduced to the status of landless labourers, many migrating to the towns where they were absorbed into the growing industries.

Those who did stay in the country found that the new techniques increased the wealth of the rich farmer but progressively made the labourer worse off. He could no longer supplement his wages with garden produce from his holding in the open fields, or graze his animals on the common lands, or collect fuel from the wastes. Further hardship was experienced by the decline of the domestic system under which the wife and children, by undertaking spinning and weaving at home, could supplement the family income.

The Act of Settlement of 1662, by making it difficult for labour to move from one village to another, further prevented wages to increase. As early as 1651 an Essex magistrate had fixed the daily wage for an agricultural worker as a shilling a day, and it remained almost static throughout the eighteenth century, failing to reflect the gradual rise in the cost of food after 1760 or the sharp rise during the years 1792 to 1815 due to the wars against France. These wages were totally inadequate even for the simple necessities of life. In 1775 Nathaniel Kent[2] pointed out that it was impossible for the labourer to live by his labour alone. He gave an example of a man with a wife and five children and concluded:

> While the present high price of provision continues, it is impossible that such a family can eat anything except bread, which is a very cruel case upon a poor man whose whole life is devoted to hard labour. On the contrary, were he allowed 18 pence a day which would be nearly the same proportion as the increase in the value of land, and price of provisions, their income would be together ten shillings and six pence a week; which, under proper management, would enable them to cloath themselves decently, and add about eight or ten pounds of coarse meat to their bread, which they are surely entitled to by the laws of nature and the ties of humanity.

In 1796 he again made the same plea, pointing out that if it costs one shilling and sixpence per day to feed, house and clothe each inmate of the workhouse, how could society expect a labourer to support himself and his family when his wage was only this?[3] Kent estimated that in the second half of the eighteenth century wages had risen by about 25 per cent, but that the cost of living had risen by 60 per cent. He advocated that wages should be fixed in accordance with the price of wheat, which would have amounted to the minimum wage urged by reformers like Samuel Whitbred.

Towards the end of the century more and more labourers were compelled to seek relief from the overseers of their parishes. The Act of 1722 authorized parishes to withhold relief from all those who refused to enter a workhouse; consequently it was found that the sick, aged and able-bodied were all herded indiscriminately into workhouses. The problem became so acute that in 1782 a further Act forbade the admission of the able-bodied unemployed and charged the parishes to find them work or, if this was impossible, provide 'outdoor' relief. In 1795 the agricultural crisis, aggravated by the war, induced the Berkshire magistrates at Speen to decide that, in order to alleviate the poverty of agricultural labourers when wages fell below a certain level of subsistence which was related to the price of wheat, the difference should be made up out of the parish poor rates. The Speenhamland system, as it was known, was adopted in many rural areas and received parliamentary confirmation shortly after. This scale allowance system failed in its objective, for whilst the provision of labour at low uneconomic wages undoubtedly kept more people employed, it took from the labourer his last shred of self-respect. Once enmeshed he could only escape from a state of pauperism with utmost difficulty and, in fact, the problem was exaggerated by the form these measures took.

The Poor Law Commissioners reporting in 1834 found that the system gave the labourer low wages, easy work and

also, strange as it may appear, what he values more, a sort of independence. He need not bestir himself to seek work; he need not study to please his master; he need not put any restraint upon his temper; he need not ask relief as a favour.

Arthur Young in 1801 puts the labourer's point:

Go to an alehouse kitchen of an old-enclosed country, and there you will see the origin of poverty and high poor-rates. For whom are they to be sober? For whom are they to save? (Such are the questions.) For the Parish? If I am diligent, shall I have leave to build a cottage? If I am sober shall I have land for a cow? If I am frugal, shall I have half an acre of potatoes? You offer no motives; you have nothing but a parish officer and a workhouse! – Bring me another pot.

Certainly the agricultural prosperity of the eighteenth century was accomplished at the expense of the agricultural labourer.

With such low wages there was inevitably a dramatic drop in living standards. Labourers lived on a monotonous and even inadequate diet – mainly of bread, cheese, butter and milk if they were lucky and only bread and water if they were not. Fresh meat, which had begun to be eaten by the poor at the beginning of the eighteenth century, had certainly been largely replaced with bread and potatoes by the end. If any meat was eaten it was usually bacon, boiled up two or three times with vegetables. Arthur Young cites Essex as a county where the consumption of potatoes had increased. In 1767 they were unknown but from that date consumption had risen, due largely to the price of meat, bread, butter and cheese. Many poor people died as the result of consuming rotten food. Henry David, in *The Complete English Farmer*, writing in 1763 cited the case of John Downing of Wattisham, Norfolk, "who had a wife and six children, who lived just as other poor people in the neighbourhood did". The family died one by one of a "dry, black livid gangmere which began at the toes and advanced more or less sometimes reaching to the thigh". On investigation it was discovered that the family had been living on mildewed wheat and rotten mutton because it was cheap. The disease, which was known to the medical men, was not an uncommon one.

The enclosure and engrossing of estates resulted in the 'closed' parish, in which the whole parish was owned by one landlord or at least by very few. The cottager, forced to sell his cottage and land to the landowner, was either evicted and the cottage immediately demolished, or his cottage was left to decay, becoming uninhabitable before being eventually pulled down. The Laws of Settlement, which made each parish responsible for the poor born within its boundaries, encouraged this destruction of all places where the poor might multiply. The squatters were dealt with in an even more harsh manner, for they were evicted and their dwellings destroyed without further ceremony. The cottagers and squatters, so forced to find accommodation elsewhere, had to procure certificates from the parish authorities which permitted them to crowd into the 'open' parishes which were not owned by one person or where there were still unenclosed or roadside wastes on which they could squat. In the open village the dispossessed often found themselves crowded into old farmhouses or old barns and sheds which were converted into cottages in order to house them. In many places new cottages – put up by small owners such as shopkeepers, innkeepers, bakers and others who relied on large groups for their livelihood – were erected and let to the unfortunate homeless at a high rent. For the first time rows of cottages began to be built, among the first being one at Boxworth, Cambridgeshire, dating from the first half of the eighteenth century. Most, however, date from the end of the century, like the row at Bletchington, Oxfordshire, dated 1794, and another at Litlington, Cambridgeshire.

Once the closed parish had been achieved the landowners and farmers removed their ultimate parish responsibility for poor rates (for there were no poor), preferring their labourers to walk, sometimes several miles, to work from the open parishes. The Laws of Settlement "did not stop the flow of labour, but regulated it in the interest of the employing class". Arthur Young,[4] writing in 1774, states that:

> When a whole parish becomes one farm, under one landlord, the power over both the poor and their habitations will centre in such landlord and tenant. The tenant pays the poor rates, and perhaps as a part of his agreement, repairs the cottages: here therefore are two strong reasons why he should drive the people away, and let their houses go to ruin, or perhaps advise his landlord to pull them down; first, he eases himself of rates, and secondly, he gets rid of repairs. As to his labour, he hires men from parishes not in the same predicament . . .

The creation of closed parishes led to emparking (a word the eighteenth century made its own) and finally, towards the end of the century, to the cult of the Picturesque. The results of emparking – the removal of entire communities and their rehousing away from the newly-built mansions of the landed class and their landscaped parks – are clear enough; the isolated church situated either in the park or near the house, and the

6. Row of timber-framed and plastered cottages with brick gables,
built about 1730 at Boxworth, Cambridgeshire.

row of identical cottages on a nearby road or on the approach to the
gates, giving the visitor a foretaste of the mansion beyond, are all
examples of such devastation.

Emparking started at the beginning of the eighteenth century. One of
the first landowners was Edward Russell, first Lord of the Admiralty
and later Lord Orford, who rebuilt the village of Chippenham, Cambridgeshire. Work began in 1696 and by the beginning of the eighteenth
century the park and artificial lake had engulfed half the village. Evidently some of the villagers were dispossessed but the majority were
housed in lines of identical semi-detached cottages forming the approach
to the park gates. The village was completed in 1712. By this time the
idea of the Picturesque had already begun to develop. Joseph Addison,
the essayist and statesman, writing in 1712, asked "Why may not a
whole estate be thrown into a kind of garden by frequent plantations? A
man might make a pretty Landskip of his own possessions." At Well,
Lincolnshire, this new approach was put into practice. The village was
rebuilt after emparking by James Bateman and although the cottages
were built outside the gates, the church, though rebuilt in 1733, was
placed inside and reconstructed as a classic neo-temple to be viewed as a

7. A pair of semi-detached cottages built by Sir Robert Walpole in about 1729 at the gates of his mansion at New Houghton, Norfolk.

decorative ornament across the grass from the mansion's windows. There was no such indulgence in the Picturesque at New Houghton, Norfolk, where Sir Robert Walpole constructed, in about 1729, two rows of sturdy whitewashed brick and pantiled cottages at the gates of his mansion, Houghton Hall, after emparking. In addition to the twenty-five cottages, contained in ten buildings, some single-storeyed almshouses and two farmhouses were also built.

At Nuneham Courtenay, Oxfordshire, built in 1761 by Lord Harcourt to replace the old village of Newnham Courtenay (the name changed on its rebuilding) which stood behind the newly-built Palladian mansion, the cottages were, like those at New Houghton, placed at intervals on either side of the road, this time not on the approach road to the mansion but on the main Oxford-to-London road. The cottages, all identical and semi-detached, were constructed of brick — one brick at the front and rear, half brick at the gables — with timber-framed gable ends. The cottages were small, originally having only two ground-floor rooms with two small bedrooms over, each lighted by a dormer. Likewise, at Milton

8. Milton Abbas, Dorset. A village of identical semi-detached cottages built between 1773 and 1786 by Joseph Damer.

Abbas, Dorset, identical rows of semi-detached cottages, broken only by the church and almshouses, were built. The rebuilding, which involved the destruction of a sizeable market town, was carried out for Joseph Damer, later Earl of Dorchester, probably by William Chambers, who had been employed to carry out extensive alterations to Milton Abbey, although Capability Brown, who laid out the park, may have been responsible for the site – a deep cleft between the downs. The village, begun in 1773 and not completed until 1786, comprised forty cottages, mostly semi-detached, set behind wide grass verges on either side of the road which gently slopes down the valley, together with a new church and reconstructed Jacobean almshouses. Each semi-detached cottage has four rooms – two downstairs and two upstairs – entered through a common front door. Between each pair of cottages was planted a horse-chestnut tree to soften the repetitive arrangement of the cottages.

Contrasting with the rows of identical or similar cottages are the model villages of Harewood, West Yorkshire, and Lowther, Cumbria. In about 1760 Edwin Lascelles, first Earl of Harewood, commissioned John Carr of York to rebuild his house and village at Harewood. Carr produced not lines of identical cottages but terraces of cottages, some built in the local West Yorkshire vernacular but others, using Palladian detail, were linked by large blank arches and with variations in height all introduced to break up the monotony of terracing. The whole appearance gives an entirely urban effect. At Lowther, in the 1760s, Sir James Lowther commissioned the Adam brothers to draw up plans for a new village. A grandiose plan was produced with two groups of cottages each around a square, based on a Greek cross, and linked by a circus. The scheme was never completed – only the left half, in a modified form, together with the circus which remained a semi-circle of two identical arms, was built. Richard Warner,[5] writing in 1802, stopped near the village

> to smile at the fantastic incongruity of its plan which exhibits the grandest features of city architecture, the Circus, the Crescent and the Square upon the mean scale of a peasant's cottage. These groups of houses were built for the labourers of Lord Lowther but from their desolate deserted appearance it should seem that no sufficient encouragement has been held out to their inhabitants to continue in them.

That these and other eighteenth-century model villages – like Thrumpton, built about 1730 by John Emmerton; Bradmore, built by Sir Thomas Parkyns also in the 1730s, both in Nottinghamshire; and Audley End, Essex, built by Lord Braybrook in the 1760s – produced in most cases, better housing is without doubt but often more by accident than by design. In 1809 the cottages at Nuneham Courtenay with their

9. Stone cottages with stone flag roofs built around the gravel-surfaced double square at Blanchland, Northumberland. The village, one of Northumberland's most attractive, was built by Lord Crewe from 1752 from the ruins of the abbey to house workers from the nearby lead mines.

10. One of the terraces of cottages built in 1760 by John Carr of York for Edwin Lascelles, First Earl of Harewood, along the approaches to the gates of Harewood House, West Yorkshire.

11. Part of the circus built at Lowther, Cumbria, in the 1760s.

four rooms was thought "just what they ought to be, comfortable but unostentatious".[6] These villages were designed rather to improve the approaches to the great houses than any particular concern for the inhabitants, whom, at the same time, would be provided with safe and sufficient employment on the estate. Stebbing Shaw,[7] visiting the village of Nuneham Courtenay in 1788, wrote

> that 40 families may here, by the liberal assistance of his lordship, enjoy the comforts of industry under a wholesome roof who otherwise might have been doomed to linger out their days in the filthy hut of poverty.

Emparking had its critics; Oliver Goldsmith's poem *The Deserted Village* is the most outspoken protest against the destruction of villages and the reorganization around the great estates. He complains:

> The man of wealth and pride
> Takes up a space that many poor supply'd:
> Space for his lake, his park's extended bounds,
> Space for his horses, equipage and hounds;
> The robe that wraps his limbs in silken sloth,
> Has robb'd the neighbouring fields of half their growth;
> His seat, where solitary sports are seen,
> Indignant spurns the cottage from the green.

It seems without doubt that the deserted village of "sweet Auburn" was

Nuneham Courtenay.[8] William Whitehead, poet laureate and former tutor and close friend of the Harcourts, came out in defence of the removal of the village with *The Removal of the village at Nuneham Courtenay*, published about 1771:

> The careful matrons of the plain
> Had left their cots without a sigh
> Well pleased to house their little train
> In happier mansions warm and dry.

Nuneham Courtenay also received criticism from the Picturesque movement which had, by the end of the eighteenth century, gained momentum. William Gilpin, one of the early advocates, wrote that

The village of Nuneham was built . . . with that regularity which perhaps gives the most convenience to the dwellings of men. For this we readily relinquish the picturesque idea. Indeed I question whether it were possible for a single hand to build a picturesque village. Nothing contributes to it more than the various styles in building. When all these little habitations happen to unite harmoniously and to be connected with the proper appendages of a village – the winding road, a number of spreading trees, a rivulet and a bridge and a spire to bring the whole to an apex – the village is compleat.

Sir Uvedale Price, who did much to establish the cult, found none of these basic essential ingredients of the Picturesque village at Nuneham Courtenay. In 1794 he wrote that

An obvious and easy method of rebuilding a village . . . is to place the houses on two parallel lines, to make them of the same size and shape, and at equal distance from each other. Such a methodical arrangement saves all further thought and invention: but it is hardly necessary to say that nothing can be more formal and insipid . . . it seems to me, that symmetry . . . is less suited to humbler scenes and buildings.[9]

Later, in 1836, John Loudon also singles out Nuneham Courtenay as a village built "too like rows of street houses" and that

in villages the houses ought never to be put down in rows, even though detached, unless the ground and other circumstances are favourable for a strictly regular or symmetrical congregation of dwellings. There is not a greater error in forming artificial villages . . . than always having one side of the buildings parallel with the road.[10]

From the 1790s, designs for Picturesque cottages appeared constantly in the pattern books published by architects, incorporating the principles previously laid down by Gilpin and Price. At first these design books showed cottages which were basically symmetrical with the ornamental detail simply added. Later they became more florid and ever more irregular. In 1798 James Malton produced his book *Essay on British Cottage Architecture* which was meant to assist builders on how to preserve the vernacular tradition "which was originally the effect of chance". Malton examined existing old cottages and from these designed his picturesque cottages; he advocated that cottages must be irregular with walls of unequal height, with bold overhanging eaves and gables, as well as porches and latticed windows so as to produce a "judicious contrast of light and shade". Another writer was David Laing who in 1801 produced his *Hints for Dwellings*. His cottages were designed "for particular Situations in which the Peculiarities of the surrounding Scenery had been attended to". His favourite designs were based on an octagon which, together with the hexagon, became during the early part of the nineteenth century one of the most favoured of cottage plans. Countless publications, containing illustrations by professional designers as well as amateur architects, continued to be produced, among the most notable being Pocock's *Architectural Designs for Rustic Cottages, Picturesque Dwellings, etc.*, published in 1807.

Many isolated romantic cottages built in the Picturesque style and adapted to the park scenery of the great estates began to be built at the beginning of the nineteenth century. Such cottages – as well as entrance lodges and casemented keepers' cottages – might be rectangular but were commonly circular, oval or polygonal, with steeply pitched ornamental thatched roofs and deep projecting eaves, scalloped and fretted barge boards, Gothic porches, fancy window casements and above all tall, slender ornamental chimneys of Tudor or Gothic influence. *Cottage orné*, as with garden ornaments and buildings some years before, began to be an indication of the social status of many landowners.

It was not until 1810, despite the economies necessitated by the Napoleonic War, that the first complete Picturesque village was built for John Scandrett Harford, the Quaker banker, at Blaise Hamlet, Henbury, near Bristol. This village, with its nine cottages, eight single and one double, dispersed about an undulating, curving central village green, was designed by John Nash in what is his most successful exercise in the Picturesque. Unlike many newly-built villages of the period it was not a replacement of a destroyed village but a desire by Harford to house his retired servants. Each cottage is different from its neighbour and has little regard for local styles; some of the roofs are tiled, others are thatched with deep overhangs and exaggerated ridges; some chimneys rise in isolation, others in clusters of three or four; all the cottages are irregular in shape. The village became the model for subsequent Picturesque villages and an important port of call to all those interested in the movement. Other Picturesque villages followed, of which perhaps

12. Cottage at Blaise Hamlet, Avon.

13. Cottages, Great Tew, Oxfordshire.

Great Tew, Oxfordshire, is the most perfect. The village – originally built by Lucius Carey, Viscount Falkland, in the mid-seventeenth century – was probably redesigned by John Loudon, who was farm steward there from 1809 to 1811. The cottages, set about a small triangular green, were probably largely rebuilt at this time and the whole village is rendered even more enchanting by the yews and laurels planted by Loudon and which have now reached maturity.

Not all early pattern books dealt with the Picturesque. Nathaniel Kent's book, *Hints to Gentlemen of Landed Property*, published in 1775, was the first to produce plans for cottages, and although he condemned the state of existing cottages he was

> far from wishing to see the cottage improved or augmented so as to make it fine and expensive . . . All that is requisite is a warm, comfortable, plain room for the poor inhabitants to eat their morsel in, an oven to bake their bread, a little receptacle for their small beer and provisions and two wholesome lodging apartments, one for the man and his wife and another for his children. It would perhaps be more decent if the boys and girls could be separated, but this could make the building too expensive and besides is not so materially necessary; for the boys find employment in farmhouses at an early age.

The smallest of his cottages, which could either be built of timber studwork or brick, comprised a principal room, 12 feet 6 inches square; with an adjoining pantry, 6 feet by 4 feet 6 inches; and cellar, 7 feet 6 inches by 6 feet; with two bedrooms, one 12 feet 6 inches by 11 feet and the other 12 feet 6 inches by 7 feet 6 inches. He also recommended that each cottage be provided with half an acre of land attached to it. The estimated cost of erecting such a cottage was £66 if constructed of brick and £58 if constructed of timber. Although the accommodation is not excessive it was probably far superior to those already existing. These suggestions and plans made by Kent were adopted by Lord Brownlow and other landowners.

In 1781 the first architectural book devoted entirely to cottages, *Series of Plans for Cottages or Habitations of the Labourer*, was produced by John Wood, the architect of Bath who designed the Royal Crescent and other terraces in that town. Before producing his designs he visited a number of cottages in the location. "The greater part of those that fell within my observation", he writes, "I found to be shattered, dirty inconvenient, miserable hovels, scarcely affording a shelter for the beasts of the forest, much less were they proper habitations for the human species . . ." Also he found a complete family – husband, wife and some half-dozen children – sharing the same bed. Wood's plans and designs were always practical, his only aesthetic requirement being regularity which he viewed as beauty. He considered that the cottages ought to be built in pairs so that "the inhabitants may be of assistance to each other in case of sickness or any other accident". He condemned the practice of placing the main windows facing north – the idea that a southerly wind brought the plague still lingered in this country and the principal openings were, therefore, often placed on the north wall. Wood writes, "Let the window of the main room receive its light from the East or the South; then it will always be warm and cheerful". He continues,

> So like the feelings of men in an higher sphere are those of the poor cottager, that if his habitation be warm, cheerful and comfortable, he will return to it with gladness, and abide in it with pleasure.

He also insisted that every cottage should have a privy – a rare feature in those days even in farmhouses – stating that "This convenience should answer many good ends, but in nothing more than being an introduction to cleanliness". Also stating that in many "villages and towns there is scarcely such a convenience in the whole place, for want of which the streets are perfect jakes . . ."

Robert Beatson,[11] in 1797 submitted plans to the Board of Agriculture of cottages with one, two or three rooms, stating that "those of four are seldom built and are more in the style of houses of a superior kind". Thomas Davis[12] considered that the smallest cottages should have three rooms on the ground floor and two above, with a skilling for fuel, and should be constructed of rough stone with a paved ground floor of stone or brick and plastered throughout with the upper rooms ceiled. Others were less generous; the smallest proposed by J. Miller[13] was of one storey having a living room 15 feet by 11 feet, a bedroom 9 feet by 7 feet, and a small closet. His plan of a two-storey dwelling is not clear and seems to have one ground-floor room with one, or possibly two, rooms above. In contrast to these John Plaw[14] advocated two downstairs rooms and at least two upstairs.

The Picturesque and model villages and cottages built during the eighteenth and beginning of the nineteenth centuries had little effect on the general housing situation of the poor. In 1775, Nathaniel Kent described the cottages as often in such disrepair that the wind and rain penetrated every part. They usually contained only one room, so that a man, his wife and family had to eat and sleep almost like animals. Kent condemned the gentlemen of landed property who bestowed more attention on their stables and kennels than on the cottages of their labourers. He continued,

> The shattered hovels which half the poor of this kingdom are obliged to put up with, is truly affecting to a heart fraught with humanity. Those who

condescend to visit these miserable tenements can testify that neither health nor decency can be preserved in them.

Thomas Davis reported similar conditions twenty years later:

> Humanity shudders at the idea of the industrious labourer, with a wife and five or six children, being obliged to live or rather to exist, in a wretched, damp, gloomy room, of 10 or 12 feet square, and that room without a floor; but common decency must revolt at considering, that over this wretched apartment, there is only *one* chamber, to hold all the miserable beds of the miserable family.

Some indication as to the housing conditions of the vast majority of the rural poor can be analysed from the evidence of the county reports for the old Board of Agriculture[15] between 1794 and 1815, as well as many topographical books produced during the eighteenth century. Broadly, the cottages of England grew steadily worse the further northwards one went, the lowest being in Northumberland. Yet in almost all parts of the country poor housing could be found.

The Home Counties, influenced by the modern practices of house-building in London, probably had the best cottages. Kent was particularly well off. C. P. Moritz,[16] a German tourist, was impressed by the order of Kentish villages

> where an uncommon neatness in the structure of the houses, which in general are built with red bricks and flat roofs, struck me with a pleasing surprise especially when I compare them with the long, rambling inconvenient and singularly mean cottages of our peasants.

William Marshall,[17] in 1798, found the houses still mainly of wood or half-timber, with the infill panels either of brick or plaster, while some were hung with tiles. Most of the newer houses were built of brick with tiled roofs. Earlier in the century, on the outskirts of the wastes of Surrey and Hampshire, there were still to be found turf cottages occupied by squatters. Later it was reported that the houses of Surrey were old and dilapidated, especially in the Weald. Sussex had the advantages of sandstone and flint and cottages were at the end of the eighteenth century constructed of these. In the Weald, Marshall found timber and weatherboarded houses roofed with thatch, tiles or 'chips'.

H. Misson,[18] a French tourist, found that the two- or three-storey farmhouses of Essex were built of brick and timber with tiled roofs, while some of the cottages were of weatherboard and thatch. Arthur Young reported in 1807 that the old cottages of wattle and daub were in poor repair and that the thatch was equally dilapidated. Modern cottages were, however, being built, those of lath and plaster being superior to those built of brick. Hertfordshire was similarly placed. In 1733 "red clay . . . by being beat and tempered with short cut straw, often supplies the place of Boards to the sides of a poor man's cottage, with the help of Hazel or other Poles".[19] Between Woodford, Essex and Little Gaddesden, Hertfordshire, brick and stud walls with straw thatch were not uncommon in 1748.[20] In Buckinghamshire, as elsewhere in the Home Counties, some of the new cottages were being built of brick, or of timber and mud with thatched roofs, but the older houses were poor, especially in the open-field parishes, while in 1813 they were reported as *good* as those found in other counties.

The improved farming methods introduced into Norfolk and Suffolk during the eighteenth century provided more substantial but, in some cases, overcrowded accommodation for the poor. The group of ten buildings containing twenty-five cottages built at New Houghton about 1729 and let by Sir Robert Walpole at a guinea a year had, some seventy years later, to house between forty and fifty families, although the rent then charged was only a shilling. *The Annals of Agriculture* for 1793 gives details of cottages built by Thomas Coke at his estate at Holkham. Each cottage – which was built of flint with pantiled roof – housed four families, each backing on to one another, and comprised a living room 14 feet square, a one-storey extension at the end of the block with one room, 11 feet by 7 feet 6 inches, and a coal house, with probably only one bedroom above. In 1804 Arthur Young reported that the housing of the poor was generally bad in the county, citing especially Snetterton and the neighbouring parishes. He added that the poor took care of what they had, that the hedges were clipped and that the gardens, although too small, were neat. Elsewhere a similar situation was noted. One observer was certain that if twenty or thirty cottages were built at Hingham they would all be let within three months. The housing in the county may well be illustrated by the fact that in Marshland Sneeth only three cottages were built in consequence of bringing, for the first time, some eight thousand acres under cultivation. This lack of cottages was also observed by L. Simond in 1810; in both Norfolk and Suffolk he noted that large farmhouses were seen but so few cottages that he was unable to discern how or where the labourers lived.[21] So poor was the accommodation provided by many cottages that Young thought it worth commending two cottages built in Norfolk. One pair – built at Carbrooke for the cost of £130 – was constructed with walls of flint 18 inches thick, under a pantiled roof and finished inside with whitewashed clay. Each cottage had a living room 15 feet by 11 feet, with a bedroom in the loft above and a further small bedroom and wood-store in a lean-to at the back. Only one window was provided to each cottage, both the bedrooms being without windows. A cottage near Dereham was a little better; the accommodation, for one family, comprised a living room 12 feet square, a lean-to

14. 'Roundhouse', Finchingfield. Built in about 1800 as a model
cottage.

at the rear containing two rooms, and a chamber over the living room. It
was constructed of flint for £40 and let for £3 3shillings per year. Young
gives no such details for Suffolk, but comments that the cottages were
"in general bad habitations, deficient in all contrivance for warmth or
for convenience . . . in bad repair". Simond found a few villages where
the cottages, although poor enough on the outside, had casements in

good repair, and clean floors.

In the Fens of Cambridgeshire and Lincolnshire cottages were either lath and plaster or mud-and-stud, often having only one ground-floor room with one room above. The cost of these mud-and-stud cottages of Lincolnshire was only £30, while in the enclosed fens, brick cottages cost some £50 for the smallest size and eighty guineas for a pair.

The further south-westwards one went, cottage accommodation grew steadily worse. In Berkshire, although the farmhouses were of brick or stone with slate or tile roofs, cottages had broken windows, rugged thatch, earth floors and frequently only one bedchamber. In Wiltshire many of the surplus farmhouses were allowed to decay and were let to labourers, how many to each house is not stated but more than one is almost certain. Marshall states that on the Downs in both Wiltshire and Hampshire cob and thatch were commonly used, with those in Wiltshire having brick foundations and dressings. The cottages with sandstone walls between Stourhead and Sherborne were commended in the *Annals of Agriculture* for 1796 for making dry housing. Although cob was common in Hampshire, particularly to the west, all the available building materials, stone, flint, brick and timber, were all used. Charles Vancouver reported that a Mr Brimstone built in brick in spite of this general prevalence of cob cottages. Cob was probably the material used by the squatters in the New Forest who "built their little huts and inclose their little gardens and patches of ground without leave".[22] A large settlement of these cottages, many erected in a single night, were built between Beaulieu Manor and the Forest, the inhabitants being employed to cut furze for the neighbouring kilns. Gilbert White,[23] in 1789, describes the inhabitants of Oakhanger as poor but living "comfortably in good stone or brick cottages, which are glazed, and have chambers above stairs: mud buildings we have none". On the Isle of Wight the cottages, which were frequently attached to farms, seem to have been substantial dwellings, built of stone and plastered and whitewashed internally. Cob was also used in Dorset, particularly east of Dorchester, where they had walls 2 feet thick. Flint and chalk were also used for walls in those areas where it was available and many cottages had only three rooms with a ground floor of earth. In the early part of the nineteenth century the cost of building new cottages with two ground-floor rooms and two above in the roof space was between £60 and £80.

The West Country was particularly poor in housing, with the cottages of Devon being almost universally condemned. Even Simond, the most optimistic of travellers, was forced to admit that the houses were generally poor and the villages not beautiful, yet he found some comfort in the fact that the windows were clean and whole without old hats or bundles of rags stuck in. Some fifty years before a Mrs Powys[24] recorded her impressions of the cottages of Devon, which she thought were the meanest in the country. Many were, indeed, so poor as to be unsafe, and she recalls a midsummer storm when in the torrential rain twenty were demolished, the cob walls soon disintegrating, and in one cottage an old lady was drowned in her bed. At Tiverton a large number of cottages – sixty-four in the previous sixty years – had by 1790 fallen into disrepair, partly because of the decline in the wool industry and partly because of the amalgamation of small farms.

In about 1800 the Rev. Luxmoore of Bridestowe built ninety-five cottages, each with one room 16 feet square on the ground floor and a bedroom above of about the same size, with walls of stone for the first 8 feet and cob above. The cottages of Somerset were little better, the majority between Dulverton and Wiveliscombe being of cob, although cottages built of 'Lyas' limestone were to be found in some places like Somerton and Kingsdon.[25] Few of these cottages had more than one upstairs room, while even the farmhouses were poorly constructed. In Cornwall too cob was the main building material and whole villages like Sennen, near Land's End, were, at the turn of the nineteenth century, built of mud. Many cottages had fallen into decay largely because of the frailty of the materials used, yet cottages of cob were still being constructed.

In many parts of the Midlands the conditions were little better. Although in parts of Rutland stone was in general use and two-bedroomed cottages with a privy were provided by the Earl of Winchelsea for his labourers, many of the cottages in the county had walls made entirely of clay with chimneys of poles daubed inside and out with the same material, which John Boys states as "a very cheap mode of building". Similar wattle-and-daub cottages were to be found in Bedfordshire, although in the west of the county, like parts of Rutland, stone was used. On the Duke of Bedford's estate cottages of two, three and four rooms had been built. Many of the cottages of Leicestershire were of timber and plaster or mud with thatch, the most common roofing material. Stone and brick cottages were to be seen in Northamptonshire, but many were of inferior material and a great many were of mud, like Naseby, a village built almost entirely of mud. Like Leicestershire the majority were thatch and as evidence of their pre-enclosure origin were nearly all situated in villages. Some cottages with stone walls and a thatched or tiled roof were being constructed in Warwickshire, each with a large living room and two small bedrooms, but the older cottages, often referred to as miserable hovels, were of timber and mud or clay walls and thatch. William Pitt makes no reference to the older buildings of Staffordshire, but states that the new ones were built of brick with roofs of slate or tile. He gives two plans of cottages, each with a kitchen, pantry and bedroom on the ground floor and possibly two bedrooms on the floor above, estimated to cost between £80 and £100 to construct. In Derbyshire, perhaps influenced by the newly-erected factory villages, the cottages were thought to be better than those in southern England, few being thatched and nearly all being built of brick or stone with stone or tiled roofs. The cottages of Worcestershire were generally constructed of timber with plaster in-filling and thatched roofs described as "merely a shelter from the weather". Three new cottages erected near Bromsgrove provided a living room, a pantry and two bedrooms above, with one pump and a common wash and bakehouse serving all three cottages.

Of the Welsh border counties Herefordshire was perhaps the most fortunate, even though the housing was generally poor. Dr Pococke[26] found all "the old houses in Herefordshire are built with frames of wood and cage-work between, called pargiting . . ." Some fifty years later little had changed, the cottages being of humble, inferior construction and of so limited accommodation that a row of ten cottages, constructed at Holmer of brick and timber – having one ground-floor room 12 feet by 14 feet with a ceiling height of $6\frac{1}{2}$ feet, and a shed at the rear and one bedroom above – were thought to be worthy of noting. William Marshall[27] who visited Gloucestershire in 1783 and again in 1788 found that in the Vale the buildings were generally timber, either plastered or weatherboarded, although occasionally walls were of brick or stone. Cottages were still thatched, whereas on the farmhouses the slate roofs were being replaced with tiles. In the Cotswolds he found most of the cottages of stone. Some twenty years later Thomas Rudge found the cottages in the Vale dilapidated, but by then building cottages was regarded as an unprofitable investment. Despite this some cottages were built near Stow, each of which had a ground-floor room 12 feet by 12 feet 4 inches, and 8 feet high; with two bedrooms of a similar height, each 12 feet by 8 feet. There is little information about the cottages of Salop at this time, but they probably resembled those of other counties. Cottages in Cheshire were either stone or timber-framed. Between Congleton and Buxton stone was the building material, although there were few cottages, they were "mean-looking, built of coarse dark stone".[28] Elsewhere in this area the cottages were not inferior to those of other counties.

The cottages of Yorkshire were often of stone, although in the Vale of Pickering and on the Wolds brick was, by about 1800, becoming commonly used. On the Wolds chalk was often a material used for walls, and elsewhere in the East Riding mud was a material commonly employed for cottages, though by 1794 some of the farmhouses were being constructed of more substantial materials and tiled. The cottages at this time were also said to be improving, but many still had a floor below ground level and windows which could not open. Generally the cottages of the West Riding were better than those of the East and North, with those of the North rarely having more than one room. Generally, however, there was a lack of cottages for the labourers, who were mainly young, unmarried men, boarded in the farmhouses.

Lancashire was in some respects similar to Yorkshire in that most of the farms were small, rarely larger than 50 acres. To the north and east the buildings were of stone and slate, but to the west, although stone and brick were used, in the Fylde and around Garstang 'clob and clay' with wheat straw thatch was to be found. The houses in this area apparently seldom being more than one storey.

The worst housing was to be found in some parts of the three northern counties of Durham, Northumberland and Cumbria. John Bailey, in 1810, dismissed the cottages of Durham as "in general comfortable dwellings of one storey, thatch or tiled, and much the same as those in other districts". In 1725 William Stukeley's view of the cottages of Northumberland were

mean beyond imagination . . . without windows, only one storey high . . . we returned through Longton, a market town, whose streets are wholly composed of such kinds of structure: the piles of turf for firing are generally as large and handsome as the houses.[29]

Although some improvement had occurred in the towns later in the century, the rural cottage, particularly near the Scottish border, still remained primitive. William Hutchinson[30] describes these cottages in 1776:

The cottages of the lower class of people are deplorable, composed of upright timbers fixed in the ground, the interstices wattled and plastered with mud; the roofs, some thatched and others covered with turf; one little piece of glass to admit the beams of day; and a hearthstone on the ground, for the peat and turf fire. Within there was exhibited a scene to touch the feelings of the heart; description sickens on the subject . . . the damp earth, the naked rafters, the breeze disturbed embers, and distracted smoke that issued from the hearth . . . the midday gloom, the wretched couch, the wooden utensils that scarce retain the name of convenience, the domestic beast that stalls with his master, the disconsolate poultry that mourns upon the rafters, form a group of objects suitable for great man's contemplation.

Only along the Vales of the Tyne was bare-footed poverty absent. Bailey and Culley found things little better in 1797. Old cottages, built of stone and clay and thatched, still survived, but new ones of stone and lime with tiled roofs and floors of plaster were being built. These cottages still had only one room – some 15 feet by 16 feet – to live in and another smaller room – 9 feet by 16 feet – at the entrance for a cow, coals and storage. In the former county of Cumberland, cottages were generally of stone built with clay mortar but nearly always thatched. The older cottages were extremely simple, consisting of only a kitchen and parlour; "in the former the family sit, eat and do all their household work; and in

the latter they sleep, and sometimes keep their butter, milk and cheese
... the windows are mere pigeon holes". In the old county of Westmorland, cottages were built of clay, especially on the western side; and stone
elsewhere, the buildings being, according to John Houseman,[31] equal to
any in the Kingdom. Here, like the western part of Cumberland, there
were few cottages, for like the farmhouses of Yorkshire, labourers were
boarded in the farmhouse or, as the farms were small, worked by the
family.

This briefly then was the housing situation for the majority of the
rural poor, especially at the end of the eighteenth century. It is obvious
that conditions varied greatly in different parts of the country. Much
new building was taking place, even to the extent of rebuilding entire villages, but these and the model cottages so lorded by Arthur Young and
others were completely inadequate to house the families with five or
more children which were so frequent. If these model cottages, with their
limited accommodation, were so commended, one can only imagine the
state and size of the cottages which were not model or not in good repair.
Yet it was well into the nineteenth century before better housing,
advocated by the reformers during this period, increased to any notable
degree.

15. Group of model cottages built at Leverton, near Hungerford,
Berkshire, in about 1800.

16. Veryan, Cornwall. One of five round, whitewashed and
thatched cottages with Gothic details, early nineteenth-century.

'Peace and Plenty'

1815 saw the end to the Napoleonic War and with it the hope that the era of peace would bring prosperity to the nation and better living conditions for the poor. However, the period of war had made great demands on the nation's energy and largely concealed the effects of the industrial and agricultural revolutions of the previous century. The spectacular rise in the population in the second half of the eighteenth century – 7 million in 1750 to 9 million in 1801, until in 1821 it was 12 million – further aggravated the situation. Though there were many unemployed and even more under-employed at least the demands of the war had kept many at work. As the soldiers returned home looking for work unemployment mounted, while the depression among the farmers caused them to lay off men. Wages fell sharply to pre-war levels and even at these lower rates work was hard to find and even harder to keep. The war was over but the land of 'Peace and Plenty' promised by some proved a terrible mockery.

Conditions for the farm labourer after the war became even more serious and the years 1814 to 1836 have been described by Lord Ernle as "the blackest period in the history of the agricultural worker".[1] As in all times of depression it became fashionable to look back on the "good old days" and though the writers probably exaggerated the prosperity of those earlier years, there was obviously a considerable decline in the labourers' living conditions. One of these writers was William Cobbett, who in his *Twopenny Trash* compared the conditions of sixty years before with those prevailing in 1831:

All of you who are 60 years of age can recollect that bread and meat and not wretched potatoes were the food of the labouring people; you can recollect that every industrious man brewed his own beer and drank it by his own fireside; . . . you can recollect when the young people were able to provide money before they were married to purchase decent furniture for a house, and had no need to go to the parish to furnish them with a miserable nest to creep into; you can recollect when a bastard child was a rarity in a village . . . when every sober and industrious labourer had his Sunday coat . . . when a young man was pointed at if he had not on a Sunday a decent coat upon his back, a good hat upon his head, a clean shirt with silk handkerchief round his neck, leather breeches without a spot, whole worsted stockings tied under the knee with a red garter, a pair of handsome Sunday shoes.

Thomas Postans[2] wrote in a similar vein.

Thirty-five years ago the Agricultural Labourer possessed a home to shelter him, a family to comfort him and food to sustain him. In most cases he was either a resident on the farm where he laboured, or lived in a cottage in a neighbouring village. Where he was without the reach of coal, he gathered wood, furze or turf with little or no molestation . . . his garden was indeed small and ill-cultivated. The value of potatoes was neither so well known or so highly appreciated as it is at present; and the idea of subsiding upon potatoes alone, as an article of food, was not entertained by the labourer of England. Bread was made at home, which, though coarser than that in present use, was not on that account less nourishing food for the labouring man. In times of distress bread and water sustained him at his last extremity.

The Speenhamland system prospered for it was considered preferable to maintain the farm labourer on a minimum wage which was subsidized from the poor rates. In many parishes those in need of parochial relief were formed into the roundsmen system; the labourers were sent round from one farm to another, each farmer maintaining a certain number for a certain length of time, and so they went round from one to the other. The farmer, knowing that the difference between the wage he was prepared to give and the recognized minimum would be supplemented from the parish, kept wages to a minimum. This system flourished for forty years from the Act of 1795, which confirmed the scale allowance system, to the Poor Law Reform Act of 1834. Russell M. Garnier[3] describes the detrimental effect of this system:

As soon as the scale allowance system was adopted in any parish, all fared alike, whether industrious or idle, and a struggle commenced among the occupiers which had for its primary object the equal distribution of the rate on the labourer. In some parishes the whole of this class was paid from the poor rate; in others after a certain portion of it – according to the acreage – had been distributed among the occupiers by mutual consent, the remainder was paid out of the rates. The men thus receiving "scale pay" were employed as roundsmen, or allotted to the occupiers according to the extent of each occupation. Acre by acre, a whole administrative centre became in this way a convict colony. Family by family, its entire labouring population degenerated into paupers, bound to toil, but labouring, as it was pointed out, "with the reluctance of slaves and the turbulence of demoralized freemen for their bankrupt master, the parish" . . .

The scale allowance had other effects. It applied equally to children as to adults and the labourer got loaves – or the equivalent of so many loaves – for each child, and so there was an advantage to have children, whether illegitimate or not, for whom the allowance could be obtained. There is one case of a Swaffham woman with five illegitimate children obtaining an allowance of eighteen shillings a week,[4] while a labourer could earn only half of this. While the system had obvious advantages to the large employer of labour, for the ratepayer who needed little or no labour the poor rate became an intolerable burden.

By 1815 much of the land had been enclosed, and although enclosures continued, the impetus of the previous fifty-five years declined. However, the effects of the enclosures were still to be felt. William Cobbett describes the situation that prevailed in Hampshire in 1826:

> There are along under the north side of that chain of hills which divide Hampshire from Berkshire . . . eleven churches . . . the chancels of which would contain a great many more than all the inhabitants, men, women, and children, sitting at their ease with plenty of room. How should this be otherwise when, in the parish of Burghclere, one single farmer holds by lease, under Lord Carnarvon, as one farm, the lands that men now living can remember to have formed fourteen farms, bringing up, in a respectable way, fourteen families. In some instances these small farm-houses and homesteads are completely gone; in others the buildings remain, but in a tumble-down state; in others the house is gone, leaving the barn for use as a barn or as a cattle-shed; in others the out-buildings are gone, and the house, with rotten thatch, broken windows, rotten door-sills, and all threatening to fall, remains as the dwelling of a half-starved and ragged family of labourers, the grandchildren, perhaps, of the decent family of small farmers that formerly lived happily in this very house.

This Cobbett observed was, with few exceptions, the case all over England.

These conditions, which caused much discontent among the agricultural workers, finally erupted in 1816. During the famines of the war years there had been numerous food riots and, like then, after the war bread was still the main cause of unrest. Food prices did fall but in years of scarcity they fluctuated violently. Protests against poverty, inadequate wages, unemployment and restricted parish relief were followed by riots among the agricultural labourers. In 1816 there were incidents in Essex, Suffolk, Cambridgeshire and Norfolk. At Downham Market, following a raid at a flour mill and butcher's shop in which flour, meal, loaves and meat were taken, the mob had to be dispersed by the yeomanry. At Littleport the rioting was worst, the labourers demanding money from farmers and shopkeepers and wrecking the home of the vicar before setting off to Ely. There they intimidated the magistrate, forced innkeepers to feed them and attacked the millers and shopkeepers before the military finally put down the revolt. At the assizes twenty-four men were sentenced to death, of whom nineteen were later reprieved, and many were transported for life. Similar riots spread from one place to another and behind all these outbursts was the discontent of the labourer with his lot. After the hangings and transportations of 1816 only isolated incidents, mainly of a local nature, occurred. The last major labourers' revolt was in 1830 and was not directed against farmers, shopkeepers and millers like so many of the earlier riots but against the threshing machine which had recently appeared on the arable farms of East Anglia and southern England. As it reduced winter employment it was considered by some as one of the major causes of unemployment. The destruction of these machines, together with rick-burning, spread throughout Kent, East Anglia and elsewhere. The revolt was, however, brought to an end with the help of the military; some 400 threshing machines were destroyed and the retribution for these crimes in which no one lost their lives was that nineteen men were hung and 500 transported.

At the end of the Napoleonic War there was concern for the improved housing for the poor. Richard Elsam,[5] writing in 1816, pleaded:

> Now the blessings of peace are restored to these happy isles by the united efforts of our countrymen, who have bled in the field of battle to protect our civil rights and independence, it is the happy moment when we should turn our eyes towards the condition of the poor, and . . . as monarchs, statesmen and philosophers of all ages have concurred in opinion, that the riches of a nation are the people, it is doubtless the duty of those in whose hands Providence has placed the means, to assist in promoting their welfare. The comforts and advantages derived in Society by their laborious exertions, make it absolutely necessary that the greatest pains should be taken to improve their condition. It is therefore a subject of deep concern that the miserable state of their habitations in many parts of these countries has never been seriously taken into consideration.

Yet for all these hopes and ideals little was achieved; the landowners and farmers, also affected by the agricultural depression and with the burden of the poor rates, were either unable or unwilling to build new or repair existing cottages. Yet despite all this the cult of the Picturesque continued to flourish and did so until at least 1870. Complete villages were built, the most notable being Selworthy, Somerset, built in 1828 by Thomas Dyke Acland, tenth Baronet Holnicote, as a refuge for his estate pensioners. He had no architect to advise him over his 'New Cottages' but there is evidence that he was influenced by P. F. Robinson's *Rural Architecture* (1823), for a copy survives from his library much marked and underlined in pencil. Robinson advocated that ". . . in making provision for the aged and infirm" it was "pleasing to render their cottages or humble habitations, objects of interest . . . as picturesque features in the landscape". This was certainly achieved at Selworthy with its group of cottages, all with cob walls and thatched roofs, set along a meandering path around the green in the shelter of the tree-clad slope of Selworthy Combe.

Some indication of the state of existing cottages can be seen from

17. One of the cottages at Selworthy, Somerset.

Francis Steven's book *Views of Cottages and Farmhouses in England and Wales, etched from the Designs of the Most Celebrated Artists* (1815), which "affords a specimen of domestic architecture in every county in England and Wales" for "those who delight in contemplating the rural beauties of our isle". Few could have associated these "rural beauties" with the plight of old cottages with gaping walls, broken windows and decayed thatch found within the pages of this book.

Although by 1825 the *Quarterly Review* claimed that it "is now rare in the country to see a cottage without a brick or stone or wood floor, without stairs to the chambers, without plastering on the walls and without doors and windows tolerably weathertight", in many parts of the country such basic amenities did not exist. William Cobbett in his *Rural Rides* comments on the "miserable sheds in which the labourers reside" found at Knighton, Leicestershire, in 1830:

Look at these hovels, made of mud and of straw; bits of glass, or of old off-cast windows, without frames or hinges frequently, but merely stuck in the mud wall. Enter them, and look at the bits of chairs or stools; the wretched boards tacked together to serve for a table; the floor of pebble, broken brick, or of the bare ground; look at the thing called a bed; and survey the rags on the backs of the wretched inhabitants.

Conditions were better in some parts of the country. In Suffolk,

Cobbett did not see "in the whole county one single instance of paper or rags supplying the place of glass in any window, and did not see one miserable hovel in which a labourer resided". The living conditions of the agricultural worker in the North was different and a little better than that of his counterpart in the South. Cobbett found at North Shields that the

> working people seem to be very well off; their dwellings solid and clean, and their furniture good; but the little gardens and orchards are wanting. The farms are all large; and the people who work on them either live in the farm-house, or in buildings appertaining to the farm-house; and they are all well fed, and have no temptation to acts like those which sprang up out of the ill-treatment of the labourers in the south.

The life of the poverty-stricken cottager from the end of the Napoleonic War until the Poor Law Reform Act of 1834 was for many accepted as inevitable, worthy of charitable assistance but not of an adequate wage or proper housing. Yet when all were poor, or at least the vast majority were poor, the conditions were accepted by rich and poor alike. During these hard times the poor found happiness in family life and the small achievement of a good fire and a full plate. William Howitt[6] wrote of English cottage life:

> I often thank God that the poor have their objects of admiration and attraction; their domestic affections and their family ties, out of which spring a thousand simple and substantial pleasures; that beauty and ability are not the exclusive growth of hall and palace . . .

The Housing of
the Victorian Rural Poor

That the old Poor Law saved many labourers in the Midlands and South from starvation is without doubt, but as the population in need of employment increased so too did the burden of the poor rates. In 1785 the total cost of administrating the Poor Law was a little less than £2,000,000; by 1803 it had increased to over £4,000,000; and it continued to rise until in 1817 it had reached a total of almost £8,000,000, which represented a cost of approximately thirteen shillings and three-pence per head of the population or about one sixth of the total public expenditure. Although it fell in the subsequent fifteen years it did not fall as much as prices, and in 1832 it stood at £7,000,000. Some parishes were particularly affected by the burden. One Buckinghamshire village, for instance, reported in 1832 that its expenditure on poor relief was eight times what it had been in 1795 and more than the rental of the whole parish in that year.

Richard Malthus noted that the increase in the population was linked with the increase in the poor rates, deducing that it was not the rise in the population that caused the rate increase but rather that the payment of the poor rates encouraged the poor to breed. It was a popular proposition for those not wishing to pay the poor rates, but it was the pressure from the ratepayers, who felt the effects on their pockets, that persuaded the Government to intervene. In 1832 a Royal Commission on the Poor Law was set up and the proposals embodied in the Poor Law Amendment Act, 1834. The new Act proved unpopular with the middle classes because it reduced the control over their own parishes and disastrous for the agricultural labourer, removing his remaining rights which had in any case been steadily eroded over the previous fifty years. The main aim of the Act was to reduce drastically outdoor relief by helping only those willing to enter the workhouse. To discourage too many entering the workhouse the conditions inside were made 'less eligible' than those for the least prosperous labourer in employment outside. Considering the condition of most of the poor at this time this was quite difficult. The harshness of the workhouse probably stimulated an exodus of labourers from depressed agricultural areas into towns.

65

The Act obviously had some effect on employment for almost immediately the farmers, who had previously declared that they could not provide full employment, at any rate if they had to pay adequate wages, for all the available labour, began to absorb it. In 1836 the Lords' Committee on the State of Agriculture was told that in Hampshire the previously unemployed had all found work locally and indeed more men would have been useful. The following year a Sussex farmer told the Commons' Committee that thirty or forty men in the parish who had formerly had to be provided with work or paid without working had all found employment. Many were not so fortunate; women and children, who had once drawn the bread allowance, had to work on the farms to help to bridge the gap between wages and the cost of living. They were sometimes employed in gangs under a foreman, who contracted with a farmer to pick fruit, lift potatoes or simply weed or pick up surface stones from the fields. The hiring of children was restricted to those over the age of eight by the Gangs Act of 1867.

The early years of Queen Victoria's reign was for most agricultural workers little better than it had been in the previous fifty years. Wages were low and, unable to obtain relief from the parish, the families' diet also deteriorated. This was particularly true of the South where the miserable wages paid and subsequent poor diet contributed to the labourer's inferior strength and energy, resulting in more men being employed than required in the North. In 1851, James Caird, in a survey of English farming for *The Times*, calculated that the wages in the North were on an average some three shillings a week or 37 per cent higher than those in the South. There are many reports of families living on nothing but potatoes and bread. Alexander Somerville[1] tells of a family at Dunford, Sussex, that would have died during the winter had it not been for the potatoes grown in their garden. In addition to potatoes they ate only bread. In Somerset he noted that the wages of a labourer in 1852 was seven shillings and sixpence a week and

for years past their daily diet is potatoes for breakfast, dinner and supper, and potatoes only. This year they are not living on potatoes because they have none (the crop failed), and the wretched farm labourers are now existing on half diet, made of barley meal, turnips, cabbages and such small allowance of bread as small wages will procure.

James Caird[2] observed that in 1850 where wages were lowest the staple food was bread, potatoes, and occasionally cheese with hot water poured over burnt crusts. In 1867 the Report of the Select Committees stated that the most underfed counties were Dorset, Kent, Chester, Salop, Staffordshire and Rutland. As the century progressed labourers' wages increased and towards the end of the century, with the import of cheaper food, there was a marked improvement not only in diet but also his general living standard.

Whether housing improved much during the Victorian era is difficult to say. The period 1840 to 1870 was one of comparative prosperity for landlords and farmers, with the years 1852 to 1863 being described by Lord Ernle[3] as "the golden age of English agriculture", and this prosperity is reflected in the number of cottages built during this time. The Union Chargeability Act of 1865 abolished the poor rates and with it the reasons for the closed parish where cottages were allowed to be pulled down or left to decay. In the latter part of the nineteenth century when farm rents and profits fell drastically, due to increased foreign competition for food stuffs and to an extraordinary succession of severe weather conditions that marked the twenty years from 1874, both landowners and farmers often lacked the money to repair old cottages or to build new ones. As Rider Haggard[4] pointed out

no one can afford to build houses which return no interest; because also the land cannot reward the labourer sufficiently to enable him to build his own or by the payment of an adequate rent, to make it profitable for anyone else to build it for him.

Rural housing was never plentiful during the nineteenth century. New cottages were built, particularly on the large estates, to replace old ones, but the motives of many landowners were mixed. Good cottages added respectability to the estate as well as to the reputation of its owner. Also they attracted to the estate good tenant farmers who were concerned in getting the best labour. The Picturesque still attracted some landowners – the villages of Sulham, Berkshire, built by the Wilder family in 1838; and Old Warden, Bedfordshire, built about 1850 by Lord Ongley, being two of the most notable. The cost of *cottage orné* was so high, not only in the initial cost but also in the cost of repairs, that most landowners built in a more practical and economical style.

The Agricultural Society of England, formed in 1839, among other things took an interest in conditions for labourers and concentrated the attention of the rural landowners on the need for good, practical designs in cottage-building. From 1840 the new building journals (among them the *Builder*), as well as numerous pattern books, published specimen plans and informative articles dealing with new cottages. The large landowners, particularly the Duke of Bedford, set an example in cottage construction which inevitably influenced, through the publication of their designs in illustrated papers, the kind of cottage built elsewhere. So large were the Duke of Bedford's estates and so keen his interest in the need for good cottages that the plans were rationalized so that doors, windows and stairs could be mass-produced

18. Picturesque cottage at Old Warden, Bedfordshire, formerly a group of three cottages.

during the winter for inclusion in the cottages the following summer, and so making economic use of both labour and materials. The cottages were plainly but substantially constructed with 9-inch-thick brick walls, the inside face being whitened and not plastered. The only ornamental feature was a concrete slab bearing the ducal crest. Each cottage had two ground-floor rooms, one fitted with a copper, the other with a kitchen range, and two or three bedrooms upstairs as well as an outbuilding for fuel. They were built in rows with a common oven to each row. Each cottage cost from £80 to £100 and let at one shilling or one shilling and sixpence a week according to whether they had two or three bedrooms. Considering the economical method these cottages were built and that there was no site costs, the 3 per cent return on outlay tends to support the claim by other landowners that building cottages for labourers was not a viable proposition.

Elsewhere in the country landowners large and small built new cottages. Lord Wantage built some; none with less than three bedrooms, the largest 15 feet by 12 feet, the others 12 feet by 8 feet and a living room 15 feet square and 8 feet 6 inches high, with a back kitchen. In Norfolk, Coke of Holkham built cottages with a living room, kitchen and pantry on the ground floor and three bedrooms above. The Duke of Manchester built some good cottages at Graffham, Cambridgeshire, each with three good bedrooms, a living room and kitchen. At Livermere, Suffolk, cottages with two living rooms and pantry downstairs and three small bedrooms above, as well as a wood-house, common oven and wash-house at the rear, were described as the "usual type of . . . new cottages which are rising in these villages". The Duke of Norfolk had built new three-bedroomed cottages in Sussex, while at North Stoke, Lord Leconfield had built four-bedroomed cottages with living room, kitchen and large garden which were let at one shilling and sixpence a week. At Beaulieu, Hampshire, every cottage had a living room, scullery and pantry and two or three bedrooms with a good water supply and drainage, a pigsty and a large garden which Lord Henry Scott charged a shilling a week rent. In the 1850s the Rev. W. H. Kerslake built some cottages near Crediton which had a living room 13 feet by 11 feet 4 inches, a scullery 14 feet by 6 feet, together with a porch, pantry and closet downstairs, and three bedrooms, the smallest 10 feet by 7 feet, upstairs. These and many others are typical of the new cottages built during the Victorian era on the estates.

In contrast to these were the cottages built in the open village by speculators. In the first half of the nineteenth century many cottages in these open villages were built for speculators anxious to take advantage of the growing population and making quick profits from high rents. Cheapness was their only concern, and so cottages without foundations, with no damp-proof courses, with half brick walls of porous bricks and without any kind of drainage were built. Dr J. Simon[5] in his report to the Privy Council for 1864 condemns these cottages:

> In the open village, the cottage-speculators buy scraps of land which they throng as densely as they can with the cheapest of all possible hovels. And into these wretched habitations (which even if they adjoin the open country, have some of the worst features of the worst town residences) crowd the agricultural labourers of England.

In spite of these new cottages the majority of the rural population of England during the nineteenth century were not living in either an estate cottage or a new cottage of any kind. They remained in their old cottages, built by their ancestors and repaired and extended over the years by themselves. These little cottages with roses and ivy creeping up their crooked, crumbling walls and over the ragged thatch may have looked picturesque but the romantic exterior of these rustic hovels concealed the intolerable squalor inside. Throughout the country those who knew what lay behind these picturesque exteriors reported on the deplorable conditions that existed within. From the evidence of the reports of the various Royal Commissions, beginning in 1842 with Edwin Chadwick's *Report on the Sanitary Conditions of the Labouring Population*, and from contemporary writers, it is clear what conditions were like. Edwin

Chadwick's report is a catalogue of scandalous housing conditions which today would precipitate a public outcry but which in 1842 evoked little interest. It describes cottages that "are neither wind nor watertight . . . where water has been running down the walls and light to be distinguished through the roof"; with floors of earth "full of vegetable matter . . . there being nothing to cut off its contact with the surrounding mould"; or with "springs bursting through the mud floors . . . and little channels cut from the centre under the doorways to carry off the water"; with windows stuffed with rags and old hats, of polluted wells and open sewers. Yet in spite of these conditions no kind of legislative action followed nor was much expected, although for the first time it was brought to the Government's notice that at least 75 per cent of all labourers' cottages were slums.

Alexander Mackay writing in the *Morning Chronicle* of the 24th October 1849, describes a typical labourer's home in Buckinghamshire and the neighbouring counties:

The cabin is so rude and uncouth that it has less the appearance of having been built than of having been suddenly thrown up out of the ground. The length is not above 15 feet, its width between 10 and 12. The wall, which has sunk at different points, and seems bedewed with a cold sweat, is composed of a species of imperfect sandstone, which is fast crumbling to decay. It is so low that your very face is almost on a level with the heavy thatched roof which covers it, and which seems to be pressing it into the earth. The thatch is thickly encrusted with a bright green vegetation, which, together with the appearance of the trees and the mason-work around, well attests the prevailing humidity of the atmosphere. In front it presents to the eye a door with one window below, and another window – a smaller one – in the thatch above. The door is awry from the sinking of the wall; the glass in the window above is unbroken, but the lower one is here and there stuffed with rags, which keep out both the air and the sunshine. As you look at the crazy fabric, you marvel how it stands. It is so twisted and distorted, that it seems as if it never had been strong and compact, and as if, from the very first, it had been erected, not as a human abode, but as a humble monument to dilapidation. But let us enter.

You approach the door-way through the mud, over some loose stones, which rock under your feet in using them. You have to stoop for admission, and cautiously look around ere you fairly trust yourself within. There are but two rooms in the house – one below, and the other above. On leaving the bright light without, the room which you enter is so dark that for a time you can with difficulty discern the objects which it contains. Before you is a large but cheerless fireplace – it is not every poor man that may be said to have a hearth – with a few smouldering embers of a small wood fire, over which still hangs a pot, recently used for some culinary purpose. At one corner stands a small ricketty table, whilst scattered about are three old chairs – one without a back – and a stool or two, which, with a very limited and imperfect washing apparatus, and a shelf or two for plates, tea-cups, etc., constitute the whole furniture of the apartment.

He continues by describing the sleeping accommodation:

These are above, and are gained by means of a few greasy and ricketty steps, which lead through a species of hatchway in the ceiling. Yes, there is but one room, and yet we counted nine in the family! And such a room! The small window in the roof admits just light enough to enable you to discern its character and dimensions. The rafters, which are all exposed, spring from the very floor, so that it is only in the very centre of the apartment that you have any chance of standing erect. The thatch oozes through the woodwork which supports it, the whole being begrimed with smoke and dust, and replete with vermin. There are no cobwebs, for the spider only spreads his net where flies are likely to be caught. You look in vain for a bedstead; there is none in the room. But there are their beds, lying side by side on the floor almost in contact with each other, and occupying nearly the whole length of the apartment. The beds are large sacks filled with the chaff of oats . . . The bed next the hatchway is that of the father and mother with whom sleeps the infant, born but a few months ago in this very room. In the other beds sleep the children, the boys and girls together. The eldest girl is in her twelfth year, the eldest boy having nearly completed his eleventh, and they are likely to remain for years yet in the circumstances in which we now find them. With the exception of the youngest children, the family retire to rest about the same hour, generally undressing below, and then ascending and crawling over each other to their respective resting places for the night. There are two blankets on the bed occupied by the parents, the others being covered with a very heterogeneous assemblage of materials. It not unfrequently happens that the clothes worn by the parents in the day-time form the chief part of the covering of the children by night. Such is the dormitory in which, lying side by side, the nine whom we have just left below at their wretched meal will pass the night. The sole ventilation is through the small aperture occupied by what is termed, by courtesy, a window. In other words there is scarcely any ventilation at all. What a den in the hour of sickness or death! What a den, indeed, at any time!

Let it not be said that this picture is overdrawn, or that it is a concentration for effect into one point of defects, spread in reality over a large surface. As a type of the extreme of domiciliary wretchedness in the rural districts, it is underdrawn. The cottage in question has two rooms. Some have only one, with as great a number of inmates to occupy it. Some of them, again, have three or four rooms, with a family occupying each room; the families so circumstanced amounting each, in some cases, to nine or ten individuals. In some cottages, too, a lodger is accommodated, who occupies the same apartment as the family. Such, fortunately, is not the condition of all the labourers in the agricultural districts; but it is the condition of a very great number of Englishmen – not in the back woods of a remote settlement, but in the heart of Anglo-Saxon civilization, in the year of grace 1849.

Similar conditions survived elsewhere. Another report by a journalist of the *Morning Chronicle* and quoted in the *Essex Standard* of 18th January 1850, gives an insight of the conditions in Essex:

Along the whole line of country from Castle Hedingham to Clavering there is an almost continuous succession of bad cottages. Among the worst of these might be mentioned those in the neighbourhood of Sible Hedingham, Wethersfield, Bardfield, Wicken and Clavering. Great numbers of these cottages are situated in low and damp situations, and their heavy and grass-covered thatches appear as if they had almost crushed the buildings down into the earth. Little or no light can ever find its way into the wretched, little windows, many of which are more than half stopped up with rags and pieces of paper. In point of fact there are many of them which, but for the possession of a chimney, would be nothing superior to many of the most wretched cabins which I have witnessed in Tipperary and many other parts of Ireland. At Manningtree also there are a considerable number of wretched one-room cottages, and those which are larger are generally tenanted by as many families as there are rooms.

Reports like these are to be found everywhere clearly indicating the condition of many cottages. It was not, however, only the condition of these cottages but also the inadequate number that caused concern. Throughout the nineteenth century there was a general shortage of rural cottages. Dr Hunter in the *Seventh Report of the Medical Officer of the Privy Council for 1864* enquires into this problem. In the 821 parishes taken in the enquiry the inhabitants had increased from 305,567 in 1851 to 322,064 in 1861, while the number of dwellings had decreased from 69,225 to 66,109. The number of inhabitants per dwelling had risen from an average of 4.41 to 4.87. In the 5,375 cottages included in the enquiry there were 8,805 bedrooms to serve 13,432 adults and 11,338 children, in other words an average of almost three persons per room. The law required an air-space in the bedrooms in common lodging houses to be 240 cubic feet per person, the Poor Law authorities required 500 and the Board of Health some 800 cubic feet, but in the average labourer's cottage at this time it was only 156. All over the country a great number of single-bedroomed cottages survived. In Lincolnshire, in the 1860s, in some eight parishes there were twenty-five cottages with three bedrooms, 193 with two bedrooms and 178 with one bedroom. In the Union of Swaffham, in 1867, in thirty-three parishes there were 303 cottages with three bedrooms, 1277 with two and 471 with only one. Considering the large number in most families the vast majority provided inadequate accommodation. Even where there were two or three bedrooms it was not always occupied by one family. Milton Abbas, built as a show village in 1786, where each cottage of four rooms was built to house

19. Cottages at Edensor, Derbyshire. Built by the Duke of Devonshire in 1838 after he visited Blaise Hamlet in 1835. The cottages and houses were larger than most of those in earlier Picturesque villages.

one family, was sixty years later inhabited by four families.

The lack of suitable drainage and sanitation arrangements, bad water-supplies, damp and draughty accommodation, the indifference in removing rubbish and the close proximity of farm animals all produced conditions in which disease could multiply. *The Report of the Royal Commission on The Employment of Women and Children in Agriculture*, 1843, gives one example:

In the village of Stourpain, in Dorsetshire, there is a row of several labourers' cottages, mostly joining each other, and fronting the street, in the middle of which is an open gutter. There are two or three narrow passes leading from the street, between the houses, to the back of them. Behind the cottages the ground rises rather abruptly; and about three yards up the elevation are placed the pigsties and privies of the cottages. There are also shallow excavations, the receptacles apparently of all the dirt of the families.

The matter constantly escaping from the pigsties, privies, etc., is allowed to find its way through the passages between the cottages into the gutter in the street, so that the cottages are nearly surrounded by streams of filth. It was in these cottages that a malignant typhus broke out about two years ago, which afterwards spread through the village. . . . I hardly visited a cottage where there were any attempts at draining. The dirt of the family is thrown down before or behind the cottage; if there is any natural inclination in the ground from the cottage, it escapes; if not, it remains till evaporated. Most cottages have pigsties joining them; and these add to the external uncleanliness of the labourer's dwelling.

James Caird,[6] the *Times* Commissioner, describes similar conditions in the village of Wark Castle, Northumberland, in 1850:

the very picture of slovenliness and neglect. Wretched houses piled here and there without order — filth of every kind scattered about or heaped up against the walls — horses, cows and pigs lodged under the same roof with their owners, and entering by the same door — in many cases a pigsty beneath the only window of the dwellings — 300 people, 60 horses and 50 cows, besides hosts of pigs and poultry — such is the village of Wark.

In 1875 the Public Health Act was implemented which applied to rural districts in a way that previous legislation had not. Charles Dilke, chairman of the 1885 Royal Commission on Housing, wrote on returning from the west of England that: "Enormous good seems to have been done by the working of the Public Health Act in these villages which were undoubtedly very bad indeed some years ago." The Commission found that, although some drainage schemes had been undertaken, they were not generally recommended for cottages and where they had been carried out the waste was usually conducted into the nearest ditch, often resulting in the pollution of water supplies. For the majority there was a privy, placed over first one and then another hole in the ground, which also contaminated the sub-soil and consequently the water supply. By the end of the nineteenth century it was generally recognized that the earth closet offered the best solution to the problem in the country, but unfortunately it was "very difficult indeed to get cottagers properly to use it"[7].

Early water-supplies, like early sewage-schemes, were often a hazard to health. J. L. Green describes one village where the mains water was obtained directly from the river and fed to the village, some two miles away, by gravity. Not only were the pipes blocked up from the debris drawn into them, but also further up the river another village, with a population of some 447, emptied all the slop water and liquid refuse into the river. In addition, drainage from privies, cowsheds, stables, farmyards and the like entered the river by means of small water courses. This was worse than the many other villages which took their water from a

20. Model cottages at Cambo, one of Northumberland's most attractive estate villages, begun by Sir Walter Blackett in the middle of the eighteenth century and added to later in the nineteenth century.

nearby pond or from the roadside in the winter.

Such conditions remained in many parts of the country throughout the century. *The Royal Commission on the Housing of the Working Class*, whose report was published in 1885, describes a state of affairs not very much different to that described in the *Reports of the Sanitary Condition of the Labouring Population* some fifty years before. Dr John C. Thresh, an Assistant Agricultural Commissioner, reports on the housing in the Chelmsford and Maldon district of Essex in 1893:

In nearly every parish there are so-called houses which are so structurally defective that they can never be converted into comfortable healthy dwellings, and which are becoming so decayed from age and neglect that they are really unfit for habitation. In many such instances neglect rather than age has been the cause of the dilapidated condition. In cottages, as with men, neglect leads to premature decay. These old places are built of a timber framework, studded outside with laths, and daubed over with plaster, or with a mixture of clay and chopped straw. Many of them have not been lined with lath and plaster inside, and consequently are fearfully cold in winter. The walls may not be an inch in thickness, and where the laths are decayed the fingers can easily be pushed through. Every time also a piece of plaster falls off outside the interior is exposed. The floors downstairs usually are of brick, laid directly on the ground, and are almost invariably damp, often indeed reeking with moisture. The bricks also get broken, the floor becomes uneven, and the bare earth may be exposed. To obtain some slight degree of comfort bits of board are laid down and several thicknesses of sacking and mats are laid upon the floor. These have to be renewed periodically, as the damp causes them to rot and become useless.

The roof is of thatch, which, if kept in good repair forms a good covering, warm in winter and cool in summer, though doubtless in many instances it serves as a harbour for dirt, for vermin, for the condensed exhalations from the bodies of the occupants of the bedrooms, and where persons suffering from the various fevers are nursed therein, possibly also for the infectious material which propagates such diseases.

The bedrooms in such houses are almost invariably in the roof, and if there be more than one, the one is usually entered from the other. The windows are small, formed of small panes of glass let into a leaden framework. These windows are usually of the most rickety description, and often do not open, but this defect is atoned for by the ease with which the air can obtain access to the room around the side of the defective frame. The utmost care has to be taken when cleaning them to avoid pushing them out. In fact, in many cases I do not know how the housewife contrives to rub the panes without someone pushing against them outside to prevent a catastrophe. Where a back window has been so pushed out the opening is usually found covered over with a piece of matting. The doors are of the rudest description. Probably when originally made there was some pretence to 'fitting', but there is none now. To keep out the draught bits of listing or pieces of wood have been nailed along the edges or over the cracks, but the result is rarely satisfactory. The fireplace also, and usually there is only one in the whole house, is of the most primitive character. A few iron bars are set in the brickwork, and as if further to prevent any economy in fuel, the bricks at the back crack and crumble away and rarely get replaced. The chimney corners are large and the chimneys wide, admitting sometimes of freer ingress for the external air than of egress for the air inside and the smoke from the fire.

Complaints are made of the draughtiness of even the best of these cottages. Often in winter the candle or lamp is said to be blown out, and yet it is impossible to tell where the draught came from. The ceilings are usually not underdrawn, and when the bedroom floor is in holes one can see into the room below. To prevent this, or to avoid the foot of the bed going through when moved, pieces of wood or of old iron are nailed over the apertures. I came across an old man who tripped over one of these holes (or a piece of wood which had been nailed over it, I forget which), and broke his leg, an accident which I only wonder is not more common.

Very few of these cottages have more than two bedrooms, many of them have only one, and usually, from their being placed in the roof, it is only possible to stand upright in the middle. The living rooms are low, many only from 6 feet to 6 feet 6 inches in height, yet the floor space is usually larger than the majority of the more modern cottages.

Apparently at the time when they were erected such conveniences as ovens, coppers, or sinks, were considered luxuries which the poor man could very well dispense with, but it is difficult to conceive how the tenants get along without them. Sometimes a bakehouse with brick oven has been provided for a group of cottages, but these are now little used, or used only as storerooms for wood, etc., if, indeed, they are not too dilapidated even for such a purpose. In many cases an attempt has been made to render these dwellings more habitable by putting down a wooden floor to the living rooms and substituting modern sash windows for the old leaded ones. Without an occasional coat of paint these window frames rapidly decay and in many cases they are now nearly in as bad condition as the ones then displaced. The floor boards are usually laid upon or within a few inches of the damp earth beneath, without ventilation under, and they speedily rot. To have raised them some inches above the level of the ground outside would have caused the rooms to be too low for an average adult to stand upright in, and to have removed some inches of the sodden earth and have laid a bed of concrete before putting in the floor would have entailed too great an expenditure, hence the present condition of things.

When these cottages were erected there were no sanitary authorities to prevent their being built anyhow and anywhere and consequently we often find them in the most unlikely and most unsanitary positions, in old gravel or marl pits, on ground which is constantly waterlogged, and far from any source of water supply except as can be obtained from polluted ponds and ditches.

Not all housing was so bad. Even by 1850 there were a number of reasonable cottages to be found on the large estates, although there were a great many more which we would condemn as unfit for human habitation. From 1850 to the end of Victoria's reign there was a slow but steady improvement. The three-bedroomed cottage, which had been rare at the beginning of her reign, had by the end become firmly established and most of the new ones were of this type. The *Report of the Royal Commission on Labour*, 1893, clearly shows this improvement and reveals that more attention was by then being paid to sanitary arrangements, the purity of water supplies and the removal of waste rubbish. It is equally clear, however, that not enough new dwellings had been built, and that a great number of labourers continued to be housed in older cottages, survivals from an earlier period, some of which had only one or two rooms.

Housing for All

The exploitation of the farm-worker – in places the agricultural wage was at the beginning of the twentieth century still at the eighteenth-century level of eleven shillings a week and only rose to fourteen shillings a week by 1914 – and the need for decent housing attracted the attention of both writers and politicians. Numerous investigations into wages, working conditions, and housing were made but the flight from the land continued and became a public issue. The number of farmworkers, which reached its peak in 1851 when 1,284,000 males and 199,000 females were employed in English agriculture, fell to around 665,000 by 1911. On the eve of the First World War, *The Land*, an unofficial report of the Liberal Land Enquiry Committee, appeared and severely criticized both landowners and farmers for the lowness of the wage, the bad working conditions and not only the state but also the scarcity of housing for labourers. In reply the Land Agents' Society, in their report *Facts about Land*, was critical of the generalization made, pointing out that many labourers preferred to have part of their wages in kind and that many were well housed and liked the security of a tied-cottage. It is also true that, during the first part of the twentieth century, farm labourers were better off than they had been earlier. Wages had increased and the price of ordinary foodstuffs had fallen and the vast improvement in both the labourers' diet and general living standards clearly indicates this. By 1902 a Board of Trade Report indicated that the diet of many farm-workers was equal to if not above that of the majority of workers in the country. They were eating more meat, bacon, cheese and sugar and drinking more milk and tea. In spite of this and although there was an improvement, the diet was still inadequate.

Of the many reasons Rider Haggard[1] found that poor housing was the principal one for the continuing drain of workers from the land:

> Of course the lowness of the wage and the lack of prospect will always cause a great number, perhaps a majority, of the more enterprising spirits to desert the land, but I am convinced that there are large numbers who would bide in their villages if only they could be sure of constant work and find decent homes in which to live . . .

Although the Housing Act of 1890 gave rural district councils power to build houses, and the Housing and Town Planning Act of 1909 gave the Local Government Board authority to encourage councils to begin building houses, only 315 had been constructed in rural areas between 1909 and 1912. It was still thought that private landowners and speculative developers could provide the housing needs of the population, but the building of new cottages was still uneconomical, for the rent which the labourer could afford did not provide an adequate return for the cost of the building. A cottage which could be built for £150 – the average cost of a three-bedroomed cottage in the years before the First World War – had to be let at between three shillings and sixpence and four shillings a week to give a reasonable return on the investment and provide a small sum for repairs. Considering that the agricultural wage at this time was not more than fourteen shillings this was a considerable amount to pay in rent.

Architects and builders took up the challenge to provide cheap rural housing and the building of Letchworth Garden City provided an excellent opportunity for them to experiment. One cottage – designed by F. W. Troup and built of studwork on a concrete raft – in the Letchworth exhibition of 1905 had two bedrooms, a living room and a parlour and could be built, it was thought, for £110. In 1913, Arnold Mitchell in response to a challenge in the Press, gave details of three-bedroomed brick cottages he had built at Merrow at a cost of £110. Built of 9-inch brick walls with a pantiled roof and a concrete raft foundation it had on the ground floor a living room 14 feet by 9 feet 11 inches, a parlour or bedroom 9 feet 2 inches by 8 feet 2 inches, and in addition a washhouse, larder and earth closet, which was approached from the outside but was placed next to the larder; on the first floor there were two bedrooms, built entirely in the roof space, one 12 feet by 9 feet 11 inches and the other 12 feet by 8 feet 3 inches. The ground-floor ceiling, which had a height of 7 feet 5 inches, was not plastered, the joists and the floorboards being exposed. In 1914 *Country Life* had a competition for a pair of three-bedroomed cottages which would not cost more than £250 the pair. It produced a number of interesting designs, the winner being one designed by W. Alex Harvey and H. Graham Wicks which only kept within the £250 stipulation by the use of reinforced concrete for the walls. Unfortunately many who built to this and the other designs found that they cost well over £300.[2]

In spite of all this the number of houses built by private enterprise was insufficient and it was finally left to the Government to act. In 1913 the need for new cottages became so great in many rural areas that the Government announced plans for building houses for the agricultural worker by the State in order to arrest the exodus from the land. Unfortunately this was on the eve of the First World War which curtailed house-building in both the public and private sectors. After the war Lloyd George made his plea for "homes for heroes to live in" but, like Richard Elsam's plea some hundred years before, little was achieved.

The demand for rural cottages also declined; the gradual improvement in farm machinery meant that fewer men were needed and with the bicycle and motor cycle becoming more common the need to build houses near the farms declined and the new ones were built in the villages. Local councils became the major builders of rural housing, often with a total lack of imagination and disregard of the local vernacular. Many council houses built in the villages in the late 1930s were still being constructed without bathrooms and water closets.

For many, however, there remained the older cottages, many of which were in poor repair. To assist in the repair of these cottages the Local Authority had power under the Housing (Rural Workers) Act of 1926 to give grants for the reconditioning of obsolete but structurally sound rural cottages. These grants remained in operation until after the Second World War, although they were not extensively used. In 1935 the Overcrowding Act, the first act to offer a special subsidy for the houses of agricultural workers, was passed. It set out a penal standard to be incurred if the number of persons per room exceeded a certain limit, and provided a subsidy to overcome such overcrowding.

During the second half of the twentieth century there has been a great improvement in rural housing. For the first time many cottages had mains water and electricity laid on. In the villages sewage schemes began to be built and elsewhere cesspool and septic tank drainage replaced the earth closet. Local Authority grants became available to improve and repair old cottages to bring them up to modern standards. New council houses, preferred by many farm-workers to their old cottages, continued to be built, while many of the old cottages were purchased by urban immigrants who had the money to repair them. Although perhaps detrimental to village life, these immigrants have done much to preserve many of our ancient cottages which would have otherwise been destroyed, helping to maintain this rich part of our rural heritage.

21. Nineteenth-century Picturesque cottage at Swan Green, Lyndhurst, Hampshire.

PART TWO

The Cottage – Its Development
and
Construction

Timber-framed Cottages

Until some four hundred years ago, with possibly the exception of Cornwall where no suitable timber was available, the use of wood as a building material in England was almost universal, even in areas where other materials, such as stone, were readily available. Timber was then plentiful, cheap and easy to handle, with the added advantage that every tree felled or woodland cleared provided additional land for cultivation. Although cottages with mud walls have always existed, it was only towards the end of the seventeenth century that timber was replaced, in some districts, by stone and later by brick as the principal building material. It is now difficult to believe that up to the seventeenth century, and sometimes later, the majority of English towns, including London, consisted almost entirely of timber-framed buildings.[1] Even Manchester remained a town primarily of timber-framed buildings well into the eighteenth century.

In medieval England much of the land was covered with forests with over sixty recorded in the thirteenth century.[2] By 1688 Gregory King estimated that the total acreage of coppices and woods in England amounted to some three million and, considering the depletion of the forests in the previous century for shipbuilding, fuel and building, it seems likely that at the commencement of the fifteenth century there were over four million acres of woodland.[3]

Oak, which thrives on deep clay, was the predominant timber used in building for its strength and durability was unbeatable and if allowed to dry naturally improved and hardened with age. At first its use was restricted entirely to buildings of the rich and it was not until the latter part of the sixteenth century that it was gradually introduced into humbler dwellings. William Harrison writing in 1577 states:

In times past men were contented to dwell in houses built of sallow, willow, plum-tree, hardbeam and elm, so that the use of oak was in manner dedicated wholly unto churches, religious houses, princes' palaces, noblemen's lodgings, and navigation; but now all these are rejected and nothing but oak in any whit regarded.

Generally the oak was not seasoned, its peculiar nature and the large scantlings required made it impracticable to dry out each baulk before use, and was used as soon as possible after it had been felled, being left to season in position. This probably explains the sag, warp and twist of many old buildings. Even when oak has been fixed in a building for centuries it will warp and twist, as if new, when cut up and used again. When oaks were plentiful the heart of the timber was used, later, with the depletion of the country's oak trees, builders were forced to economize not only in the size of scantlings used but also in the quality of timber for particular framing. This constraint probably explains the lack of uniformity of studs sometimes observed in some late sixteenth-century houses, and the use of rafters, particularly in cottages, where the bark has been left on.

Considering the limited and crude tools available to the early carpenters the skill in which they wielded them was remarkable. The oaks were felled with a narrow axe, although if the tree was large it was usually first cut around with a broad axe before the narrow axe was used on the heartwood. The larger trees were split into baulks by means of an axe and iron wedges, while they were cut into suitable lengths by a cross-cut saw, called a 'twart-saw'. This was a two-handled saw managed by two men. For the principal timbers (the posts, wall-plate and bressummers) these baulks were simply shaped by means of the broad axe and finally trimmed with the adze – an attractive feature on the timbers of many old houses today. For the smaller timbers (the studs, rafters, joists and floor boards) it was necessary to cut the baulks along their length to the required scantling. This was undertaken with a pit-saw worked by two men, one below and one above, with the baulk of timber being set over a pit. Two types of pit-saw were in common use: one, the great pit-saw, was similar in shape to the twart-saw but was longer with larger teeth set to facilitate cutting along the fibres of the timber – a rip-saw; and the other, the framed pit-saw, comprised a narrow blade fixed in the centre of a large rectangular frame to keep the blade taut, its principal use being for cutting boards. With the timber so prepared it was then necessary to cut the joints. All joints were mortice and tenon; the tenons being cut with a hand-saw – a one-handled tool with a scimitar-like cutting edge – while the mortices were formed either with a mallet and chisel or with a series of holes bored by an auger with the remaining wood being chopped away with a twibill.

All of this work was carried out at the carpenter's workshop or yard – the 'framynplace' – the timbers being framed on the ground and the components incised at the joints for assembling on site. These carpenters' numerals (*See* 22) were based on a system of Roman numerals, although not strictly Latin they were simple and effective. In Tudor times they were cut with a tool used for cutting straight lines, called a 'scribe', but later in Jacobean times, when the marks were smaller, they were cut with a gouge or chisel. The system was based on various combinations of I, V and X with the Roman IV becoming IIII, and IX becoming VIIII. This was necessary because on site the timbers could become inverted with IV being mis-read as VI and with IX being read as XI. Other variations were

22. Medieval carpenters' numerals.

$$\mathcal{X} \quad X \quad \mathcal{X} \quad \mathcal{X} \quad X$$

23. Medieval carpenters' marks.

that Vs were often cut upside down, while they also made one cross-cut do when both X and V were used together, or when two or more Xs were used. To assist in locating the various timbers to different parts of the building, carpenters' marks (*See* 23) were added to the Roman numerals. These were a series of circles and segments made with the use of a 'scribing compass', each mark denoting a particular section of the dwelling, such as the front, the rear, the sides, the floors, the roof trusses and so on. This enabled the timbers to be sorted easily prior to erection.

Once framed at the yard, the timbers were dismantled and transported to site and re-erected. The joints were in addition secured with heart of oak pegs, often referred to in medieval times as 'trashnails',[4] which were driven into holes, already bored by an auger at the yard, and left slightly projecting. Iron bolts, screws and nails were rarely used, for iron was then too precious to be employed. Moreover, had they been used the acid in the unseasoned oak would have soon corroded them, and although the dipping of bolts and nails was practised the expense involved restricted it to work of greater importance. The use of galvanized iron was unknown before the eighteenth century. However, whether the carpenters of the period were aware of the effect of unseasoned oak on untreated iron is unknown, but heart of oak pegs tightly fitted would have been equally effective as untreated bolts and more so than nails. So strong were these pegged joints that in 1530 John Palsgrave wrote "I shall pynne it so faste with pynnes of yron and of wodde that it shall laste as longe as the tymber selfe."[5] There is evidence that from the eighteenth century onwards nails began to be used, but by then softwood was in frequent use and even if oak was used the scantlings would have been small and easily seasoned. There is evidence that the timbers were not at first permanently fixed during erection. Joseph Moxon[6] states that plenty of play was left for the easy insertion of the summer and other beams, with the sills and posts not immediately pegged together but temporarily held by means of long tapering wooden pins, shaped rather like a tent-peg, called 'hook-pins'. These could not be driven in too far and consequently could be easily loosened and withdrawn.

Few medieval timber-framed buildings survive today and certainly no cottage for these, being constructed of inferior timber, have long since disappeared. Some small timber-framed houses do, however, survive from the thirteenth or fourteenth centuries but, although today they would be regarded as cottages, these buildings would probably have been the houses of yeoman farmers and other men of means and have, over the years, slipped down the social scale. At Boxted, Essex, there is a thatched cottage which, based on evidence of the notch-lapped joints used, has been dated back to some time in the thirteenth century and like the fourteenth-century cottage at Didbrook, Gloucestershire, would have been constructed for someone of some substance. Two small half-timbered cottages at East Bilney, Norfolk, which date from the beginning of the fifteenth century were, in fact, built to house the Bishop of Bilney.[7] At Treeton, Yorkshire, C. F. Innocent found a cruck cottage occupied by a coal-miner which had, five centuries before, been a manor house.[8] The number of surviving examples increase from the fifteenth century (at Shell, Himbleton, Hereford and Worcester, there is a thatched cottage which is in fact a diminutive fifteenth-century hall-house with every detail of medieval design in miniature) until they reach their peak in the great period of rebuilding in the second half of the sixteenth and first half of the seventeenth centuries. After the reign of Elizabeth timber-framed buildings were generally restricted to buildings of lesser importance and increasingly so until entirely confined to cottages.

Later, in the seventeenth century, the supply of home-grown timber decreased. This was due only in part to the Elizabethan housing boom, for the use of wood as a fuel had been widespread not only for heating but also for use in the iron-working furnaces and forges, particularly in the Mayfield and Ashburnham areas of Sussex. Also there was the ever-increasing demand for the building of ships, both for the navy and merchant fleet, started by Henry VIII and continued by Elizabeth. These factors, coupled with the failure to replant the felled trees, lead to the depletion of the forests of the South and Midlands. Even by the end of Elizabeth's reign timber was becoming scarce and it is reported that the price had risen by as much as 25 per cent in a few years and, in 1608, John Norden deplored the lack of oak, elm and ash which he called the "three building trees". The scarcity of oak was more acute in some areas than in others particularly in the eastern coastal areas, for instance in the Lincolnshire Fens where in the sixteenth and seventeenth centuries

24. Cruck cottage, Didbrook, Gloucestershire.

various species of timber, including poplar, lime and hornbeam, were often used. In the Breckland of Norfolk – the area around Thetford now covered with acres upon acres of fir plantations – it was ordered in 1604 by royal proclamation that all new houses must have their walls and window-frames constructed of brick or stone and that the cutting of trees for fuel must also cease. Therefore, in this area, as in other areas where timber was scarce, as timber-framed buildings decayed they were replaced by buildings constructed of other materials, until in some districts no timber buildings remained. During the Elizabethan and Jacobean periods oak was often taken from old buildings, which were for some reason being demolished, cut up into smaller sections and re-used, either in the construction of a larger building or two or more smaller ones.

By the eighteenth century building in half-timber began to decline. The country's forests were so depleted that it became of increasing necessity to import softwood from the Baltic and Scandinavia supplemented later, in the nineteenth century, with supplies from Canada and the United States. These softwoods, although easier to work than the traditional English hardwoods, were inferior in their structural capacity. Cottages using softwood framing continued to be built well into the nineteenth century, its use being fostered by the tax on bricks first imposed in 1784 and not finally abolished until 1850.

Today few towns, except for Chester and Shrewsbury, have more than isolated examples of timber-framed buildings their distribution being concentrated mainly in rural areas. The two main areas of distribution are the counties east of the limestone belt extending northwards to central Norfolk and Cambridgeshire, and the counties west of the limestone belt and north of the Severn estuary extending northwards to the east of the Pennines, through Nottinghamshire to York, and west of the Pennines into central Lancashire. In addition to these two main areas there are many other isolated pockets distributed amongst areas which are predominately stone or brick. There is, however, within the two major areas considerable variations not only in density but also in construction.

CRUCK-FRAME CONSTRUCTION

The distinguishing features of cruck construction is the use of inclined timbers, which rise from the ground to meet at the apex and serve as the truss of the roof, in contrast to other forms of construction where the roof is a separate structure carried on walls. Today, most crucks are to be found in cottages or barns and this has brought about the belief that cruck construction was restricted to the poorer classes. This is far from the truth, for most of those that have survived from the thirteenth and fourteenth centuries are far superior, both in size of scantlings and the quality of finish, to those of later centuries, and were constructed for the upper classes. This is not to say that in this period cruck construction was restricted solely to the upper classes, only that the inferior timbers used for general housing, not only in the quality of timber but also in the size of scantling, would have been less substantial and therefore have not survived. Also most of these early surviving crucks are what are known as 'base crucks', in which the crucks, although rising from ground level, are truncated well below the apex and are joined together at the head by

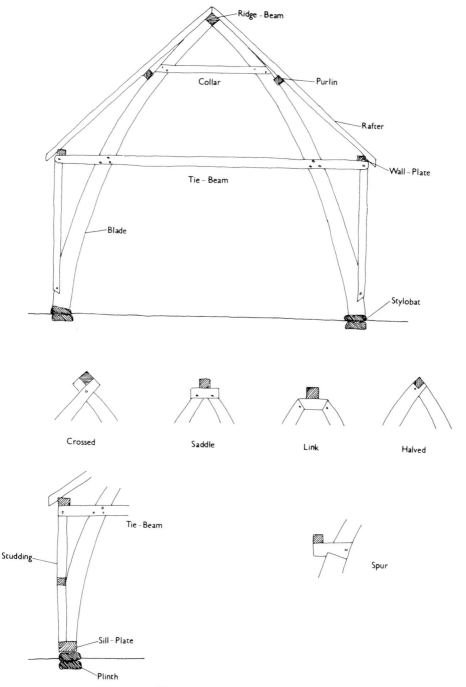

Ridge - Beam

Collar

Purlin

Rafter

Tie - Beam

Wall - Plate

Blade

Stylobat

Crossed

Saddle

Link

Halved

Tie - Beam

Studding

Sill - Plate

Plinth

Spur

25. Cruck construction.

means of a tie-beam or collar on which is fixed the roof structure. Very few true crucks survive from this early period and those that do are to be found in less ambitious upper class dwellings. By the mid-fifteenth century the use of crucks had been abandoned by the upper class and their use slowly slipped down the social scale until, by the end of the sixteenth century, they were restricted to those of humbler means, their use continuing in some areas into the seventeenth and early eighteenth centuries.

The most primitive forms employed in simple cots were of light construction. A pair of inclined poles, their butt ends charred and set into the ground, were lashed together, sometimes at the apex or sometimes just below the apex so that they crossed. Each cot comprised two or more pairs of poles with each pair linked at the apex with a lighter pole, called the 'ridge-beam', and lower down on each side by one or more additional poles, called 'purlins', which supported the covering of straw, brushwood or heather which reached to the ground.

From this form of construction developed what is known as cruck construction (*See* 25). Like the simple cot, early cruck construction made no distinction between roof and walls. The crucks timbers, commonly known as 'blades', were either cut from trees with, whenever possible, a natural curve, or from a tree trunk split in two halves to ensure a symmetrical arch. The shape of the timbers varied and could be straight, or elbowed (as in Dell Cottage, Harwell, Oxfordshire, and the cottage at Wilsford, Wiltshire) or with a smooth single curve (as the cottage at Dymock, Gloucestershire). Although the blades of the internal frames were always perfectly symmetrical, the outer ones, at the gable end, were sometimes constructed of unmatching blades. At first these blades were burnt and either placed on or set in the ground, but later they were supported on a stone foundation or 'stylobat', which gave the ends greater protection from rising damp. Later a continuous stone plinth was provided, on which was laid a timber sill-plate, framed at the corners, into which the ends of the blades were framed. At the top the blades were either simply butted or halved and crossed with each other, forming a cleft in which the ridge-beam could sit. In the simplest cottages two pairs of crucks would be employed, one at each end of the building, with the space between each pair being known as the 'bay'. The length of a bay was commonly 16 feet, although there are many exceptions recorded, and may be as little as 9 feet. Secured from cruck-frame to cruck-frame and running parallel to the ridge-beam were the purlins on which the roof was built. When the crucks were placed on a stone foundation a tie-beam was introduced, being fastened at a height of between 6 and 9 feet from the ground, and secured to each blade with oak pegs to ensure stability and prevent the feet of the crucks moving out. The gable ends were constructed of a simple framework filled in with wattle and daub and

26. Dell Cottage, Harwell, Oxfordshire.

into one was incorporated the door, which was at one time probably the only opening. The appearance of these early buildings can be seen from the illustration of the cottage which stood near Scrivelsby, Lincolnshire. It consisted of four straight inclined wood members, one at each corner, each standing directly on the ground and supporting the ridge-beam. The vertical gable walls were composed of wooden studs filled in with wattle and the whole overlaid with mud and plaster. It was a cottage of one bay and was, both in shape and size, not dissimilar to early cruck cottages corresponding closely to the recorded dimensions of a fourteenth-century booth in the village of West Auckland, Durham.[9] It was not, however, a survival of medieval times but was of comparatively

27. Cruck cottage, Wilsford, Wiltshire.

28. Cruck cottage, Dymock, Gloucestershire.

29. 'Teapot Hall', Scrivelsby, Lincolnshire.

recent construction, being built, it is believed, in the nineteenth century by a retired captain of a tea-clipper – hence its name, Teapot Hall. The building was, unfortunately, fired in 1945 to celebrate VJ Day.

Early cruck cottages were single-storey, but later, with the introduction of the tie-beam, it was possible to insert an upper floor. Reached by ladder, this upper storey would have been convenient for sleeping or for storage but would lack headroom. To overcome this problem the tie-beams holding the blades were increased in length until their ends were directly above the base of the blades. Vertical posts tied back with oak pegs to the foot of the blades – were introduced, which supported the ends of the tie-beams, and so for the first time it was possible, to have vertical walls while still using crucks. Wall-plates were carried on the ends of the tie-beams, from cruck to cruck, forming continuous beams on which the ends of the rafters could be fixed. Vertical side walls could then be provided, formed of a brick or stone plinth on which could be fixed a timber sill-plate with studding framed between this and the wall-plate. The walls were, however, entirely independent of the roof, which was held up by the tie-beams and cruck-frames, enabling the timber walls to be removed at a later date and replaced with brick or stone without disturbing the crucks or roof. The crucks could further be strengthened by the introduction of a collar situated close to the apex; and sometimes an additional collar, lower down but above the tie-beam, was also fitted to support the ends of the purlins. Because of the shallower pitch of the roof compared with that of the cruck-frame, it was necessary to provide a separate cantilevered bearer, or sometimes a duplicate blade, to support the lower purlins. Similarly, when the tie-beam was omitted to gain more headroom, bearers, called 'cruck-spurs', were also introduced to support the wall-plates.

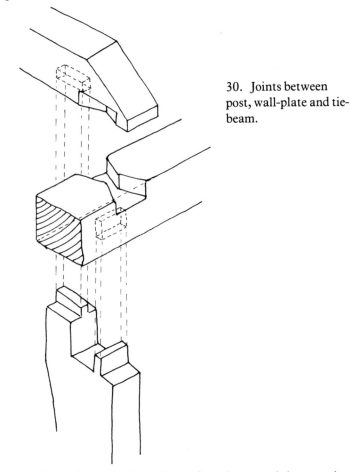

30. Joints between post, wall-plate and tie-beam.

It is evident from the incised markings found on cruck houses that the cruck-frame was assembled on the ground, jointed with oak pegs, and reared, one by one, into a vertical position so that the ridge-beam, purlins and wall-plates could be fitted into the sockets provided in the frame to link the crucks together. Because of the rearing process it was necessary to provide a substantial joint at the apex of the cruck-frame. The problem was overcome by various methods, the most common being the 'saddle', in which the blades were joined by a short piece of timber pegged at each end to the blades and onto which the ridge-beam sat. A simple cruck cottage could be erected very quickly and could be dismantled with ease and moved to a new position, and there is evidence that this did occur on occasions. The gable end of the fourteenth-century cottage at Didbrook, Gloucestershire, shows the complex development of cruck construction, the original cruck having been preserved within an enlarged post-and-truss structure of a later date. The original roof lines and the height of the former walls can clearly be seen.

There are two kinds of true crucks; the full cruck, where the blades start at ground level and meet at the apex; and the raised cruck, where the blades meet at the apex but start not at ground level but from some way up a solid wall. The two forms are similar in all other respects and often full crucks are referred to as raised crucks because the starting point at the foot, being concealed within the wall, is uncertain. The other principal form of cruck construction is the 'jointed' or 'scarfed cruck', in which a cruck-like form is obtained by jointing a vertical post and an inclined blade, of which neither are crucks. There are other forms of cruck construction which although not true crucks, are obviously related in some way to the cruck family. These are the 'raised based' or 'truncated raised cruck' where only the centre – the curved part of the cruck – is used, and the 'upper cruck', in which the blades rise to the apex from a tie-beam at or near eaves level. Like the base cruck, however, these other forms of cruck construction have little significance in cottage construction.

Although some of these other forms of cruck construction are found in other parts of the country full crucks are only to be found in the Midlands, North and West. This form of construction is entirely absent from the south-eastern counties of Cambridgeshire, Essex, Kent, South Humberside, Lincolnshire, Norfolk, Suffolk and Sussex, with only isolated examples being recorded in Surrey, Bedfordshire and Hertfordshire. It is also only found occasionally in the south-western counties of Devon, Dorset, Hampshire and Somerset. Clearly its scarcity in the south-western counties and absence from certain parts of East Anglia, Cambridgeshire and Lincolnshire can be attributed to the lack of suitable trees, but the reason for its absence from the other south-eastern counties of Essex, Kent and Sussex, where there were considerable forests, is not easily explained and several theories have been put forward. One is that the South and East were always influenced by the Continent, where this form of construction was never prevalent. This, coupled with the fact that the South-east was always more advanced and agriculturally richer than other parts of the country, suggests that this system was probably abandoned while still in use elsewhere. Even in areas where crucks survive the distribution varies greatly, both in number and date of construction. The social development of the country was not evenly spread, so that in one area, which was more prosperous, crucks were being replaced with other forms of construction, but in other areas they were still being built. Hence, while cruck construction was abandoned in most areas by 1700, in parts of Lancashire and Yorkshire cruck construction continued after this date. In Cumbria, around the Solway Firth, crucks, although of small scantling and not matching pairs, were still being used at the beginning of the nineteenth century.

Today more cruck-frames survive than is generally thought, for many have been either incorporated within enlarged buildings, hidden beneath a cladding of brick, stone or mud, or simply plastered over. This situation is particularly relevant to Cumbria, Derbyshire, Lancashire, Leicestershire and North Yorkshire, all with a relatively large number of cruck-framed buildings of which few are exposed, while in Devon, Dorset, Somerset, Nottinghamshire and Northamptonshire, although all with fewer examples, the same applies. However, there are within these areas some exposed crucks, particularly in Leicestershire, for example, at Cossington, Newtown Linford and Rothley. Hereford and Worcester is the county where most visible cruck-frames survive, particularly in the north-west of the county around Weobley, Dilwyn, Eardisland, Pembridge and Eardisley, an area now unrivalled in England. At Weobley, adjacent to the Red Lion Inn, is a cottage which has in one gable a remarkably well-preserved cruck-frame. This cottage, once part of a barn, is reputed to have been built in the fourteenth century. To the south, in the former county of Worcestershire, although a reasonable number of cruck-frames exist, few are exposed. Other counties where cruck-framed buildings can best be observed are: Salop, where they have even been incorporated in three churches — at Acton Round, Munslow and Stoke St Milborough; Staffordshire, with a good example at Haughton; Warwickshire where Woodbine Cottage, Maxstoke, also incorporates an original framed stack; and Cheshire, which, in common with other counties along the Welsh border, possesses a number of cruck-framed cottages. Many of these buildings can also be found in the northern part of Gloucestershire, in the area adjacent to Hereford and Worcester, in such villages as Ashleworth, Dymock and Sandhurst; while the Severn Valley is another area where a number survive. Cruck-framed buildings can also be observed in Berkshire and the adjacent areas of Oxfordshire, Wiltshire and Buckinghamshire. Ten cruck-framed buildings survive at Harwell, Oxfordshire, with Dell Cottage and Le Carillon having been dated by the radiocarbon process as 1445 and 1425 respectively; while in the northern part of Wiltshire at Urchfont, Pewsey and Wilsford cruck-frames can be seen, and further west at Lacock there is another excellent example.

Jointed crucks, the other form of cruck construction used in cottage building, are restricted to a smaller area than the true cruck for they are only found (except for a few isolated cases elsewhere, and then only in more important buildings) in Devon, Dorset and Somerset. In east and north of these counties they far outnumber true crucks, but are almost entirely absent from south Devon with only one example being found in Cornwall. In Dorset and Somerset they are predominately late medieval, while in Devon their use extended to the sixteenth century.

POST-AND-TRUSS AND BOX-FRAME CONSTRUCTION

The vast majority of timber-framed cottages in this country are not of cruck construction but of either post-and-truss or box-frame construction. Although to the casual observer these two types of construction may look similar, there are, in fact, some fundamental differences.

Post-and-truss, sometimes called post-and-panel, is to be found mainly in the West, Midlands and North – the area where most of the cruck construction occurs. It is closely allied to cruck construction, and follows the same basic principle, in that the weight of the roof is transferred to the ground by means of transverse frames spaced at determined intervals. Of the many variations of this form of construction, the most common consists of a pair of posts, one on either side of the building, held together at the top by a tie-beam. On this beam are fitted the principal rafters, held together, about half-way up, by a collar which is supported by two vertical struts, one end framed into the tie-beam and the other into the collar. These timbers form what is known as a 'tie-beam truss'. The weight of the roof is supported, like that in cruck construction, by purlins, which are framed into the trusses and wall-plates. Supported on these are the common rafters which in turn support the roof coverings. Diagonal bracings between the vertical posts and wall plates provide greater stability. Consequently the wall between the vertical post has no structural importance and is, therefore, generally of light construction formed with a combination of studs, braces and struts; the variation of pattern is unlimited.

Box-frame construction differs from post-and-truss construction in that the roof loads, instead of being transmitted to the ground by means of transverse frames, are taken on framed external side walls. These side walls provide a continuous bearing, there being no posts or division into bays. Consequently it was not necessary to provide trusses or purlins, the roof often consisting of pairs of rafters jointed near the apex by a collar.

The characteristic of box-frame construction is the predominance of vertical studs extending the full height of each storey wall, forming tall narrow panels. This arrangement differs from post-and-truss construction where, with the greater use of horizontal members, the panels are often square or almost square. In larger buildings ornamental timber work is also found within these panels, the quatrefoil being frequently used. This is not to say, however, that all buildings with closely spaced studs are of box-frame construction, or that all buildings with square panels are post-and-truss construction. Close studding belongs to the period 1475 to 1600 and was a typical Tudor extravagance. In the sixteenth century the studs of the box-frame construction began to be spaced further apart and it is, therefore, in some cases more difficult to distinguish between the two types. In these cases it is necessary to observe the gable-end of the building, for in post-and-truss construction the purlins protrude beyond the face of the gable (although sometimes on larger houses they are covered with a barge board) and are usually linked by a horizontal collar-beam across the face of the gable. In box-frame construction the purlins, although sometimes used, are less essential with the collar-beam less prominent and in most cottages are omitted completely.

Although there are these differences and, of course, many local variations, the two forms of construction have many essentials in common. First there is the plinth built of local material, either stone, flint, brick or occasionally baulks of oak, laid in a shallow trench directly on the subsoil with no foundation or damp-proof course. On top of this are the sill-beams framed together at the angle which, as long as they remain sound, acts as a kind of damp-proof course. Into these sill-beams are set the studs, framed into them at the bottom and at the top to the wall-plates, if the house is of one storey, or to the summer or bressummer if it carries the floor joists of an upper floor. The vertical timbers, both posts and studs, were often inverted with the butt-ends uppermost, a practice which, it has been suggested, helps in the preservation of the wood by allowing the sap to dry out by the same route as it entered the wood. Up until the middle of the sixteenth century these studs were placed at intervals approximately equal to their own width, but later, owing to the need to economize, the studs were set wider and wider apart. The spacing and scantling of the studs is generally a good indication as to the age of the building – the closer the studs and the larger their scantling the greater the building's age. Wind-braces were often incorporated in the walls. Early braces were curved and of smaller depth than the studs, being framed into the post and wall-plate or bressummer and halved over the intervening studs. Later ones were generally the same scantling as the studs and were straight with the studs being cut and framed into the braces. Floor joists, like studs, were, up until the early part of the sixteenth century, generally heavy beams about 8 inches wide and 5 inches deep and were laid on their side, broad side horizontal. After the early sixteenth century these, like studs, decreased in size, while at the same time were spaced wider apart. It was not, however, until into the seventeenth century that the practice of placing floor joists on their sides was superseded by the improved carpentry technique of placing them on their narrow sides. Where there is no jettying the beam carrying the floor beams is called the 'bressummer', and is often decorated with twisted leaves, running foliage, especially vines, and dragons, whose long bodies are suited to the narrow face of the beam. Where jettying (the projection of an upper storey beyond the one below) is employed, a beam, called the 'summer', carries the joist and is situated at the back of the overhang. Generally the ends of the joists were shaped into a quarter-round and left exposed, but in early jettying the ends were often concealed behind a fascia board. These are now rare for later their use was discontinued and once decayed they were not replaced. These fascia boards were often decorated with designs similar to those used on the bressummer. One of the few examples of a fascia board to be found today on a cottage can be seen on the row of late fifteenth-century cottages situated close to the church at Clavering, Essex. The present row of five cottages were originally one house and were converted, in the eighteenth century, to almshouses before being used as a workhouse in the early part of the nineteenth century.

Jettying is one of the most attractive features of timber-framed buildings. It can occur on one or more sides of a building and even, on occasions, on all four sides, projecting in some cases as much as 4 feet; though houses of the fifteenth century have sometimes only moderate projections with the South-east rarely attaining the boldness of the West. When the jettying was to one side only the construction was simple in that the floor joists were cantilevered over the wall below, but where two adjacent sides projected the process was a little more complex (*See* 32). It was necessary to change the direction of the floor joists, and to enable this to be undertaken one floor joist was replaced by a larger horizontal cross-beam, to which was framed another horizontal beam, called the 'dragon-beam', which ran diagonally to the corner. Into this beam were framed the floor joists, each pair set at right-angles, although sometimes the last few were framed at an angle. The outer end of the dragon-beam rested on and was framed into a massive corner post which was sometimes finely carved and often had a curved bracket to support the outer end of the dragon-beam. Additional supports to the jetty along its length were sometimes given by further curved brackets, occasionally carved, framed into the vertical studs. Once the floor joists were in position the framing of the next storey would continue as the floor below with the sill-beam being laid along the ends of the floor joist. Jettying was not restricted to one storey and if there was another one this too could be jettied as the floor below.

The reason for jettying has caused much speculation and at least four explanations could account for its use.

1 To increase the floor area of the building, which was certainly

31. Cottages at Clavering, Essex.

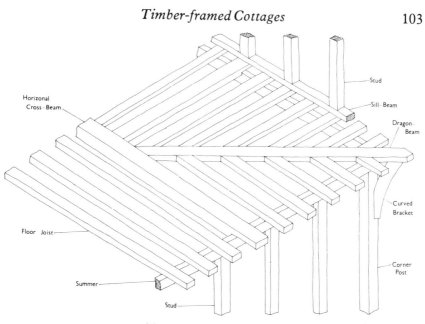

Horizonal Cross-Beam

Floor Joist

Summer

Stud

Stud

Sill-Beam

Dragon Beam

Curved Bracket

Corner Post

32. Jetty construction.

desirable in towns, without increasing the land on which the building sat. However, jettying was not restricted to towns and can be seen frequently in the depths of the country where there is no shortage of land. This can be explained by the desire of the country builders to follow a practice which had become fashionable in the towns.

2 The necessity to protect the building from damp. There were, of course, no gutter or downpipes in those days and without jetties much of the rainwater would, on windy days, pour off the roof and be blown back onto the face of the building. It is obvious that a building constructed of timber with wattle and daub infilling would not last long if incessantly soaked by rainwater.

3 Possibly the reason was purely structural. It has been suggested that jettying was used to overcome the difficulty of obtaining posts long enough to run the full height of the building, for with jetties it was only necessary to have posts of one storey height. Certainly it alleviated the difficult joint of three mortices from three directions at one point at the junction of the ground- and first-floor studs and floor joists with the bressummer.

4 Another structural reason is that the weight of walls and roofs transferred to the cantilevered end of the floor joist counteracted the possible sag in the floor joists caused by the weight of furniture, particularly as these were placed on their broad side.

All or any of the above explanations could be why jettying was used, although it could be simply that people who could afford it could not resist its obvious charm.

Jettying was first introduced in the fourteenth century – the earliest example is perhaps the row of low timber-framed cottages in the Goodramgate, York, next to the archway leading to Holy Trinity Church, built about 1320 for the chantry priests – and remained popular until the latter part of the sixteenth century when its use began to decline. By this time oak for building was becoming scarce and expensive and there was a need to economize in the amount of timber used for building. Jettying was considered wasteful and by the beginning of the seventeenth century had been replaced by a more economical method of construction in which the walls reached from ground to eaves. Robert Reyce,[10] writing in 1618, states that the wastage of timber had encouraged

> a new kind of compacting, uniting, coupling, framing and building with almost half the timber which was wont to be used, and far stronger as the workmen stick nott to affirme, butt the truth thereof is nott yett found outt soe.

Examples of this form of construction are commonplace throughout the areas where timber-framed buildings are to be found. Many of these cottages are of one and a half storeys, that is with the first floor in the roof.

Both the crown-post and queen-post roofs were used in early timber-framed buildings, but from the late sixteenth century, particularly for cottages, the collar-rafter roof was commonly employed in box-frame construction, while on post-and-truss a simple tie-beam truss was frequently used. The rafters of these roofs, like the floor joists, were laid on the broad side and, as with joists, the practice of laying them on their narrow side came later in the seventeenth century.

The process of re-assembling both post-and-truss and box-frame buildings on site varied from that used in cruck construction. Although there is some evidence that on cottages and small houses the gable ends, excluding the roof timbers, were assembled on the ground and reared – at Peterborough in 1541 payment was made "to Robert Hackman the wryght for rerying up grovyl end",[11] grovyl being a medieval name for gable – generally each member was erected separately. Palsgrave, in 1530, wrote "My housed is framed all redye . . . it wanteth but setting up".[12] The principal posts were erected on the sill-beam propped in position and many buildings have wedge-shaped sockets cut in their posts, approximately 6 feet from the bottom, into which these props were placed during erection. The wall-plates were then dropped onto the tops of the posts while the tie-beams were fitted to tie together both posts and wall-plates. The studs were placed into position at the same time, the temporary hook-pins withdrawn and the permanent oak-pegs driven in and left slightly projecting.

In discussing the distribution of the timber-framed cottage it is probably easiest to divide the country into three sections – the eastern counties, the southern counties and the West and Midland counties – but it must be remembered that there is no demarcation line and one area intermingles with that of another. The study of vernacular architecture should be on a basis of geological regions and not related to county boundaries.

The eastern counties comprise East Anglia with the adjacent counties of Essex, Hertfordshire and Cambridgeshire spreading westwards into Buckinghamshire and Bedfordshire. Unlike other areas, exposed timber work is less evident here, but one should not come to the conclusion that little exists, for hidden behind a coat of plaster is timber framing equal in craftmanship to any other in the country. This is particularly true of the villages of Suffolk and Essex, which possess a high proportion of timber-framed buildings generally covered in plaster, weatherboarding or, on occasions, refronted with brick, a common practice in Georgian times. This does not mean, however, that there are no exposed timber-framed buildings, for many villages have at least one, but perhaps most are to be seen at Lavenham, Suffolk's most resplendent wool town of medieval half-timbered buildings. In Butcher's Lane, Boxford, there is a delightful range of timber-framed cottages, while at Bildeston there is also a long row of attractive closely timbered houses. However, more typical are the villages of Cavendish (one of Suffolk's prettiest), Kersey, Nayland and, further east, Coddenham and Debenham, all of which contain mostly plastered cottages. Essex probably contains more timber-framed buildings than any other county, for *The Royal Commission on Historical Monuments* refers to about 750 buildings built before the Reformation. The inventory, which is in four volumes, contains all buildings built before 1714 and some villages, like Felsted, contain over one hundred entries. Once again, a large proportion of these are clad with plaster but exposed timber can be seen throughout the county in places like Clavering and Newport, which includes Monk's Barn, a Wealden house with diagonal brick-nogging. Both in Suffolk and Essex such features as jetties soon leave little doubt as to what is underneath. Timber-framed cottages are still quite numerous in the southern half of Cambridgeshire but once again, like its neighbours Essex and Suffolk, most are entirely masked under a coat of plaster. Typical are those at Barrington, Lode and Linton, many of which date from the seventeenth and eighteenth centuries. In the Fens, never rich in its supply of wood, timber-framed buildings are rare. Similarly, in the northern and western parts of Norfolk there are few, and where they do occur they are of fifteenth- or sixteenth-century date, built before the decline in timber, as at Little

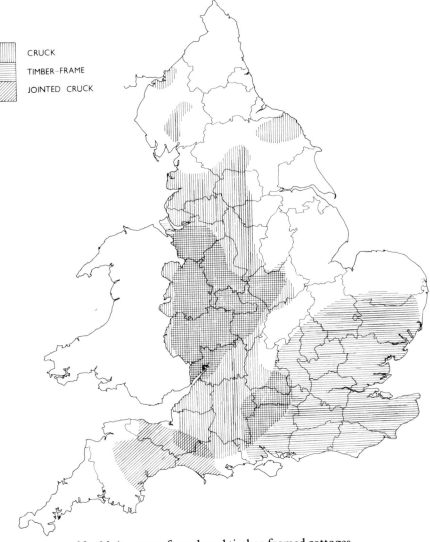

CRUCK

TIMBER-FRAME

JOINTED CRUCK

33. Main areas of cruck and timber-framed cottages.

Walsingham; while in the south in villages like the Pulhams they follow much in the traditions of those of Suffolk.

In Hertfordshire the transition from the plaster-clad cottages of East Anglia to the exposed timber-framed cottages of the Midlands takes place. In the eastern part of the county, at Ashwell, Barkway, Braughing and Westmill, with its attractive group of Tudor cottages standing between the green and the church, cottages are generally masked by a coat of plaster, or sometimes clad with weatherboarding, or on occasions a combination of both. In the central part the cottages are often of exposed timber and plaster infilling, like the sixteenth-century cottages around the green of the secluded and picturesque village of Bennington. Further west most of the cottages have exposed timbers, usually with brick-nogging like those near the village stocks at Aldbury. Although not rich in timber-framed cottages, Bedfordshire has a good number, mainly in the south and east, and like Hertfordshire has a mixture of both clad and exposed. In the villages of Buckinghamshire scores of timber-framed cottages are to be found intermingled with ones of brick. Generally of sixteenth- or seventeenth-century date with exposed timbers and brick-nogging, these cottages are to be found at Whitchurch, Newton Longville, Stewkley, Padbury and Weedon. Perhaps, the best group of villages, however, are the Claydons – Middle, Steeple and East, together with the hamlet of Botolph – of which East Claydon is perhaps the best, with several timber-framed cottages mainly of seventeenth-century date.

In the southern counties of Kent, Surrey, Sussex, Hampshire, Berkshire, Oxfordshire, Wiltshire and Dorset, timber-framed cottages are to be found in all areas east of the limestone belt. In the south-eastern counties of Kent, Surrey and Sussex there are plenty, except along the coast where the climatic conditions were too severe for much timber-building. Inland, especially in the Weald, timber cottages abound and there are many more than at first might be thought; as in the eastern counties, much of the half-timbering is masked over. Cottages with exposed frames can be seen throughout Kent, but can be observed at their best at Chiddingstone, with its fine group of cottages and houses of the sixteenth and seventeenth centuries; and at Chilham, with its picturesque central square surrounded with black-and-white timbered buildings. In Sussex, exposed half-timbered cottages can be found throughout the Weald, intermingled with those which are clad, like those in the villages of Wisborough Green and Rusper and elsewhere on the Downs in villages such as Amberley, Easebourne and Steyning. Surrey too has many, often, like its neighbours Kent and Sussex, clad with tiles or weatherboarding.

Perhaps here it is appropriate to mention the Wealden house, an important local variation. The characteristic Wealden house is rectangular, generally with close vertical studding, with a central hall, originally open to the roof, in the centre between projecting jettied wings at each end. The roof, hipped and lofty, covers the entire structure, not following the line of the central recess. Over a thousand examples survive, mainly in Kent, dating from the fifteenth and early sixteenth centuries. The term 'Wealden' is, however, a little misleading, for the greatest concentration is, in fact, not in the Weald but to the east of Maidstone. This type of

34. Village street, Chiddingstone, Kent.

house is also found in Sussex, the south-east corner of Surrey and occasionally in Essex, Buckinghamshire and elsewhere. Built for the well-
to-do yeoman farmers, they cannot be regarded as cottages except perhaps for the smaller example at Bignor, Sussex, a fifteenth-century
Wealden cottage with an infilling of brick and flint.

It is surprising that Hampshire, a county so poor in good building
stone, has no important timber-framed houses, although some of the
churches near the Berkshire border contain some impressive timber
work. However, timber-framed cottages, often thatched, abound in the

35. 'The Old Shop', Bignor, Sussex. A fifteenth-century Wealden house.

36. Cottage row at
Shottery, Warwickshire.

37. Timber-framed and brick cottages, Padbury, Buckingham-shire.

38. Timber-framed cottages, Nether Wallop, Hampshire.

39. Typical timber-framed cottage found on the eastern side of the limestone belt in Wiltshire, this one at Ablington is dated 1665.

county, with some of the best being in the villages of Chilcomb, Itchen Stoke, Martyr Worthy, Tichborne, Wherwell (Hampshire's showpiece village) and the Wallops – Nether, Middle and Over – three villages strung along the willowed Wallop Brook which are, like the other villages, an enchantment of framed thatched cottages. Further west, in Dorset, timber-framed cottages are rare, surviving only here and there as at Cerne Abbas, which has an attractive row of jettied houses some with exposed timbers, and occasionally in villages like Okeford Fitzpaine, which has a pleasant group near the church. The building materials of Wiltshire are as diversified as its own geology and although the use of timber is not predominant it is found in most Wiltshire villages away from the limestone belt. Villages like All Cannings, Upton Scudamore, Horton, Wilsford, near Upavon, all have pleasant timber-framed cottages, many of them thatched. At Bishops Cannings, one mile south-east of the church, there are two thickly-thatched timber-framed cottages, and at Ablington, near Figheldean, there is another nice group, one of which is dated 1665.

Berkshire was greatly reduced in size in the re-organization of local government in 1974, with the result that many of the attractive villages to the north of the former county were transferred into Oxfordshire. Berkshire's loss was certainly Oxfordshire's gain for villages like West Hagbourne, Steventon, Blewbury and Kidmore End, as well as many others, all with many attractive timber-framed and thatched cottages, were all lost. However, Berkshire is lucky to possess such villages as East Garston, Waltham St Lawrence, and nearby White Waltham and Sonning, the prettiest of all the Thames riverside villages, all of which contain attractive timber-framed cottages. Generally speaking the frame is exposed, sometimes blackened and sometimes left in their natural state, with the panels filled in with brick-nogging or plaster, generally painted white, and the roofs thatched. Apart from the villages already mentioned, Oxfordshire has, in the south-eastern part of the county away from the limestone belt, a number of timber-framed cottages.

The Welsh border counties of Gloucestershire, Hereford and Worcester, Salop and Cheshire, including Lancashire and the Midland counties of Leicestershire, Warwickshire, West Midlands and Staffordshire, were always rich in timber, and continued to be used for the construction of cottages well into the eighteenth century[13] for unlike the forests of the South they were not so depleted by iron furnaces, shipbuilding and the like. Cottages in these areas are not only of cruck construction but more commonly of post-and-truss construction, framed in squares or with panels slightly higher than they are broad, usually plastered or filled with brick-nogging and nearly always painted white with the timber painted or tarred black, thus giving the famous 'black-and-white' or 'magpie' effect which can look uncommonly attractive. Although curved or straight bracings are not uncommon the elaborate patterning found in the larger houses of Cheshire and Lancashire are usually absent from cottages.

Today, Lancashire is generally regarded as a brick county, but this is something new for even as late as the beginning of the eighteenth century brick buildings were rare, only gaining popularity because of the growing scarcity of wood. For many centuries timber was plentiful and up to the end of the seventeenth century timber-framed buildings prevailed everywhere away from the Pennines, as far north as the River Ribble. Also, considering the industrialization of Lancashire it is remarkable how many still exist, often of cruck construction, but now generally hidden behind a later cladding of brick or stone. Timber-framed houses and cottages are abundant in Cheshire, which at one time had perhaps as high a proportion of these buildings as any other county in the country. Unfortunately during this century many of these splendid buildings have been wantonly destroyed, which indicates the number that once existed for many still survive, among them many cottages.[14] Although there are still a number of cruck-framed cottages, most are of post-and-truss construction with square or almost square panels, like those to be seen in the villages of Bunbury, Duddon, Lower Peover, Mobberley and Prestbury. Salop, like other Welsh border counties, abounds with black-and-white cottages especially in the low-lying country away from the hills. Preston Brockhurst, Claverley, Knockin, Stanton Lacy, Milson and Neen Sollars all contain typical black-and-white cottages.

Few areas in England can possess such a wide variety of timber-framed buildings as that in and around the villages of Eardisland, Weobley, Pembridge, Eardisley, Luston and Dilwyn in the north-western part of Hereford and Worcester. Here the attractive church belfry tower at Pembridge; major houses like Luntley Court, Dilwyn, The Ley, Weobley (an eight-gabled farmhouse built in 1589 and one of the most attractive in England), Bury Farm, Luston, Lower Burton Farm, Eardisland; barns like those at Cholstrey Court; dovecotes like that at Luntley Court; as well as numerous smaller houses and cottages, are all built of timber. Half-timbering is not confined to this district for elsewhere cottages, singly or in groups of three or four often with a large external stone chimney, a common feature in this part of the country, are to be seen everywhere. To the east of the county – the former county of Worcestershire – brick is more prominent, but outside the towns, in the country areas, a great amount of timber-framing still survives. Like the remainder of the county most are of post-and-truss construction and like the other counties of the West are almost entirely 'black-and-white'. Abbots Morton is a striking example, being a village predominately of black-and-white houses and cottages of an outstanding variety of design. At one end of the village street, around the church, are the larger houses and at the lower end are the smaller houses and cottages built on long narrow plots built end-on to the road. Several of the houses and cottages show alterations to their frames, either by the raising of the roof or by modernizing, which probably took place in the seventeenth century. Other villages like Chaddesley Corbett, Harvington, Inkberrow and Norton all contain many attractive timber-framed cottages.

A number of pleasant black-and-white cottages are to be found in Gloucestershire along the Severn Valley in such villages as Great Washbourne, Longhope, Longney, Redmarley D'Abitot, Woolstone and Wormington, and stretching to the escarpment of the Cotswolds, where the villages of Didbrook, Stanton, Willersey, Weston-Subedge and Mickleton mark the gradual transition from timbered cottages to those constructed of stone.

Of the four Midland counties timber-framing plays the most important part in Warwickshire and rural West Midlands, as one can see in such towns as Stratford-upon-Avon. Cottages are plentiful in all locations except to the east of the county along the limestone belt. The row

40. Old cottages at Blewbury, Oxfordshire. The tile-hung gable end to one of the cottages is a common feature in this part of the country.

41. Seventeenth-century cottages, Wherwell, Hampshire

42. Cottages, Aston Cantlow, Warwickshire.

43. Seventeenth-century timber-framed cottage, Rempstone, Nottinghamshire.

of timbered, thatched and tiled cottages at Shottery and the cottage at Salford Priors are typical of those built throughout the county. Close vertical studding, similar to that found in the South and East, can often be seen in the towns like Stratford-upon-Avon, larger villages like Alcester – which has a delightful row in Malt Mill Lane with a large overhang – and even on occasions in the smaller villages like the row of cottages at Aston Cantlow. In Staffordshire they do not survive in anything like the number which still exist in its neighbouring counties of Cheshire and Salop. However, villages as wide apart as Betley in the north-west and Alrewas (a beautiful tranquil village near the Derbyshire border) in the south-east, as well as Kings Bromley and Abbots Bromley, all have pleasant groups.

Half-timbered cottages are to be found in Leicestershire in all the villages away from the limestone belt and so one finds stone cottages to the east where good building stone was plentiful, with timber-framing being confined to the west. Villages like Birstall, Cossington and Rothley have a number, some of cruck construction. Sometimes cottages with narrowly placed studs are to be found, like the one close to the entrance to the church at Cossington which has many diagonal braces. At Hugglescote a cottage south of the church carries the date 1583 carved on one of the external beams and is, according to Dr W. G. Hoskins, the earliest dated cottage in the county. Timber-framed buildings continued to be constructed well into the seventeenth century, not only post-and-truss construction but also cruck. Evidence of the continuing use of timber can be seen in a cottage at Shearsby which has, on the tie-beam under the gable, the date 1669, but which was still built of timber with an infilling of wattle and daub.

Elsewhere in the country timber-framed buildings are rare except for isolated areas. In the South-west timber never played a significant part in domestic architecture. Apart from York, which still possesses many timber-framed buildings, including the Shambles – a medieval street so narrow and picturesque that the houses almost touch with their overhangs – West, South and North Yorkshire as well as North Humberside possess little timber-framing. Likewise, Lincolnshire and South Humberside, counties where oak was scarce by the seventeenth century, houses even with a simple timber frame are uncommon although a few mud-and-stud houses are to be found, often encased in brick, either for their entire height or up to window-sill level. Surprisingly, Nottinghamshire has few timber-framed cottages and these are to be found only in a handful of villages in the extreme south-west, like Sutton Bonnington, Rempstone and Normanton-upon-Soar, in the valley of the Soar and Trent. As one would expect, in the North-east timber-framing is absent and it is of some surprise to find in the North-west some in places like Kendal and Hawkshead, Cumbria.

44. Seventeenth-century cottage at Eastwood, near Tarrington, Hereford and Worcester.

45. Timber-framed cottage, Cossington, Leicestershire.

LATE TIMBER-FRAME CONSTRUCTION

So far, the timber-framing under review has been mainly of a substantial nature, generally constructed of oak. Even from the sixteenth century, however, timber-framed buildings using slight and inferior timbers were constructed and this was especially true of cottages. By the eighteenth century the wealthy were abandoning their old houses and converting them into tenements or else pulling them down and replacing them with more spacious houses of brick or stone. However, for the poor, timber remained an important material in all areas where it was readily available. In the Lincolnshire Wold timber-framed cottages were constructed in the latter part of the seventeenth and the early part of the eighteenth centuries, using a very slender frame with the studs rarely having intermediate rails, the only cross rail was one fixed to the inside of the frame to support the floor joists. Some of these cottages, known as 'mud-and-stud', still exist here and there in villages like Coningsby, Somersby and Thimbleby.

The size and quality of the timber used decreased for several reasons. Obviously the decline of suitable timbers and its increase in price had some bearing, but also the improved techniques in carpentry and the availability of suitable cladding materials – plaster, weatherboarding and tile-hanging – also contributed. Although many cottages, particularly in the South-east and East Anglia, are clad, there are some examples in the South, West and Midlands built in the eighteenth century, and some, like a group at Ampthill, from the nineteenth century which have their timbers exposed. The timbers used were slight and straight but the construction was similar to that of earlier buildings, though the sparing use of timber gives a somewhat different visual effect.

Often these timbers came from demolished buildings, which were cut up to provide timbers of smaller scantlings for re-use, but by the eighteenth and nineteenth centuries, with the availability of imported softwood of uniform section and the manufacture of cheap machine-made nails, oak was no longer regarded a necessity and the elaborate joinery techniques of earlier timber-framed buildings were no longer required. The technique used was similar to box-frame construction in that there were no load-bearing posts, the wall comprising of studs of approximately the same section spaced at about 18 inches apart to form one continuous load-bearing wall. Sill-plates and wall-plates were used in a similar manner to box-frame construction with intermediate noggings introduced for greater stability. Window and door openings were simply formed in the studwork; an extra large or a double stud being introduced at each side, with a larger timber over them to form a lintel. As previously

46. Cottage, Sledge Green, Hereford and Worcester.

mentioned joints were generally omitted, the timbers being nailed together. Cottages using this method were quick and cheap to erect, particularly when clad with weatherboarding. Examples of these cottages, built in the eighteenth and early part of the nineteenth centuries, can be found throughout the South-east – in Kent, Sussex and Surrey, principally in the Weald and especially at Groombridge, Kent, an outstanding village in an area rich in attractive villages, which has numerous eight-eenth-century cottages around a triangular village green, and Hawk-hurst where, in the newer part, eighteenth-century weatherboarded houses intermingle with its shops. They are also to be found in the eastern counties of Essex, Suffolk and particularly Cambridgeshire, in the villages of Fen Ditton, Lode and Swaffham Bulbeck, which has a number of terraces of single-storey cottages with attics, framed in softwood and plastered (many incised to simulate ashlar), built in the first quarter of the nineteenth century.[15]

WEATHER-PROOFING

Two basic methods of weather-proofing timber-framed buildings were used; one by infilling the open panels between the studs and the other by cladding the entire building.

INFILLING

Although local variations exist, the earliest and by far the most common form of infilling was what is known as 'wattle and daub' (*See* 47c). To provide adequate support for the daub it was necessary to introduce additional timber into the open panels. This timber was called the wattle and many local variations were used. Where the panels were square it was usual to have upright staves, usually of hazel, cleft chestnut or oak, which were pointed at one end and shaped at the other and sprung either into holes in the upper horizontal member and a groove in the lower one or into grooves top and bottom. These staves were generally fixed at about 10 or 12 inches apart, although they could be up to 18 inches apart, and between them were interwoven pliable wands, usually unbarked hazel or ash sticks, to form a hurdle-like panel. In better class work riven oak or beech laths were substituted for the hazel or ash sticks. In the days of close studding often only uprights were used, sometimes merely wedged between the horizontal members but more often fixed in a similar method as staves. Sometimes when the panel was tall a short cross-piece was wedged between the studs, on which were tied the uprights. The materials used for tying these uprights varied greatly; tendrils of wild clematis, green willow withes, thick string composed of twisted grass, and thin strips of leather were all used. Alternatively the uprights were omitted and horizontal sticks were used, slotted into grooves in the studs. In the sixteenth century when the studs began to be placed further apart, stout cross-pieces were fixed horizontally between the studs and into V-grooves cut into their sides. To these, upright wands were either woven or tied. This last method was commonly employed in East Anglia. All these various methods of wattle, with the possible exception of laths,

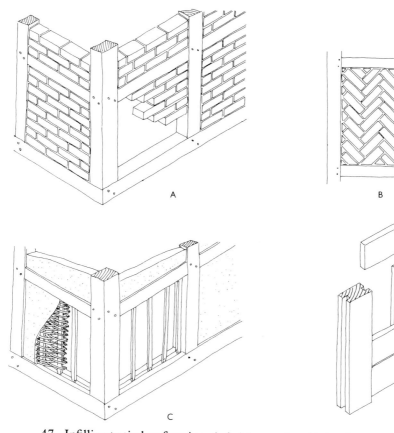

47. Infilling to timber-framing: A. brick-nogging; B. herring-bone;
C. wattle and daub; D. slab infilling.

were constructed and inserted without the use of nails.

To this rough panel was applied the daub. Its consistency varied from
district to district, but generally comprised wet clay or mud mixed with
chopped straw or cow-hair with sometimes the addition of cow-dung.[16]
The materials were carefully mixed and, where available, lime was also
added as an ingredient. In 1530 Palsgrave stated that "daubing may be
clay onely, with lime plaster, or lome that is tempered with heare or
strawe".[17] The daub was then thrown onto both sides of the wattle at the
same time so as to fill in the interstices between the sticks. It was then left
to dry before successive layers were applied to reach the required thickness. Although the daub set hard, it was liable to shrink or swell in dry or
wet weather and to overcome this, where possible, the panels were finished
with a thin coat of plaster – a mixture of lime, sand and cow-hair –
and then limewashed. In cottages, however, an earth ochre wash, usually
yellow or deep red, had often to suffice.

From the seventeenth century bricks were becoming cheaper and more
widely used. Consequently when the old wattle and daub became

decayed it was often removed and substituted with an infilling of brick (*See* 47a). First the practice was restricted to larger houses, but later, as bricks became cheaper, it was also used on many cottages. It is difficult to say why this transition took place for old bricks were usually more porous than good plastered daub, so that dampness was encouraged, while the weight of the bricks often caused structural problems as well. One explanation for this transition is that by the end of the seventeenth century the old craft of daubing, which was a specialized one, was declining, as more and more houses were constructed of brick. This changeover to brick-nogging, as it is called, took place at different times in different areas. There is no proven evidence of its use before the seventeenth century[18] and, in fact, much is Victorian, probably being a replacement of earlier defective brickwork. Today brick-nogging is found in all areas where timber-framed buildings survive.

Although brick-nogging was used as a replacement for wattle and daub, in the seventeenth and the early eighteenth centuries small houses and cottages using both a timber frame and brick-noggings were erected. Today it seems curious that a timber frame was considered necessary when constructing in brick. At Nuneham Courtenay, Oxfordshire, when Lord Harcourt had the new village constructed in 1761, a timber frame was incorporated into the gable ends of the brick cottages. Today these frames have mostly gone, but on some the remains, forming trusses, can still be seen. The group of semi-detached brick and timber cottages at Ampthill, Bedfordshire, dated 1812 to 1816, comprises vertical studding with a cross-rail above the ground-floor windows and long straight braces from post to post. The main studs are 4 inches wide, the subsidiary ones 2 inches wide with the studs spaced approximately 1 foot 2 inches apart. The cottages originally had a main front room, and a narrow service room at the rear with a staircase leading to the attic above. The entrance door was originally in the gable end with the fire in the party wall.[19] In all these timber-framed buildings the framing was slight in comparison with earlier framing.

On cottages the bricks were generally laid in stretcher bond, although sometimes they were laid in a haphazard manner with no consistent pattern. Herring-bone pattern (*See* 47B) was another common pattern and the most attractive, its use being, however, generally restricted to larger houses. Often a combination of stretcher bond and herring-bone pattern was used. In Essex and Suffolk the brickwork was often recessed and plastered, while in Cheshire, Salop, Hereford and Worcester and Warwickshire the brickwork was usually limewashed.

Although wattle and daub and brick-nogging were the two commonest forms of infilling, many other local materials were used. Local building stones were employed; at Albury, Surrey, there are some cottages with Burgate stone infilling, while in the same county, at Ash, as well as at

Prinsted, near Southbourne, flint is found. At Bury, Sussex, under the South Downs, there are some cottages with chalk filling. Tiles, slates and slabs of stone were also used in close-studded buildings; here the studs had grooves in their sides in which these were fitted horizontally, one above the other (*See* 47D). In West Yorkshire, and occasionally in Lancashire, sandstone flags were used, while the infilling around Stamford, Lincolnshire, was often Collyweston slates plastered both sides. Oak boards, placed vertically where the studs were spaced close together and horizontally where the studs were spaced wide apart, were also employed, and at Penshurst, Kent, by the churchyard, an example still survives of vertical board infilling. In all these forms of infilling, where slabs fitted into grooves, it would have been necessary for them to be inserted at the time of erection of the timber frame and not, like wattle and daub or brick-nogging, inserted afterwards.

The exposed timber-framing between the panels if left untreated weathered to a silvery hue. Whether this was general practice throughout the country is unknown, but it certainly was in East Anglia and the south-eastern counties. In the Welsh border counties, as well as Lancashire, Staffordshire and Warwickshire, much of the timber work is blackened, with the infilling whitewashed, giving spectacular results, especially in villages like Abbots Morton, Hereford and Worcester. It is doubtful, however, how many, if any, of these 'magpie' buildings received this black-and-white treatment when first erected. Certainly the practice is old, for John Gage,[20] writing in 1822, quotes from the household account of Sir Thomas Kytson for 1574: "To plastering and whitening the fare front of my Mr his house ... with the blacking of the timber work, xlijs, vjd". No permanent black, however, became available until tar and pitch were manufactured from coal in the nineteenth century. It therefore seems likely that most of these houses, especially the cottages, were treated in Victorian times or later. Such is the passion for black and white buildings in this area, and increasingly so elsewhere, that one finds brick buildings treated to simulate timber-framing. In Essex, Kent, Suffolk and Sussex most of the exposed timber is left untreated and with the plastered panels often colour-washed, they produce a softer effect than those of the West.

CLADDING

A timber-framed building always moves, expanding in wet weather and contracting in dry. With an infilling of wattle and daub, which often shrank, decayed or came away as the house settled, or brick-nogging, which could not be adequately bonded to the timbers, the house was often draughty and damp. To overcome this problem it was necessary to devise some method of cladding the face of the building to keep out the

48. Nineteenth-century timber-framed cottage, Lode, Cambridgeshire.

49. Timber-framed and thatched cottages were at one time common in the southern and western parts of Lancashire. This one, dated 1665, is at Hale, near Liverpool.

weather. This was achieved by three methods – plastering, tile or slate hanging, and weatherboarding.

The external plastering of timber-framed buildings was generally confined to the eastern part of the country and, although found fairly frequently in the northern part of Kent and to some extent in Surrey, it is in Suffolk and the surrounding counties of Cambridgeshire, Essex, Hertfordshire, Norfolk and, further westwards, in southern Bedfordshire, that most is to be found. Within this area it is in the villages of Essex and Suffolk that it can be seen at its best. In the villages of central and southern Suffolk in such delectable villages as Boxford, Kersey, Clare, Nayland, Hartest and Cavendish, not much timber-framing is exposed yet nearly every house is built of wood. Similarly in Essex, in villages like Finchingfield, Great Bardfield, Wethersfield and Manuden, most of the timber-framed buildings are plastered externally. In the southern and western parts of Cambridgeshire again many of the cottages, particularly those built around the seventeenth and eighteenth centuries, like those around the exceptionally large green at Barrington, are plastered. These plastered timber-framed cottages are also found in North-east Hertfordshire where Ashwell, a village of well-preserved timber-framed cottages, is perhaps the best.

The plastering of half-timbered houses began in the sixteenth century, and by the latter part of the seventeenth and eighteenth centuries had become common practice in East Anglia and the South-east, coinciding with the improved quality of lime plaster and the availability of wooden laths. William Harrison, clearly indicates that on larger houses it was widely used providing greater comfort to the inhabitants:

In plastering likewise of our fairest houses we use to lay first a line or two of white mortar, tempered with hair, upon laths, which are nailed one by another . . . and finally cover all with the aforesaid plaster, which, beside the delectable whiteness of the stuff itself, is laid on so even and smoothly as nothing in my judgement can be done with more exactness . . . whereby the rooms are not a little commended, made warm, and much more close than otherwise they would be.

It is obvious that during this period many old houses were clad, but those erected during the eighteenth century, when building in timber was in decline and inferior quality timbers of smaller scantlings were used, were frequently intended from the outset to be plastered. Today there is a desire by some restorers of old buildings to strip away the plaster and expose the underlying timbers which were in many cases, in fact, never intended to be exposed. It means, however, that even buildings where the timbers were originally meant to be exposed, the subsequent plastering process, which often necessitated the driving in of numerous

50. Seventeenth- and eighteenth-century timber-framed cottages,
Barrington, Cambridgeshire.

51. Timber-framed and plastered cottages, Euston, Suffolk.

nails to secure the laths, leaves unsightly holes disfiguring the face of the timber.

The walls would generally be plastered externally and internally. In these cases the walls were hollow and in some areas the voids were filled with chaff. Riven laths were closely spaced and nailed to both faces of the studs and if necessary, for additional support, intermediate members were introduced (*See* 52). The plaster would then be applied to each face. Plastering of the exterior, however, was sometimes combined with wattle and daub infilling. This form of construction was found during renovations, in 1951, of an early eighteenth-century cottage at Pebmarsh, Essex.[21] Here the cross-pieces of the wattle were nailed to the external face of the studs with the staves set behind and tied to them. On the inside a thick layer of daub was applied to the wattle, while on the outside a thin coat, extending over the whole surface, was keyed to the wattle and subsequently plastered over.

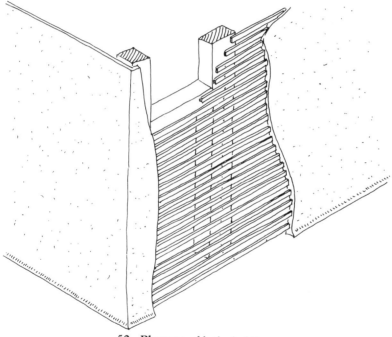

52. Plaster and lath cladding.

In the Lincolnshire Wold a similar technique, known locally as 'mud-and-stud', was used. As previously mentioned the cottages here were constructed with slender timber frame with the studs, visible occasionally on the inside, merely having intermediate rails and the only cross rail was to support the floor joists. The panels were therefore of considerable size and were covered with thin staves fixed to the outside of the frame with the daub being carried across the outer face of the timber to protect them. At Great Cotes, Lincolnshire, these cottages "were formed by driving in rows of stakes and then trampling in with the feet, between the stakes, wrought clay mixed with chopped straw".[22] Like the other methods the whole face was subsequently covered with a coat of plaster. Some cottages using this form of construction still exist, particularly in the southern part of the Wold, in such villages as Coningsby, Somersby and Thimbleby. This technique of daubing the panels between the framework and at the same time extending it over its face had been practised to some extent from the Middle Ages, particularly in towns, as a precaution against fire.

A similar form of construction is found on the Lancashire plain and known as "clam-staff and daub". Here, however, unlike the mud-and-stud walls of Lincolnshire, which always incorporated a complete timber-frame, the houses are generally of cruck construction with no frame, the walls being built of clay stiffened with thin studs morticed to the wall-plate and sill. An example of this form of construction can be found at a cottage at Diglake, Scarisbrick.

Early plastering was of poor quality but by the seventeenth and eighteenth centuries it had improved. Various mixes were used but ideally a mixture of compounded common lime and coarse sand – normally in the proportion of three to six times the quantity of sand as lime – mixed with some admix for additional strength. These admixes varied from area to area, with sometimes one or more being incorporated to bind the mixture together. Chopped straw was often used, as was cow-hair, cleaned of dust and finely teased, horse-hair, when it could not be sold for upholstery, or even feathers. Road-scrapings or fresh cow-dung might also be included, so too was stable urine. Water was then added, the ingredients beaten, carefully mixed and blended to produce a thick plaster as "tough as leather".

This toughness and thickness of the plaster made it possible to form ornamental enrichments to the face of the plaster, known today as pargetting – a term which originally described any form of external plaster sheathing. The art of pargetting, an English craft little known or practised outside this country, developed in the sixteenth century, reaching its zenith in the late seventeenth century. As plastering was the main method of weather-proofing buildings in East Anglia and the surrounding counties, it is naturally found more often in this area than others, but it can be found elsewhere on occasions. There is a house in York, another in Maidstone and a few isolated examples on houses in Salop and North Hereford and Worcester. At The Leys, Weobley, a sun head and a spray of thistles and oak leaves can be seen on one of the gables.

Two forms of pargetting exist; one, incised work which appeared first;

and the other, raised work which many would call true pargetting. Many examples of this raised work survive in East Anglia, particularly in North-west Essex and South-west Suffolk. In Essex there is Colneford House, Earls Colne, dated 1685; the former Sun Inn, Saffron Walden; Crown House, Newport, a house built about 1600 and enriched in 1692 with a shell-shaped hood over the door and much excellent pargetting arranged in moulded panels, left blank at ground floor but filled in with foliage and swags above, with a crown in high relief over the front door; while Garrison House, Wivenhoe, the ornamental floral strap-work covers the entire wall at first-floor level. Notable examples in Suffolk are the Ancient House, Clare, a house of 1473 on the south side of the churchyard which, in fact, is a renewal of the original seven-teenth-century work, and Sparrow's House, Ipswich, perhaps the most ornate, dating from about 1670. At Ashwell, Hertfordshire, there is a group of houses in the High Street, one dated 1681, noted for their raised pargetting. However, these more ambitious forms of pargetting were re-served for the houses of the well-to-do and are displayed for all to see mostly on houses in towns and large villages and seldom on houses stand-ing in isolation. Only on Bishop Bonner's cottages at East Dereham, Norfolk, can this more ambitious form of pargetting be found on what may be called a cottage. Here there is an elaborate coloured vine, star and rosette pargetted frieze, running along the front of the cottages which, despite a 1502 date, is probably seventeenth century. The date is probably the date of erection for roofs of very steep pitch are almost always of pre-Elizabethan origin. Their original use is unknown, and equally uncertain is their connection with Bishop Bonner, Mary Tudor's ruthless but conscientious persecutor of the Protestants, who came to East Dereham as Rector in 1534, some time after the cottages were built, and stayed there until 1540. Fortunately they escaped the devastation of the town by fire in 1581 when 350 houses were destroyed. These cottages are not probably of true cottage status and have recently been converted into a museum.

Pargetting on cottages usually took the form of incised work, also known as 'stick-work' or 'combed work', but here again most sixteenth- or seventeenth-century work was restricted to larger houses. It remained in favour, however, much longer than raised pargetting, continuing to be used well into the eighteenth century when it fell into the Georgian con-cept of cottage-building. The process was simple and the implements required were home-made – either a pointed stick, a group of sticks tied together to form a fan, a wooden comb with five or so teeth, or simply a large nail. The process was to impress a pattern into the surface of the wet plaster with the use of one or more implements. Sometimes the whole face of the building would be covered with one design, but more fre-quently the walls would be divided into rectangular panels of various

53. Plastered cottages, Great Bardfield, Essex.

54. Plastered cottages, Kersey, Suffolk.

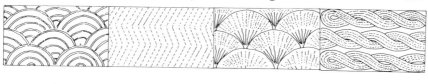

A   B   C   D

55. Pargetting patterns: A. fan; B. herring-bone; C. scallop; D. cable.

sizes to suit the windows and doors. Each panel had a slight border with the remainder filled in with one of a variety of patterns (*See* 55), a process known as 'pinking'. The patterns commonly used were semi-circles, scallops, zigzags, fans, scales, cables, herring-bones and basket-work. Another, the simplest form of decoration and one frequently used on cottages, was 'sparrow-picking'. This consisted simply of holes formed by a tool formed of a triangular piece of wood with teeth on one side and a handle the other, which was stabbed over the face of the plaster. Although not very effective, it broke up the plain face of the plaster. This, like other forms of pargetting, lost its sharpness with each successive coat of lime or colour-wash. Today, due to the renovation and alteration of old buildings and the deterioration of the old plaster over the years, little of the original pargetting of the seventeenth and eighteenth centuries survives. The art of incised pargetting is still carried on today on renovated buildings, but the hardness of the plaster, which often has cement added, results in a less pleasing effect than that obtained with the original softer plaster. The mix commonly employed today for external plastering comprises one part of cement to two parts of lime to nine parts of sand.

Examples of incised pargetting – some original, others replacements of the seventeenth and eighteenth centuries – can be seen in numerous villages in the eastern counties, but once again the villages of South-west Suffolk and North-west Essex preserve the greatest quantity. Hertfordshire, particularly in the eastern part around Bishop's Stortford in villages like Braughing and Little Hadham, is another area where the craft flourished at one time. Norfolk has some, but only in the southern part, while in Kent, although less common than in Suffolk and Essex, it is not rare.

One of the most attractive aspects of these plastered buildings is the colour-wash applied to them. Traditionally white, cream or buff were used, but in some areas it is found that a particular colour is employed, for example in Suffolk various shades of pink have long been popular and are known as 'Suffolk pinks'. Today, with a greater variety of colours available, many colours are used and sometimes to good effect, as can be seen at Elm Hill, Norwich, a cobbled street of mainly sixteenth-century buildings generally timber-framed and all but one plastered, all recently restored and colour-washed in blues, greens, pinks and yellows as well as white.

Weatherboarding, sometimes called clapboarding, is another method of rendering a building water and draught-proof (*See* 56). Its use in preference to tile-hanging or plastering for cladding a timber-framed building was probably the need for economy and is, therefore, found principally on small houses; cottages, farm buildings, windmills – post and smock – and watermills. Surviving examples of weatherboarding suggests its use on barns and other farm buildings commenced from about 1600, but the technique never became popular on domestic buildings until the eighteenth century. Even then its use was generally restricted either to the slight timber-framed cottages built at the end of the eighteenth century in South-east England or, like other cladding materials, applied long after they had been built to the face of old timber-framed houses when being modernized.

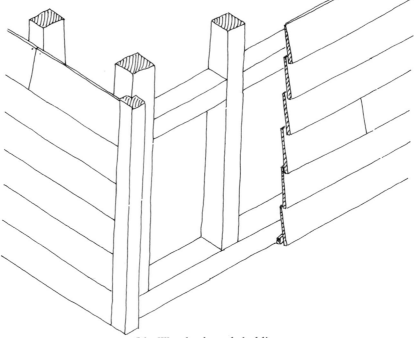

56. Weatherboard cladding.

The use of weatherboarding continued into the nineteenth century. At Cobham, Kent, there are a number of pleasant weatherboarded cottages dating from the beginning of the nineteenth century as there are at Boughton under Blean, Ickham and Newnham. Timber-framed cottages clad with weatherboarding were, in fact, still being constructed at Tillingham, Essex, as late as 1881.

57. Cottages at Dalham, Suffolk.

58. An old tarred weatherboarded cottage at West Mersea, Essex.

59. Weatherboarded cottages, Upshire, Essex.

60. Weatherboarded cottage near Bures, Suffolk.

Early weatherboarding was oak or elm, pegged to the frame and left untreated, but later, especially on cottages, softwood was used nailed to the studs. Various types of boarding were used, sometimes it was square-edged boarding chamfered along the lower edge, but generally it was feather-edged boarding – boarding tapered across its width. Later, in the latter part of the eighteenth and early part of the nineteenth centuries, a beaded bottom edge was given to the boarding. The weatherboarding was fixed horizontally, each board covering the board below with a single lap, with the boards being usually fixed directly to the studwork without battens. At the corners a vertical batten was provided up to which the boarding was fitted, while at the reveals to windows a similar but smaller batten was fixed to provide a stop for the boarding. The cottages are invariably painted white or cream, but in Essex, particularly along the coast in villages like West Mersea, the boarding is occasionally covered with black tar as a protection against the weather. This form of protection is to be found on weatherboarded barns and farm buildings throughout East Anglia and South-east England.

Weatherboarding is indigenous to the three south-eastern counties and occurs more often in the Weald of Kent than perhaps anywhere else in the entire country. In and around such villages as Biddenden (a beautiful village with weatherboarded weavers' cottages), Tenterden, Smarden and Rolvenden, numerous examples exist, sometimes clad the full height or sometimes with only the upper floor clad, like the row of cottages at Plaxtol. Perhaps not found in such numbers as in the Weald of Kent, many weatherboarded cottages survive in Sussex. They are found along the county boundary with Kent in such places as Burwash, Northiam and Rye, while further west they can be found at Heathfield, where the entrance to the church is flanked by pretty weatherboarded and chequered brick cottages. They can also be found in Cuckfield and Wisborough Green, a village with cottages in the usual Weald vernacular of brick, half-timber, tile-hanging and a few terraces of weatherboarding. Surrey has the least number of weatherboarded cottages of the three south-eastern counties, but they are by no means rare, although they are not concentrated into one area and are found throughout the county. The village of Capel is where it can be seen at its best. It is interesting to find that eighteenth-century weatherboarded cottages still survive in places like Mitcham and Epsom, which have long become urban or suburban. Weatherboarding also occurs fairly frequently on cottages in Essex, where its use was restricted more to the cladding of cottages erected in the eighteenth and nineteenth centuries than the cladding of older timber-framed buildings. Although found throughout the county, these weatherboarded cottages are more common in the southern part, particularly in the villages of Epping Forest, like Upshire; in and around Ongar, in the Rodings, a group of eight farming villages along the valley

61. Weatherboarded cottages near Smarden, Kent.

62. Weatherboarded and stone cottages, Plaxtol, Kent.

63. Thatched timber-framed plastered and weatherboarded cottages, High Roding, Essex.

64. Timber-framed, plastered and weatherboarded cottages, Cottered, Hertfordshire.

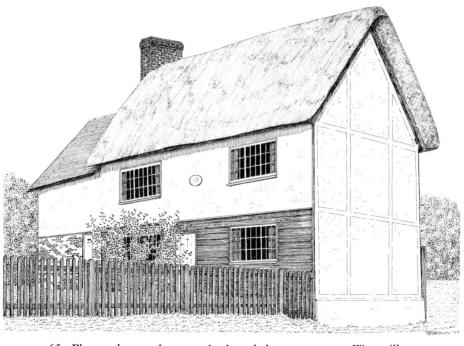

65. Plastered and weatherboarded cottage, Westmill, Hertfordshire.

66. Pair of nineteenth-century weatherboarded cottages at Hadleigh Heath, Suffolk.

of the River Roding; along the coast in such villages as Leigh-on-Sea, Tillingham, Tollesbury, West Mersea and Churchend, near Paglesham; while further inland there are to be found in the villages surrounding Colchester, among them Dedham, Ardleigh and Eight Ash Green. Weatherboarding is also found, but to a lesser extent, in Hertfordshire, Suffolk (in villages like Walsham le Willows), and Buckinghamshire.

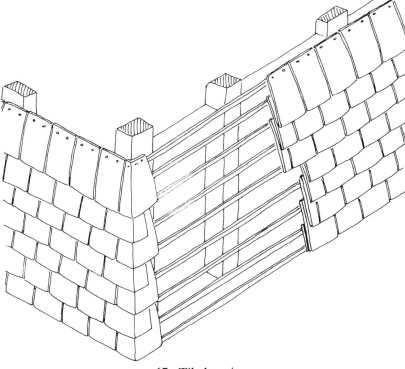

67. Tile-hanging.

Naturally in the eastern counties weatherboarding is found combined with plaster. In Essex and Suffolk the gable ends of cottages were often weatherboarded, with the front and rear plastered, like those at High Roding, Essex, although today this is found less frequently than in the past. In Hertfordshire, weatherboarding is sometimes used up to the ground-floor window-sill, in which case it is frequently tarred. This type of construction can be seen on the delightful row of timber-framed cottages at Cottered and also in such places as Much Hadham, while on a cottage at Westmill the boarding is carried up to above the top of ground-floor windows. On a cottage near the church at Thaxted, Essex, weatherboarding is employed on the gable ends as well as the lower part of the front and rear walls, the only plaster being that from the window-sill up to the eaves.

Another method of weather-proofing timber-framed buildings was to tile-hang the walls (*See* 67). First appearing in the South-east in the last quarter of the seventeenth century it remained popular throughout the next century, when an abundant supply of hand-made tiles became available, and well into the second half of the nineteenth century when machine-made tiles became available. Needless to say, the regular shapes of these tiles are less pleasing than those of the hand-made ones, each with a slight curve, slightly different in size, shape, colour and texture, forming a wall of great charm compared with the depressingly monotonous appearance of the machine-made ones.

Sometimes applied as a covering to brick walls, it was on the face of timber-framed buildings where most tile-hanging was employed and was, like weatherboarding, a speciality of the three south-eastern counties; Kent, Sussex and Surrey. It did spread to some extent into parts of Hampshire and Oxfordshire in some of the villages under the Downs such as the Hagbournes, the Hendreds, Harwell, Blewbury and Aston Tirrold. In Somerset, at least near Bridgwater, they were also used at the beginning of the nineteenth century to cover the fronts of houses to make them waterproof, which the Rev. Edmund Butcher thought better than building in brick.[23] Elsewhere, in East Anglia, the West and the Midlands, the practice is rare except for isolated exceptions like the farmhouse at Takeley, Essex. It is, however, in the Weald of Kent, Sussex and Surrey that tile-hanging can be observed at its best. At Goudhurst, Kent, the village is mainly tile-hung, with the houses and cottages, some with exposed timbering, some with bricks below, in picturesque groups. A long, nearly but not quite uniform row of attractive eighteenth-century cottages are situated in The Walks, Groombridge, Kent, with red and blue bricks or weatherboarding below and plain tile-hanging above. A pleasant group of tile-hung cottages stand near the churchyard at Lenham, while at Matfield there is a short row of cottages, red brick and blue bricks below and tile-hung above, which still keep all their original fitments, even the window-catches. However, tile-hanging is found in all the delightful villages of the Kent Weald, among them Biddenden, Tenterden, Yalding and Chiddingstone. Surrey too has many tile-hung villages such as Alford, Chiddingford (one of the largest and loveliest of the Wealden villages), Brook, Newdigate, while Witley is probably the most typical Surrey village in its proportion of tile-hanging, brick and half-timber. Detillens Cottages, Limpsfield, is a pleasant row of six sixteenth-to eighteenth-century timber-framed and tile-hung cottages and at School Hill, Merstham, there is a long irregular terrace of very humble tile-hung cottages. Tile-hanging is to be found throughout the Sussex Weald from Burwash in the east to Fernhurst in the west, but it is perhaps in the north in villages near the Surrey border, namely Plaistow, Loxwood, Lurgashall, North Chapel, Rudgwick and Rusper, that it is

68. Brick, weatherboarded and tile-hung cottages at The Walks,
Groombridge, Kent.

most prevalent.

Plain tiles were at first used for tile-hanging and these were the same as for roofs, though sometimes slightly thinner. When applied to timber-framed buildings horizontal oak battens were fixed to the studs to which the tiles were hung to give a triple lap, each tile covering two others. The upper ends of the tiles were often bedded solid in lime and hair mortar to make a satisfactory and permanently waterproof wall and might also be secured by wooden pegs, generally of oak, hazel or willow, or later nailed. Special tiles were manufactured for corners and jambs, but on cottages these were often substituted for vertical timber battens. Occasionally the vertical joints would be filled with mortar, but generally these were left open, giving a more attractive appearance. Generally the tiles were restricted to the upper floors and gable ends, these being the most exposed parts of the building, but not infrequently the whole building would be clad, or sometimes simply the whole front or one side.

The use of tile-hanging was not only restricted to the cladding of old timber-framed buildings but also, like other cladding materials, was an appropriate finish for the slight timber-framed buildings developed in the South-east during the eighteenth and early part of the nineteenth centuries. When the tiles were applied to an existing timber-framed building which had a jettied upper floor, the opportunity was sometimes taken to build a new brick wall outside the timber frame and flush with the tile-hanging above.

The clays of the Weald produced the beautiful terracotta tiles seen today, which over the years have mellowed and toned down yet still retain their glowing red, for, unlike roof tiles which often remain wet for days, these tiles hung vertically soon dry and discourage the growth of lichen and moss. In other parts of the country dark reddish-brown tiles were often used.

The plain rectangular tile, slightly curved on the face, was the tile most frequently used, but patterned tiles of considerable variation of design were also employed to give decorative effects. These decorative tiles could be used individually or combined with plain tiles – a number of rows of patterned tiles and then a number of rows of plain tiles were often used. Not only shaped tiles were used to produce a decorative effect, but patterns were derived from the use of tiles of differing colours used in a variety of diaper patterns. These tiles were sometimes of the same make and colour when manufactured, but before being fired they would be dabbed with the bristles of a stiff brush, producing a rough surface which weathered quicker than the ordinary hand-made tiles and thus, after a while, formed a pattern.

While fish-scale and other patterned tile-hanging appears in Kent and to a greater extent in Sussex, it is in Surrey that most occurs, in places like Ewhurst, Hascombe, Haslemere, and Witley. In all three counties,

69. Cottages, Alford, Surrey.

however, the majority of patterned tile-hanging belongs to the Victorian period. These ornamental tiles can look charming although they can produce a monotonous and distracting effect.

Often used as a cladding material in Cornwall, Devon and the North-west, slate-hanging was rarely employed on timber-framed buildings, for in these areas where it is found timber-framed buildings are uncommon or even, as in Cornwall, unknown. There are, however, odd examples, the most famous perhaps being the group of old houses at Dunster, Somerset, known as The Nunnery. The ground floor is of red sandstone, while the upper two floors are timber-framed, and hung with slates, with the slates arranged in a diamond pattern between the windows of the upper floor. Fixed in a similar way to tiles (nailed to battens spanning the studs), they may have single or double lap according to the exposure of the situation.

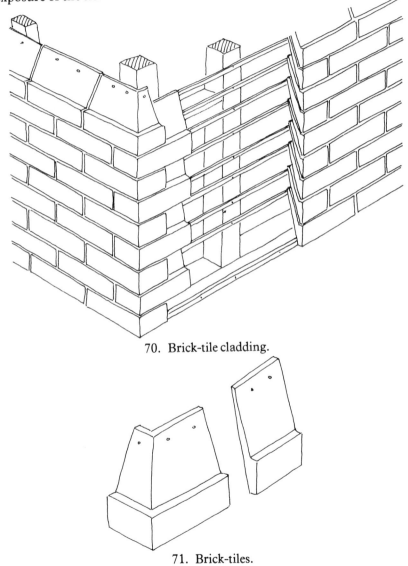

70. Brick-tile cladding.

71. Brick-tiles.

The Brick Tax encouraged the manufacture and use of another cladding material – the brick-tile (*See* 71) or, as they are often called, the mathematical tile. These imitation bricks were hung vertically like tile-hanging, but were shaped in section to give the appearance of brickwork on the face (*See* 70). They were hung or nailed to timber battens fixed between the vertical studs in the same manner as tile-hanging but with the joints bedded and pointed in mortar like brickwork. Special return tiles were sometimes used at the corners to maintain the bond and preserve the illusion of brickwork. So skilfully were these tiles made and hung that sometimes only an expert can distinguish between them and true brickwork which they intend to resemble. This illusion is often dispelled, however, for they were frequently confined to the front wall, the side walls being covered with tiles or some other material, with a vertical timber batten at the corners.

Brick-tiles introduced in the middle of the eighteenth century, were not cheap and were not originally introduced to save money but to give an inexpensive 'face-lift' to old timber-framed buildings. However, with the introduction of the Brick Tax there was a strong incentive to use them for cladding new buildings as well and were used like other cladding materials, on the slight timber-framed buildings constructed in the South-east in the first part of the nineteenth century. Although they are found on occasions elsewhere in the country, it is in the counties south of the Thames where most are to be seen. Within this area Kent and Sussex have most, in the southern and coastal parts of these counties. Examples can be seen at Canterbury, Hythe and Tenterden, all in Kent, while in Sussex further examples are to be found at Lewes, Rye and Brighton.

72. Cottages at Ewhurst, Surrey.

Mud Cottages

The use of mud or unbaked earth as a building material has been known from medieval times, not only as daub used in conjunction with wattle but as an important building material in its own right. The use of turf as a building material was presumably widespread in England in medieval times although there is little archaeological evidence of its use outside the South-west where the buildings consisted of turf, lined on the inside with wattle hurdling.[1] There is documentary evidence of its use elsewhere. In the Isle of Axholme, a low-lying area between the Yorkshire Ouse and the River Trent in Humberside, peasants in the fourteenth century had the right to cut turf for walling as well as fuel;[2] while at Whitwick, Leicestershire, in 1604, a "poor man, a wisket-maker, made a cot of stickes and turffes".[3] Its use continued until the nineteenth century for there is a reference to a turf cottage in White's *Directory of Leicestershire and Rutland* for 1846.

More recently three principal methods using unbaked earth have been employed: clay mixed with straw and used without moulds or shutters, called 'clob', 'clom', or more commonly by its Devon name, 'cob'; earth or clay used with moulds in shutters, called 'pisé'; and clay shaped with moulds into rectangular blocks left to dry naturally and laid in puddle clay mortar and called 'clay-lump' or sometimes 'clay-bat'. The chief advantage they had over other forms of construction was that they were cheap to build, requiring only limited skills, and could, if need be, be carried out by the cottager himself. Another advantage was that with the thick walls insulation was good, being warmer in the winter and cooler in the summer. Although occasionally used for more important buildings, all these materials were generally confined to cottages, small farmhouses and farm buildings.

As early as 1212 it is known that houses in London were constructed of mud walls, and there are also medieval references to mud walls at Leicester, Bridport, Southampton and Hedon,[4] while there is evidence of its use in Buckinghamshire, Cornwall, Devon, Cambridgeshire, Lincolnshire, Norfolk and Northamptonshire, as early as the thirteenth century.[5] Its use was widespread throughout the country, even in areas where other building materials were available. When Celia Fiennes travelled through Cumberland in 1698 she saw cottages "daub'd with mud walls";[6] while further south in Westmorland cottages of 'clay daubin' were common in 1775 but by 1794 had almost disappeared.[7] In the seventeenth and eighteenth centuries, according to Dr Norman Davey in his book *A History of*

73. Cob cottage, Dunsford, Devon.

Building Materials, clay-lump was used in the West Midlands, particularly at Lye, near Stourbridge, which was known as 'mud city'. At the end of the eighteenth century when the Earl of Dorchester rebuilt the village of Milton Abbas, Dorset, cob was the material chosen. At Naseby, Northamptonshire, in 1792, the buildings consisted almost entirely of a kind of kealy earth, very durable, and reported to be capable of lasting 200 years.[8] In Leicestershire, in 1809, road scrapings were considered to make the best mud for walls of cottages and these cottages were often built and thatched by the labourers themselves.[9] Three years later W. Stevenson also reported that road scrapings were used in Dorset for cottage walls.[10] This method of construction was still practised in Oxfordshire, around the Banbury district, in the middle of the last century and presumably in many other areas.[11] The use of mud in the construction of walls continued until this century when many architects in the 1920s, under the leadership of Clough Williams-Ellis, believed that a system based on mud was highly suitable for low-cost housing. In fact some were built and in South Norfolk two council housing schemes were undertaken between the two wars in the villages of Blo'Norton and Garboldisham using clay-lump.

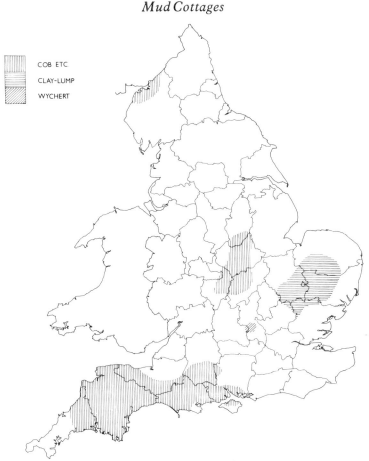

74. Main areas of distribution of mud cottages.

The distribution of the mud cottage was evidently widespread and still exists more extensively than generally thought. Many have now been covered with plaster or limewash, making them indistinguishable from other cottages, particularly in East Anglia where so many of the timber-framed buildings are clad with plaster. Others have been clad with stone or brick and it is reported that many of the cottages in Norfolk that appear to be brick are, in fact, built of clay-lump faced with a half brick skin.

The largest and by far the most important area today is in the South-west, and in that area Devon has more than any other county, some buildings dating from the sixteenth century, more from the seventeenth century, but the majority are from the eighteenth and early nineteenth centuries. Here the use of cob was not restricted to cottages but also several other buildings of considerable size were constructed, the most famous being the E-shaped sixteenth-century manor house at Hayes Barton, near Exeter, birth-place of Sir Walter Raleigh. It was, however, in cottage construction that cob was mainly used and can still be seen at its best. The picturesque villages of Dunsford (a charming village whose winding streets climb to the church), Cheriton Fitzpaine (a village high in the hills with its cottages clustering around the church), and Zeal Monachorum (with its winding street of cottages), as well as such villages as Awliscombe, East Budleigh, Iddesleigh and Whimple, are all typical of many cob and thatch villages to be seen throughout Devon, whitewashed in the north, often colour-washed in the south.

Cob cottages are not restricted to Devon. They are also to be found in Somerset, especially in the southern and western parts in such villages as Selworthy, now owned by the National Trust, Bratton and the old part of Minehead and, although some parts of Dorset have few or no cob buildings, on the chalk belt many do survive. Bryant's Puddle, Milton Abbas and the Winterbournes, as well as other villages, all preserve cob cottages with cob garden walls which are still, on occasions, capped with thatch. Its use also spread into the neighbouring counties of Wiltshire, Hampshire and Cornwall. Another area where a number still survive is in the Midlands, particularly in Leicestershire and the surrounding parts of Northamptonshire, Nottinghamshire and Warwickshire. In the North, Cumbria, and in particular the area around the Solway Firth, still possess a number, 105 clay buildings surviving there in 1956,[12] although the number has since declined. In Buckinghamshire, in a small area to the west of Aylesbury, there are also a number of buildings constructed with mud walls built of 'wychert', a chalky clay. East Anglia, where clay-lump was used, is probably the second most important area where unbaked earth was employed. The area takes in the southern part of Norfolk, where the villages of Blo'Norton, Garboldisham, Kenninghall in the south, and Shipham further north, are built almost entirely of clay-lump. It also includes most of Suffolk, apart from the extreme east; all of southern Cambridgeshire; the northern part of Essex, spreading as far south as White Roding, where a good example stands south of the cross-roads near the brick tower mill; and into Hertfordshire in such villages as Ashwell, near Royston.

The building of a mud or cob cottage was by the very nature of the material a laborious process and had, of course, structural limitations. Although probably requiring semi-skilled labour, the work was, more often than not, carried out by the cottager himself, for the only implements required were a dung-fork and a shallow shovel, known as a 'cob parer', which resembled a baker's peel – the shovel for removing bread from the oven. With the material being dug on site construction costs were minimal. The stuff consisted of loamy earth, containing sufficient lime to enable it to set, mixed with water and a little chopped straw – a process known as tempering – to act as reinforcement. It was carefully mixed and trodden by horses, oxen, or more often by the labourers themselves, into a sticky consistency. The mixture was then placed in position, trodden down and allowed to dry before the next layer was placed in position. Consequently the process was of necessity a lengthy one but although it is said that a two-storey cottage, if constructed well, could take up to two years to complete, there is evidence that the period was shorter. In 1962 a man who actually constructed cob buildings in Northamptonshire stated that six months was sufficient to erect a cottage.[13] In 1812 it was estimated that about a week was needed between each layer before the next was laid[14] and this would suggest an overall building period for the walls of about six weeks. In wet weather, when the period between each layer might have been several weeks, a temporary capping of thatch was sometimes used to give the walls some protection.

There were local variations in the methods of construction and in the North each layer was separated by a layer of straw. S. O. Addy,[15] writing in 1898, describes the composition of the mud walls he examined at Great Hartfield, Humberside:

The walls are built of layers of mud and straw which vary from five to seven inches in thickness, no vertical joints being visible. On the top of each layer is a thin covering of straw, with the ends of the straws pointing outwards, as in a corn stack. The way in which mud walls were built is remembered in the neighbourhood. A quantity of mud was mixed with straw, and the foundation laid with this mixture. Straw was then laid across the top, whilst the mud was wet, and the whole was left to dry and harden in the sun. As soon as the first layer was dry, another layer was put on, so that the process was rather a slow one. Finally the roof was thatched, and the projecting ends of straws trimmed off the walls. Such mud walls are very hard and durable, and their composition resembles that of sunburnt bricks.

In Devon the first layer was some 2½ feet high laid all round the foundation and subsequent layers were about a foot high. Each layer was known as a 'raise'. One of the labourers, called the 'cob-mason', stood on the wall to tread each layer down as another labourer threw on the cob, the excess, which projected beyond the face of the wall, being pared off by means of the cob parer. Lintels for doors and windows were fitted into the walls as the walls were raised but the openings were cut out later. The whole operation was undertaken without the aid of shutters, consequently these cottages have an undulating but charming appearance. To avoid cracking during the drying out of the wall, always a hazard with cob walls, the external angles were generally rounded. The walls were always thick, seldom less than 2 feet, often 3 feet and even occasionally 4 feet. The walls were left, sometimes for many months, to enable them to dry out before being smoothed and roughcast, plastered or simply lime-

75. Cob cottages, Minehead, Somerset.

washed. The fireplace, flue and chimney stack were the only parts of the structure, as in most mud cottages, to be built of stone or brick.

Mud walling was also used in conjunction with timber. In the North-west, particularly in Cumbria at Burgh-by-Sands and elsewhere around the Solway Firth, a cruck-frame was often incorporated within the walls. The walls of these cottages were sometimes completed in a single day, the whole village turning out to work together for a newly married couple, ending the day with a celebration. A ballard, published in 1805, called *The Clay Daubin*, describes the process and the celebrations. In Devon, Somerset and parts of Dorset, cruck-frames were also incorporated within cob walls. In the cob buildings of West Somerset the gables were made of rough poles fixed up-right and across these, split sticks were nailed to serve as laths on which daub or very rough mortar was applied. This work was known as 'split-and-dab'. Similarly, masonry was also used with cob. Sometimes, as at the row of five almshouses at Cheriton Fitzpaine, Devon, the lower half of the front wall is of stone with cob above, while others, as at Great Creaton, Scaldwell and Clipston, all in Northamptonshire, have stone at the front and cob to the rear. Occasionally brick was also used in the same building as unbaked earth but few examples survive.

The thickness of these cob walls varied considerably from area to area. As already mentioned walls in Devon were seldom less than 2 feet thick. White Cottage, Beaulieu, Hampshire, a small house constructed in about 1800, has cob walls only 1 foot 4 inches thick, while a lean-to, probably added later in the nineteenth century, has walls only 1 foot 1 inch thick.

The consistency of cob varied in different parts of the country accord-ing to the materials locally available. The use of road scrapings as an ingredient for mud walls has previously been mentioned, and although there is evidence of its use in the nineteenth century in Dorset, Leicester-shire and Oxfordshire, where walls were produced of such durability that it was almost impossible to demolish them with a pick, its use as a build-ing material was not new. In 1587, at Lamport, Northamptonshire, sev-eral people were brought before the court for having "digged and taken upp menure and gravell lyeing in the streates of Lamporte and in the Quenes highway there for the mending of their mowndes and howses". In Cornwall cob was called 'clob' and was composed of two parts of clay to one part of 'shilf' (small pieces of broken slate) with barley straw added afterwards. In the sandy and heathy districts of Dorset, loam, gravel and sand were used and heather was substituted for straw as a binding material. Where chalk was available, in Wiltshire and Dorset and the adjoining parts of Hampshire and Berkshire, this was considered to be an invaluable ingredient. The chalk would be crushed and mixed with water, mud and straw, usually in the proportion of three parts of chalk to one part of clay,[17] though the higher the proportion of chalk the greater the durability. Thomas Hardy in a letter to *The Times* in 1927 describes the process in his native Dorset.

> What was called mud-wall was really a composition of chalk, clay and straw
> – essentially unbaked brick. This was mixed up into a sort of dough-pudding
> close to where the cottage was to be built. The mixing was performed by
> treading and shovelling – women sometimes being called in to tread – and
> the straw was added to bind the mass together . . . It was then thrown by
> pitchforks on to the wall, where it was trodden down to a thickness of about
> two feet, till a rise of about three feet had been reached. This was left to settle
> for a day or two . . .

A similar mixture of chalk and clay is found occurring naturally in Buckinghamshire in an area south-west of Aylesbury and extending westward towards Long Crendon, in all some six miles in length and a mile wide. Known as 'wychert' – sometimes spelt *wichert* or *witchit* – it is found some 2 feet below the surface and when mixed with water and straw, is used in the same manner as cob, without shutters and with each layer trodden down. This material can be seen at its best at Haddenham, where almost all the older buildings are constructed of it, with unrendered wychert garden walls capped with pantiles. In this village even the more important buildings were constructed of this material; the large Baptist Chapel, built about 1810, was constructed entirely of wychert, while the Wesleyan Methodist Chapel was formed with a combination of wychert and brick. Other villages where wychert can be seen are Dinton, Cuddington and Lower Winchendon.

Walls were sometimes constructed entirely of chalk. Here the water was added to the chalk, the mixture 'pugged' and then poured into position between shutters, rammed, trodden down and consolidated before being left to dry. The result was a wall which resembled cob but was considerably stronger and comparable to the consistency of clunch.

In the New Forest the walls of mud-built cottages were formed of clay mixed with chopped straw or stones, packed down between boards or hurdles which were later removed when the clay had dried.[18] This form of construction was similar to that employed in *pisé* for it entailed the use of shutters, but the mixture comprised gravelly or sandy earth with a little clay added, while it was essential that the material remained dry. The mixture was placed between the shutters and rammed down with a heart-shaped rammer, which was formerly of hardwood but later of iron. As the material was kept dry the process was faster than that of other mud or cob walls and a height of 9 feet was sometimes reached in a single day. Although much of the soil in England was suitable for this type of construction, the method was never as popular in this country as it was on the Continent, particularly in France. Why this was is not known, but it is thought that the use of shutters not only increased the costs but also

76. Late eighteenth-century thatched and wychert cottage, Haddenham, Buckinghamshire.

required greater skill. Also, as the mixture had to be kept dry our damp and unreliable weather probably affected its popularity. Said to have been introduced into this country at the end of the eighteenth century by Henry Holland, the fashionable architect of the period, it was used by him in the construction of some estate cottages at Woburn, although these have since been demolished. According to the *Cyclopaedia* published in 1819, *pisé* was widely used in the southern counties and perhaps some still survive there hidden beneath a coat of plaster.

Although not so picturesque as the cob cottages of the South-west, the clay-lump cottages of East Anglia were technically the most advanced of all mud cottages. First introduced in the early part of the seventeenth century, it remained in common use into the nineteenth century and was even, as previously stated, used on occasions in the present century. Its use was confined almost solely to East Anglia, although it did occur elsewhere from time to time. The soils of East Anglia, particularly the Boulder Clay in South Norfolk and North Suffolk, were all suitable for this form of construction, while further west, in the chalk areas of Cambridgeshire, chalk marl was often employed. The method of construction was a simple one. The earth was generally dug out near the site of the building, but this was not always the case for it was apparently sometimes obtained indiscriminately. It is recorded that, in 1838, one John Cornell was instructed by the Swaffham and Bottisham Drainage Board to desist from making clay-lumps out of mud dug from the ditch belonging to their lands which he occupied in Quy Fen. Whether he manufactured them for his own needs or for someone else is not known. After being dug out the clay was spread into a layer about a foot thick, all large stones, over about an inch diameter, removed and the clay watered; then short straw, or sometimes grass, was spread over it and trodden in, usually by horses, to bind the materials together. The clay was then pressed into wooden moulds and left to dry for a few days before being taken out and turned up on end. The bats were finally placed on a platform to finish drying out, generally for a month or two depending on the time of year. Sometimes the clay was raised in the winter for use in the following spring. The bats were naturally larger than fired bricks, but varied considerably in size. Usually they were about 18 by 9 by 6 inches although 18 by 12 by 6 inches were sometimes used, while in Essex bats measuring 12 by 6 by 6 inches have been recorded. Bonded in a similar manner as brickwork, they "were carried up in a rather rough manner to ensure key, and the angles protected by angle beads" being jointed in puddle clay mortar. The method was much faster than that of a wet mud or cob wall and, once the bats had been made, was relatively easy to construct. Even though the walls were much thinner than cob walls the insulation was equally efficient. Walls of clay-lump are generally rendered externally and it is therefore seldom seen unless the rendering has been neglected, although it can often be observed on some of the dilapidated farm buildings in Norfolk.

It was essential that all these unbaked earth buildings were kept dry if they were to survive, for once subjected to long periods of damp they soon disintegrated. Kept dry they would last for centuries, often increasing in strength over the years. There is an old Devon saying that "all cob wants is a good hat and a good pair of shoes" – that is, a good foundation and a good roof. The foundation would be in the form of a plinth, generally between 1 and 2 feet high, made of local materials. Flint in Norfolk (where it was called 'pinning'), stones and pebbles in Devon, chalk in Buckinghamshire, boulders from the Boulder Clay or rubble limestone in Leicestershire, and sandstone in Cumbria were all used. In later years, particularly in East Anglia and Cambridgeshire, these local materials were replaced by brick. Often, to give the wall added protection against the damp, the plinth would be tarred. Not only was it essential to have a good foundation to prevent rising damp, but also to resist "the inroads of vermin". Thatch, the lightest form of roof covering, was almost the universal material, and by far the most appropriate one, for these cottages.

77. Cob cottage, Zeal Monachorum, Devon.

In East Anglia, particularly Norfolk, pantiles, also being a light roof, were commonly used. It was essential that when thatch was used a large overhang was provided at the eaves, enabling the rain to be thrown well clear of the walls.

Not only were a "good hat and a good pair of shoes" required, but also the external face of the wall required some protection to prevent dampness from penetrating the wall. As previously stated it was necessary for the walls to be thoroughly dry before any application could be undertaken. A cob wall, over 2 feet thick, would take a considerable time, possibly over a year, before the wall was dry, but a clay-lump wall, which had at least been partly dried before erection, required less, and a *pisé* wall none at all – an advantage with this type of wall. The easiest and traditional covering was limewash. The material was cheap and easy to apply and being porous enabled any rising damp within the wall to dry out. It was applied, generally by the cottager, every year or two with brushes tied to long poles. So many coats have been applied over the years to some of the cob cottages of the South-west and the clay-lump cottages of East Anglia that a coating has been formed so thick that they could be taken as being rendered. Another cheap but less attractive method was to apply a coat of tar to the face of the building. This usually occurred, and can still be seen in Norfolk, on farm buildings. On cottages the tar was generally sanded and a coat of colour-wash applied. In Norfolk an outer coat of clay slurry was applied to the wall prior to the application of the tar. Roughcast, known in Devon as 'slap-dash', mixed with chalk when available, was commonly used, but in Norfolk plaster was composed of either good clay mixed with road sand or silt or, more frequently, old clay and magden well kneaded together, and in Cambridgeshire chalk marl mixed with straw were all frequently used. However, the most pleasing and, perhaps, most widely used, particularly in East Anglia, was lime plaster.

What is the future of our surviving mud cottages? They are, of course, the most vulnerable of all our vernacular buildings and every year a few more are condemned and disappear from the scene. Once neglected they soon deteriorate and once dilapidated are difficult to repair. It is now almost impossible to repair a cob wall effectively once the wall has become defective, for we no longer have the knowledge to undertake such work. With walls constructed of clay-lump, repairs can be undertaken with comparative ease, for a defective bat can be cut out and replaced and even larger openings can be rebuilt. It seems likely, however, that unless some action is taken to protect all these buildings their numbers will continue to decline slowly.

Stone Cottages

Although stone was used in the late Middle Ages for important secular and ecclesiastical buildings, its employment in cottages and other minor buildings is usually a fairly recent practice. While there were always cottages made of mud, timber remained the almost universal vernacular building material for cottages until well into the seventeenth century, by which time, with the rising price of timber due to the depletion of the forests, stone could, for the first time, compete with it. Even in the South-west, where timber was scarce, the earliest cottages were of turf, and in some areas of Cornwall and Devon cob was, until quite recently, preferred to that of surface granite, so abundant there. Throughout the North, which now is associated with stone, timber-framing had been preponderantly in use, even now surviving here and there among the later stone dwellings of some Lancashire and Yorkshire villages.

It is clear from archaeological research that in almost all stone-producing areas, like Berkshire, Cornwall, Devon, Dorset, Gloucestershire, Humberside, Lincolnshire, Northamptonshire, Somerset, Sussex, Wiltshire and North Yorkshire, during the late twelfth and thirteenth centuries buildings with timber walls were being replaced with ones built of stone. The transition did not occur at exactly the same time all over the country, happening first in the South and South-west, then, later in the thirteenth century, in the North. The reason for this change is not clearly understood, and several theories have been put forward; the most probable being the decline of suitable timber within a reasonable distance of the village. Likewise, in the South-west the changeover may have taken place due to the shortage of suitable turf for, with the increase in cultivation, the peasants, like those in wooded areas, would have to travel further afield from the settlement to collect turf. The stone used for these early medieval buildings was always close to the village and, with the exception of chalk, was either picked from the surface of the ground, or extracted from river-beds or from the boulder clay.[1]

The walls of these peasant buildings were between 2 and 3 feet thick, generally built without foundations, being laid directly on the ground and, because of the irregular shape of the stones used, were seldom built straight, neither at right angles nor parallel to each other. The use of lime mortar is very rare but, on the other hand, clay mortar was very common. In most mountainous and moorland areas of England it is obvious that cottages were built of dry walling for many continued to be built into the nineteenth century. On Dartmoor and parts of Cornwall, cottages, barns and the like can still be seen built of 'moorstone', picked from the surface of the ground, laid without mortar and frequently whitewashed. Celia Fiennes, in 1698, found cottages at Land's End, the Lake District and further north, near Carlisle, built with "drye walls".[2]

Stone dwellings like these were later replaced, and although some small sixteenth-century stone houses often of two rooms can be found on Dartmoor, in places like Chagford, Buckland and Shaugh Prior, elsewhere it is not until the middle of the seventeenth century that any great numbers appear. Then all along the limestone belt, from Dorset to Humberside, a great deal of building was in progress and by the end of the century stone became the accepted building material, even for cottages. This is clearly evident in Northamptonshire where many of the cottages carry date-stones of the seventeenth and eighteenth centuries, such as at Rockingham, that enchanting ironstone village which contains many cottages dating from this period. In Lancashire and North Yorkshire small stone houses did not appear before the end of the seventeenth century, with cottages appearing even later. William Marshall, writing in 1788, reports that ". . . oak is now almost wholly laid aside as a material for the house carpenter except for door and window lintels, wall-plates and some few other purposes".[3] This clearly indicates that the transition from timber to stone had by this time almost been completed. In other parts of the North small stone-built houses are of an even later date. In Northumberland the majority of houses date from the latter half of the eighteenth century, with cottages much later.

This transition from timber to stone can clearly be seen in those marginal areas which lie between the predominately stone regions and the predominately timber ones. In Cambridgeshire, in the strip which separates the stone area around Peterborough from the timber area of the south, in the villages of Yaxley, Stilton and Great Gidding both timber and stone were used, but while the larger houses were being constructed of stone, cottages, like some at Great Gidding, continued to be erected in timber. Similarly on the western edge of the Cotswolds, in villages like Didbrook, Stanton and Mickleton, the stone ones were always of a higher social status than the timber ones. The cruck cottage at Didbrook probably precedes any of the stone ones in that village. Perhaps the best village to observe this transition from timber to stone is the National Trust village of Lacock, Wiltshire, which has an impressive cruck house, together with framed and jettied houses from a later period, and from about 1600, stone houses. Clearly stone, formerly used solely for larger buildings, began to be used, where readily available, for buildings further down the social scale; while timber, although once of such importance, was confined more to cottages and other less pretentious buildings.

Up to the time of the industrial revolution builders relied on materials

78. Cottages at Stanton, Gloucestershire.

79. Cottage, Rockingham, Northamptonshire.

found in their immediate neighbourhood and so where there was an adequate supply of local stone this was used. Later, with the revolution in transport and the manufacture of cheap bricks, this reliance in local materials declined and the traditional relationship between the cottage and its environment was broken, with brick slowly replacing stone as the principal building material, often creating harsh discords in all but major buildings. By the nineteenth century, with the completion of the process, it was no longer necessary or economical to rely upon local materials and only in a few isolated places, where the railways did not spread or where there was a plentiful supply of stone in such places as Cornwall, the Cotswolds and the Lake District, did stone continue to be used.

The walling for stone buildings was either built in rubble work, which comprised blocks of stone either undressed or comparatively roughly dressed with wide joints; or ashlar, which comprised carefully dressed blocks of stone with narrow joints. Ashlar, being extremely expensive, was restricted to important buildings and so most stone cottages are of rubble work. Often there was little alternative to the use of rubble for many kinds of stone could only be used as rubble, even the more favourable ones often yielded only small pieces and so here rubble work was also employed so every piece of stone was usable. So, almost all humbler buildings – farmhouses, cottages and barns – are constructed in rubble work, either random rubble or squared rubble, depending largely on the stone used.

In random rubble the stones were quarry-dressed and, not being of uniform size and shape, required great care and ingenuity in arranging the stones so that the weight was spread over a maximum area and that no long continuous vertical joints occurred. It was necessary to bond the wall both transversely – across the width of the wall – and longitudinally – along the face of the wall. The transverse bond was obtained by the use of 'headers' – stones from each side of the wall which reached beyond the centre to overlap in the middle; and 'throughs' – stones which extended the full thickness of the wall. When the impermeability of the stone was unsatisfactory throughs were not used, as moisture would be conducted through them to the inner face. To overcome this the throughs were either replaced with three-quarter headers, or with the throughs extending to within 1 inch of the internal face, and the end covered with slate bedded in mortar.

The cheapest and roughest form of random rubble, and one often used on cottages, is uncoursed (*see* 80A). The waller selected the stones more or less at random from the heap, knocking off any inconvenient corner or projection to assist in obtaining a bond. The larger stones were laid flat and packed and wedged with small pieces of stone, called 'spalls', with the resultant spaces being filled with small stones. The stones were

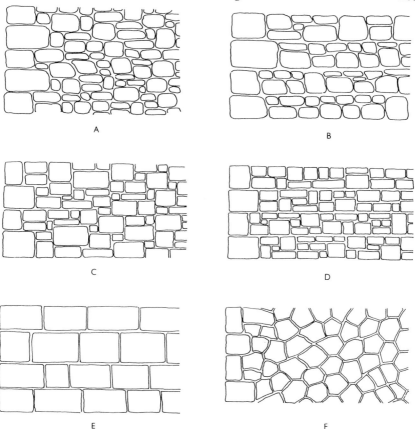

80. Stone walling: A. random rubble; B. random rubble brought to course; C. squared or snecked rubble; D. squared rubble brought to course; E. coursed squared rubble; F. polygonal rubble walling.

arranged without any attempt to form horizontal or vertical joints and the appearance varied greatly with the differing shapes and sizes of the stones. At the quoins and jambs larger stones, roughly squared with a walling hammer, were used, bonded into the wall to increase stability and also to improve the overall appearance. The other form of random rubble is built or 'brought' to course (*See* 80B) and is similar to the above except that it was roughly levelled to form courses. Large, roughly squared stones were again used at the quoin and jambs and the rubble built so that it roughly coursed in with them. The height of these courses varied according to the type of stone used and was anything from 12 to 18 inches. Walls brought to course were stronger than the uncoursed type for the long continuous vertical joints were more readily avoided, although the horizontal joints sometimes detract a little from the cottage's appearance. Because of the irregularity of the stone used in random rubble walling the mortar joints were often thick and as previously stated were bedded in clay from a very early period. This practice continued for many centuries. William Marshall, writing in 1788, states that

> formerly ordinary stone buildings were carried up entirely with 'mortar', that is common earth beaten up with water, without the smallest admixture of lime. The stones themselves were depended upon as the bond or union, the use of mortar being merely that of giving warmth to the building and a degree of stiffness to the wall.[4]

Later, although these mortars were made with lime, they were soft and less weather-resistant than the cement mortars employed later. The life of a random rubble wall depended not only on the durability of the stone but also the skill of the waller in choosing and laying the stones and the degree to which the wall was exposed to the elements. This form of construction has been used in the erection of hundreds of cottages in various parts of the country.

The stability and life of rubble walling improved if the stones were first squared before use, so that they could be bonded more accurately with thinner mortar joints than was practicable with random rubble walling. This could be achieved where the stones were found in thin beds or in thicker beds of laminated stone which could be readily split into smaller blocks and where comparatively little labour was required to form straight bed or side joints. This form of construction was known as squared rubble walling and, like random rubble, the type of squared rubble used depended on the ease with which the rubble could be squared, whether the stones could be matched for height without too much selection, and the skill of the mason. The cheapest form employed was uncoursed squared rubble (*See* 80C), often known as square-snecked rubble, in which the stones, roughly squared, were available in various sizes and arranged on face to form several irregular patterns but without continuous horizontal courses. A pleasing effect was obtained when the wall comprised a combination of four stones – a large stone called a 'riser' or 'jumper', which was also generally a bonder, two thin stones called 'levellers' and a small stone called a sneck, which were characteristic of this type of walling and used to prevent long continuous vertical joints. Squared rubble could, like random rubble, be brought to course (*See* 80D). The stones were similar to those used for uncoursed squared rubble but were levelled up in courses of varying depth and, as with random rubble, larger stones were used at quoins and jambs. In some areas the stone could be quarried in more uniform sizes and were laid in what is known as coursed squared rubble (*See* 80E). The wall was

81. Colour-washed cottage, Dunster, Somerset.

built in courses of varying height, but the stones within any one course, unlike other rubble walling, were all of the same depth. Depending on the stone, these courses varied from 3 to 18 inches but were generally of about 9 inches and were 6 to 9 inches wide on bed. In certain areas of the country, where there was available a plentiful and convenient supply of hard stone with good weathering qualities, the face of the stones could be dressed to give a smooth finish and is sometimes referred to as 'rough ashlar'.

There are many varieties of walling which can be classified as rubble work but which, due to the characteristic of the materials as well as the traditional forms of construction peculiar to any one locality, differ from both random and squared rubble walling. Perhaps the most common is what is known as polygonal rubble walling (*See* 80F) where the stone used, although strong, could be easily split but was difficult to dress. It was dressed to an irregular polygonal shape and was bedded in position to show the face joints in all directions. This type of walling is also known as Kentish rag – a limestone found in Kent and used fairly extensively for this purpose. Another local variation can be found in Cumbria, in the Lake District, which is unique and required great skill by the wallers. The stone, which was found locally, varied in size from small pieces up to about 2 feet by 3 feet and were broken and dressed to the required size and shape by the waller as the work proceeded. Two forms of Lake District masonry, as it is known, are to be found; rough-faced random, where the stones are roughly dressed and irregular in shape, and best-faced random, which resembles square-snecked rubble, the stones being squared on face with a hammer. Rough-faced random was used for humbler work and the blocks were tightly fitted together with the through stones forming a continuous course every 2 or 3 feet. The wallers worked in pairs, the more experienced man working on the outside and the other on the inside assisted in packing up the face stones with 'spalls'. The walls were built in three sections, the inner and outer faces with an intermediate 'hearting' and was built 'watershot', that is the tilting of the stones downwards towards the external face, with particular attention being given to the throughs. Both faces are nowadays partially bedded in mortar kept back from the face some 2 or 3 inches, but were originally built dry with the hearting being dry packed with small stones. This ensured that any water penetrating the outer face would pass down the dry filling to the throughs below, which being watershot would carry the water to the outside. The thickness of these external walls varied from 21 to 30 inches. This form of construction proved so effective in resisting damp penetration in a district notorious for its high rainfall that it is still employed. Like other random walling, quoins and jambs were formed of larger stones, usually limestone, and often hammer dressed.

Most stone walls of cottages were built to a thickness of between 18 inches and 2 feet and their sturdy appearance was apt to belie their powers to resist both cold and damp especially when, as was more often the case than not, the foundations were built of dry rubble with no method of preventing rising damp, with the flagstone floor laid directly on the ground. Yet, for all this, the comfort these stone cottages afforded was certainly a great advance on the timber-framed wattle-and-daub hovels of the past which many replaced. These stone cottages were, however, subject in many ways to the same limitation, both in planning and arrangement, as the old timber-framed cottages, for the builders were still unable to roof them to a depth of more than one room and so to increase the size it was necessary either to add another bay or build an out-shut to the rear or side.

The stone for these cottages was invariably obtained from a local quarry, and it is the resultant variety, not only in the colour and texture of the stone – quarries in the same locality produced slightly different stone and even stone obtained from the same quarry varied – but also the local masonry technique, which gives them much of their undoubted charm. Rocks can be placed into one of three major groups; namely, igneous, sedimentary and metamorphic. Igneous rocks are rocks formed by the solidification of molten rock, called magma, which originated at considerable depths beneath the earth's surface in temperatures in excess of 600° centigrade. It reached the surface either by means of volcanoes and lava flows or by the erosion of the surface rocks in which the magma had been emplaced. Of the igneous rocks the only one employed to any extent in building in England is granite, a stone of great strength and durability. Because of its hardness it was difficult to cut, and most of the cottages built of this stone are built of moorstone, the surface stone lying about the moors of Devon, Cornwall and Cumbria. Metamorphic rocks are either of igneous or sedimentary origin, changed from their original form by the effects of heat or long continued pressure or a combination of both. Slate is a metamorphic rock and, although used for roofing throughout England, its use in walling is, like granite, restricted to Devon, Cornwall and Cumbria. Of all the building stones of England the sedimentary rocks are by far the most important. To this group belong the limestones and sandstones, which have been estimated as constituting at least 90 per cent of the stone buildings in England and if flint is left out the proportion would be as high as 99 per cent. Limestone basically consists of calcium carbonate which occurs in various forms; some are composed entirely of the remains of living organisms, like shells and fossilized animal life; others of primitive algae and seaweed; others by the direct chemical precipitation of calcium carbonate which occurs in some circumstances on the beds of seas and lakes. Although the majority of limestone consists essentially of calcium carbonate, some limestones contain various quantities of magnesium carbonate and are known as magnesian limestones, a stone much used in Yorkshire. Sandstones are composed principally of particles of quartz, with, on occasions, other minerals such as felspar and mica, all of which are cemented together by various matrix materials. It is these matrix materials that determine the stones' durability. The strongest sandstones are those cemented together with silica, for example the Millstone Grit of the southern Pennines, but others can be calcite, dolomite, oxide of iron, or even clay.

Of the two sedimentary rocks, limestone of the Jurassic series is the more important and most widely used. The principal area is the limestone belt, comprising the Oolite limestone to the east, with the Lias limestone to the west, which spreads from Dorset in the South to North Yorkshire in the North, culminating in the Cotswolds; an area which embraces a large part of Gloucestershire, the western fringe of Oxfordshire, a north-west corner of Wiltshire, part of Avon and a small corner of Hereford and Worcester around Bredon Hill. This area is a small architectural world of its own, and though today some villages – like Broadway, Bourton-on-the-Water, and to a lesser extent Bibury and Castle Combe – are somewhat spoilt by the tourists they attract, there are others – among them Upper and Lower Slaughter, Snowshill, Ilmington, Great and Little Rissington, Longborough, the

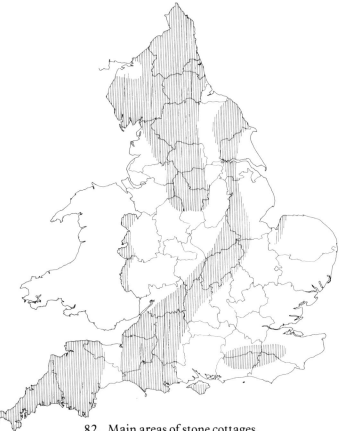

82. Main areas of stone cottages.

Duntisbournes, Stanton, Great Tew, Sherston, Little Barrington, Bledington and Church Icomb – which have survived almost unspoilt. The majority of the cottages in these villages were built in the seventeenth and eighteenth centuries, although some survive from the middle of the fifteenth and sixteenth centuries. Two important factors influenced the evolution of these villages; the prosperity of the district derived from sheep and a good supply of limestone, which was not only readily available but was comparatively easy to work when first quarried. It was the softness of this creamy or pale golden stone that rendered it possible for the many refinements seen in the Cotswolds to be undertaken. The well-moulded mullioned windows with the elaborate dripstone dropping down at each end of the windows and then neatly returning, the gable coping stones, the chimney stacks crowned with a generous cornice, the date-stones and the abundance of ornamental finials are all characteristic of the Cotswolds. Perhaps, however, the most striking feature is the dormer for, although in many cottages they are small with the dormer window simply standing on the wall or set back on the roof, in some the main wall is built to form a gable, often with a ridge as high, or nearly as high as the ridge of the main roof. A combination of all three

83. Cottage row, Broadway, Hereford and Worcester.

types of dormers can be seen at Arlington Row, Bibury, a row of seven cottages which show all the characteristic style of the Cotswolds; not only the dormers but also the mullioned windows some surmounted by a dripstone, the straight-headed lintel to doors, the chimneys with moulded cornice and the steeply pitched stone-slate roof of the same limestone as the walls, supported on several middle or upper cruck trusses. Now owned by the National Trust, this row of cottages date in their present form from the seventeenth century and were, it is believed, originally used in connection with the local cloth industry. What is most

84. Cottage row, Enstone, Oxfordshire.

85. Arlington Row,
Bibury,
Gloucestershire.

striking about the Cotswolds is the abundance of stone buildings – churches, manor houses, market-halls, farm buildings and cottages – all employing the same style, yet varying in richness according to the building's scale.

From the Cotswolds the limestone belt extends north-eastwards across most of Oxfordshire; to the north and west of the county the golden-brown stone of the Cotswolds changes to the iron-impregnated brown stones of the villages of Wroxton, Shotteswell, Cropredy and Hornton, as well as the adjacent part of Warwickshire where Warmington, built of Hornton stone, is the county's showpiece. The belt continues north-east across all of Northamptonshire, where the stone varies from the brown ironstone villages of the west – like Preston Capes, Grimscote and Rockingham – to the golden-yellow oolite stone villages of the east – like Aynho, a village justly celebrated for its beauty with a number of ancient stone cottages, some with outside stairs, and Alderton, Tichmarsh, with cottages of Weldon stone, and Polebrook, a village with pleasant limestone and thatched cottages, so typical of the neighbourhood. In the western half of Leicestershire, particularly in the former county of Rutland, the warm brown stones of Northamptonshire change to the delicate granular buffs and the yellowish pink varieties of Lincolnshire limestone. It is here that the famous quarries of Ketton, Clipsham and Casterton, together with those at Barnack, Cambridgeshire, Ancaster, Lincolnshire and Weldon, Northamptonshire, sent out choice building stone to all parts of the country. This region, with Stamford as the centre, is without doubt the second most important stone area outside the Cotswolds. Villages like Ufford, Cambridgeshire, and Collyweston, Northamptonshire, in their setting and texture of their building stone could belong to the fringes of the Cotswolds rather than to the edges of the Fens. Here all the delightful features of the Cotswolds can be found. With so much good stone available naturally cottages were also built of stone. Ayston, Ketton, Ryhall and Belton all have delightful groups, many of which are thatched, but perhaps the best are to be seen at Exton, with its delightful green with stone cottages all round.

From Leicestershire the limestone belt extends northwards into Lincolnshire, where village after village is built of rubble limestone from some nearby quarry. Unlike the Cotswolds, the stone buildings of Kesteven are of a later date; houses of the sixteenth and seventeenth centuries are relatively rare, the bulk having been built in the eighteenth century. In southern Kesteven, in villages like Barholm, the roofs are usually Collyweston slate, but further north, away from Northamptonshire, the typical Lincolnshire roofing of pantiles is equally effective. These rubble limestone buildings spread down into the Fens and, in fact, some of the finest stone cottages in the county are to be found in the Deepings, Baston and Castle Bytham, the most charming of all. To the west of the

86. Stone cottages, Boughton, Northamptonshire.

limestone ridge, in villages like Caythorpe and Hough on the Hill, the stone changes to the brown ironstone and even further west one finds cottages, like those around the church at Long Bennington, built of the blue-grey stone of the Lias. North of Lincoln and into Humberside the number of stone cottages decreases perceptibly, yet can still be found here and there like Kirton-in-Lindsey. Across the Humber the Oolitic limestone is only intermittent, but there is a narrow belt of lias limestone extending northwards. Several of the older cottages found in villages like Howsham are built of a rich orange-brown stone from this belt. Oolitic stone is found again in North Yorkshire, in and around the villages of the North Yorkshire Moors, but here the best Jurassic stone is often sandstone rather than limestone. Some of the most attractive cottages in this area are to be found at Lastingham, Thornton Dale, a charming village with cottages beside a stream crossed by small bridges; and Hutton-le-Hole, a village of scattered cottages set round a large green with a stream running through.

To the south of the Cotswolds, where the limestone belt extends into parts of Dorset, Wiltshire and Somerset, limestone cottages abound and, although few possess the refinements associated with those of the Cotswolds, they are nevertheless still attractive. In the western part of Somerset the limestone cottages are often of greyish-cream or buff stone as those at Shepton Mallet, High Ham and Mells, one of Somerset's most beautiful villages with its thatched stone cottages. Further south in the county, as well as the adjacent part of Dorset, in and around the villages of Stocklinch, Dowlish Wake, Donyatt, Montacute, Martock and Stoke sub Hamdon, are many cottages built of Ham Hill stone, a rich golden-brown stone, the surfaces of which attract lichen, giving it an attractive mottled appearance.

In the villages in the neighbourhood of Bath, among them Monkton Combe, a hamlet of ancient stone cottages, the best of the stone cottages can hold their own with any in the country. Along the Nadder Valley, in Wiltshire, cottages in the villages of Barford St Martin, Fonthill Bishop, and Fovant, as well as the picturesque villages of Chilmark and Teffont Evias (where many of the cottages are reached by delightful little stone footbridges crossing the sparkling Teff which runs beside the road) are all built from the once famous quarries of Chilmark and Tisbury. Producing limestone of almost identical fine-grained texture, these creamy-white stones were used in many important buildings in the area, including Salisbury Cathedral. Much of Shaftesbury and the surrounding district is built of greensand stone, a Cretaceous sandstone which in many cottages looks particularly pleasing chequered with flint.

Some thirty miles south of Chilmark, in Dorset, are to be found many cottages of Purbeck stone, particularly between Swanage and Dorchester, in villages like Corfe Castle and Worth Matravers. Often the cottages are roofed with heavy stone-slates from the same quarry, which causes the roofs to sag and adds charm to many old cottages. Further west in the county many cottages are built of a golden-yellow stone, like those at Stoke Abbott, Chideock, Powerstock and Symondsbury.

In the South Midlands, to the east of the Oolite limestone, are the coarser Jurassic limestones, of which Coral Rag and Cornbrash limestones are the most widely used. Cornbrash limestone, and the Great Oolite formation below it, yields inferior stones liable to spall and crumble, yet were at one time widely employed and can be seen in many villages throughout central Oxfordshire, North Buckinghamshire and along the Bedfordshire, Northamptonshire and Cambridgeshire borders; among them Marsh Gibbon, Hanslope, Thornborough and Odell. Coral rag is more durable and cottages of this rubble stone, laid with plenty of mortar, give the impression of great strength. It is found in many villages to the south-west of Oxford, from Cumnor and into Wiltshire, at such places as Faringdon, Highworth, Wootton Bassett and Calne. It is found again in Dorset to the south-west of Shaftesbury, in and around the villages of Marnhull and Todber.

On the downs and heaths of southern England, particularly the Marlborough Downs, in the villages on the Wiltshire and Berkshire borders – such as Lambourn, Ashbury, the nearby hamlet of Idstone, and Avebury – sarsen, the youngest of our sandstones (up to 70 million years old), can be found. The stones, sometimes called 'grey wethers' or 'heathstones', are unique in England, for they are sandstone boulders, of indeterminate size, found just below the surface, and are firmly cemented remnants of what was once a more continuous layer largely eroded away. Although sometimes of enormous size – the stone circle at Avebury and the larger stones at Stonehenge are all sarsens – the stone could be picked from the surface of the downs and was in some areas more readily available than chalk or flint and was often used in cottages.

The Tertiary series which yields sarsen is to be found in the Isle of Wight, but it was, however, sandstone from the Cretaceous series that was most widely used. Found on the southern side of the island, especially between St Catherine's Point and Bonchurch, it was used in the construction of many cottages on the island as well as buildings further afield. Some of the most attractive rubble stone cottages on the island can be seen at Godshill, Shorwell, Brighstone and Calbourne, where Winkle Street, with its rubble cottages, flowers and stream, is most charming.

Apart from chalk and flint, the south-eastern counties of Sussex, Surrey and Kent have little building stone and what there is is mainly sandstone. In the Weald, cottages of sandstone are to be found in many villages, among them Bepton, Bury, where more than half the cottages are built of sandstone and hardly any of flint or chalk although there is

87. Colour-washed stone cottages, Burton Bradstock, Dorset.

88. Stone cottages, Stoke Abbott, Dorset.

chalk a mile away; and Rogate, a village of yellow sandstone and tiled roofs. North of Midhurst can be found cottages built with a greenish sandstone called Burgate. It can be found at Woolbeding (where it is used with brick dressings), Amberley and Washington. Burgate is also found in Surrey in the Guildford–Godalming neighbourhood. Further to the east, in Kent, a limestone known as Kentish Rag is found. A rough, brittle stone which is difficult to work, it was used for many important buildings in medieval times, not only in Kent but also in the surrounding counties. The stone regained popularity in Victorian times and was used on the estate cottages at Linton and some two-storey cottages at Greatness, near Sevenoaks.

North of the Thames, to the west of the limestone belt, a narrow belt of sandstone called carstone can be found. It was used in Bedfordshire and Cambridgeshire, but it is mainly in Norfolk where, apart from chalk and flint, it is the only building stone in the county. Here the carstone is heavily impregnated with iron oxide, resulting in a dark, somewhat drab, brown. The principal quarry was at Snettisham, and several villages, from Downham Market northwards to Hunstanton, like Stow Bardolph, Setchly and North Runcton, as well as many cottages on the Sandringham estate, are built of this stone. Although moderate size blocks were sometimes obtained, most of these cottages are built of tiny pieces between 1 and 2 inches thick which give a more pleasing effect.

In the South-west, to the west of the limestone belt, in Devon, Cornwall and the western part of Somerset around Exmoor, although the traditional material for cottage building was cob, there are a great number constructed of stone. Around Exeter and extending northwards to Cullompton and Halberton they are often constructed of a red sandstone, but more often they are of the dark brownish-red sandstone found between Dartmoor and Exmoor. In North Devon and West Somerset the slates of the Devonian rocks are to be found intermingled with areas of sandstone and limestone. Cottages of all these materials are to be found on Exmoor and along that splendid coast from Porlock to Mortehoe. The stone cottages of Dartmoor are of granite. Built of moorstone, these cottages, sometimes incorporating very large blocks, were often built without mortar and, as elsewhere in the South-west, frequently covered with so many successive coats of whitewash that it is sometimes difficult to distinguish them from their cob neighbours. Stone is the predominate building material in Cornwall, but, whereas in the rest of the country this would mean either limestone or sandstone, here it means granite or slate. Like those in Devon, the granite cottages of Cornwall were generally built of moorstone, often built dry and whitewashed like many in the fishing villages of Polperro and Mevagissey. Cornish granite is mainly concentrated in four areas between Bodmin Moor and Land's End – around Bodmin, the Land's End peninsula, around St Austell and the area encompassed by Falmouth, Helston and Camborne. Within these areas, in villages like Camelford, Troon, Wendron and Madron, as well as elsewhere occasionally, rugged Cornish granite cottages (frequently whitewashed) can be found. The most attractive of Cornwall's granite villages is Blisland, with its stone cottages around a green, an unusual feature in Cornwall.

Slate, quarried from the Devonian rock which covers a large part of Cornwall, was also often used as walling. So plentiful was this material that it was not always necessary to quarry it, for much was readily available lying about as scree. This stone-slate tended, by its nature, to be rather long and thin, often splitting to points, so that much mortar was necessary. Some of these granite and slate-stone cottages of Cornwall and the south-western part of Devon were slate-hung as an additional protection against the Atlantic gales. The slates, basically similar to roofing slates, were usually hung on timber battens fixed to the face of the wall, the top edges of the slates being bedded in mortar. Sometimes pattern slates were introduced, either in small panels or continuous bands, but generally the entire wall, from top to bottom, was covered with rows of plain slates, the largest at the bottom decreasing in width towards the eaves. Slate-hung cottages can be seen throughout the above areas and can on occasions even be found to be whitewashed. Today the best place to observe slate-hanging is at the Devon town of Totnes.

Both slate and granite were quarried in Leicestershire, the only area between Devon and Cumbria where these materials are found. The slate was not used for walling but granite was, and today is still quarried, although now it is only used as road stone. The stone, quarried at Mountsorrel, is extremely hard and was not used much for building until 1812, when it was discovered how to work the granite. Closely related to granite are syenite and porphyry, both of which are to be found in the Charnwood Forest of Leicestershire, and together with granite are collectively often referred to as 'forest stone'. Many cottages, as well as barns, constructed of these stones, built of rubble in random fashion with brick dressing to jambs and quoins, can be seen in some of the forest villages among them Newtown Linford, Woodhouse Eaves and Croft.

The vast majority of the great stone-building area of northern England can seldom compare with the charm and mellow characteristics of those of the limestone belt and the South. The magnesian limestones, the stones of the Carboniferous series, the granites and slates which cover most of the northern region are hard stones, difficult to shape, and because of this almost impossible to carve. Yet these characteristics attribute much to the ruggedness and the simplicity of many of the cottages of the Peak District, the Lancashire slopes of the Pennines, Cumbria, the Yorkshire Dales, and the area north of the Tee which blend in perfectly with the bleak, harsher climate with which they have to contend. These

89. Slate-hung cottage, Kingbeare, Cornwall.

90. Cottages at Hovingham, North Yorkshire.

cottages are squat, built as low as possible to escape the worst of the winds in these exposed districts, with shallow pitched roofs with little or no eaves overhanging, and covered with heavy stone-slates or tiles, but rarely with thatch, although this was, up to 200 years ago, found in many parts of the North before being replaced by austere red tiles and blue-grey slates. Unlike the cottages of further south, dormers were rarely used, the cottages often being double-fronted with an unadorned chimney at each end often, as in the Lake District, protected against down draught by two pieces of slate inclined together to form an inverted V-shape. Surrounds to window and door openings were commonly made from single blocks of gritstone or granite, set projecting slightly from the face of the wall. In the Lake District, the Peak District and parts of Northumberland, particularly around Wooler and Elsdon, one finds many single-storey cottages built in the tradition of the old longhouse, with dwelling accommodation one end and byre for the animals the other, and which continued to be built well into the latter half of the nineteenth century.

The best of these stones are the magnesian limestones. Stretching in a narrow strip from Nottingham northwards, along the Nottinghamshire and Derbyshire border, into Yorkshire as far as Ripon and then in a widening triangle across County Durham to the coast between the Tees and Tyne, it provided stone for innumerable churches in the North, as well as for York and Beverley Minsters and many important buildings further afield. It is in South, West and North Yorkshire, however, that it was most widely used and can be seen in many villages like Arksey, Campsall, Hooton Pagnell, and Darrington. Like other limestones it was comparatively soft when quarried, hardening on exposure, and so it was possible to introduce some refinements.

The other limestone of the North belongs to the Carboniferous series of rocks, sometimes known as 'mountain limestone', for it is generally found in the sparsely populated mountainous regions of England. One such area is the Peak District, where it is the principal building stone of the central and southern part, and is found in most of the villages of the limestone plateau where this greyish-white stone lightens the whole landscape. Outside the Peak District, carboniferous limestone is to be found in Cumbria, on the west side of the Pennines, where Gilsland, Alston, Kirkby Lonsdale and Ravenstonedale, are typical grey stone villages. The stone could be dressed, but most walling was of rubble stone constructed of small pieces and a good deal of mortar. Dotted about the countryside, as well as in the villages and towns, these cottages are often limewashed. This stone can also be found in many villages across the border into North Yorkshire, like Deepdale, Thwaite, Wensley and Keld, a lovely grey stone village, as well as further north in and around Richmond and into County

Durham in places like Romaldkirk. In Northumberland this stone is again widespread, and like the stone of Cumbria, North Yorkshire and County Durham is a somewhat darker grey than those of the Peak District and is not infrequently whitewashed. Because of the late development of Northumberland many of the cottages date from the nineteenth century, many being part of estate or planned villages, of which Etal (where some cottages date from the eighteenth century), Blanchland and Bamburgh (with its cottages of soft grey stone below the castle), are some of the best.

The two principal formations which make up the carboniferous sandstones are the Coal Measures and the Millstone Grit. Although not the most attractive of sandstones they are unrivalled both for strength and durability. The sandstones from the Coal Measures are usually associated with industrial regions of the North: Greater Manchester, in such towns as Oldham, Rochdale and Colne; West Yorkshire, around Leeds, Bradford and Halifax; the eastern part of Derbyshire; the corner of Nottinghamshire; as well as in parts of Durham, Northumberland and Tyne and Wear. Millstone Grit, or gritstone, as the stone from this formation is often known, is more characteristic of rural areas and is found in many of the Pennine villages of Lancashire and Greater Manchester as well as in northern Lancashire. On the eastern side of the Pennines, almost as far north as Richmond, North Yorkshire, gritstone cottages can be found. Many in the north are plastered and whitewashed, which brightens the rather dark tones of these stones. Gritstone is the principal building stone of the southern Pennines, extending to the east of the central limestone plateau along the great sweep of the Derwent valley and its tributaries the Ashop and Noe, in such villages as Bamford, Baslow and Darley Dale, and to the west of the Dove valley into Staffordshire and Cheshire. In many villages, like Hulme End, Longnor, Sparrowpit, the Hucklows and Eyam, along the edge of the limestone plateau, cottages are to be found with both limestone and gritstone incorporated into the same building.

Granite and slate-stone cottages can still be found in Cumbria. Granite is mainly found in and around Eskdale, where cottages, like those of the South-west, were not infrequently built without mortar and likewise were often whitewashed. Slate-stone walling is also found in the Lake District and even today, because it blends so well in its mountainous setting, is still used. Built as previously described, these walls were often built without mortar, and today the mortar is kept back from the face of the wall in order to give it this appearance. The stone-slate was obtained from the waste material from the production of roof slates, called 'greenstone', although it is not always green. Often both slate-stone and granite can be seen together, as the row of early nineteenth-century cottages at Elterwater, near Ambleside, where the walls are of slate-stone with large

91. Harome cottage at Ryedall Folk Museum, Hutton-le-Hole. A typical cottage of North Yorkshire, built in the second half of the eighteenth century, based on an old cruck cottage. Moved from Harome in 1972.

92. Cottages at Thornton Dale, North Yorkshire.

uneven granite slabs as lintels and quoins and smaller ones to the jambs of windows and doors. Many of the cottages around Hawkshead, Staveley, Bowness, Windermere and Ambleside are constructed of Silurian stone, an extremely hard material which was relatively cheap and readily available. Normally used as rubble, its severe colouring of sombre greys, blacks and browns are not attractive and like so many of the cottages of Cumbria are often roughcast and whitewashed, and as at Hawkshead are occasionally slate-hung, although the practice is less common than in the South-west.

Apart from these stones much of the North, particularly the western half, is covered with New Red Sandstone. In Cumbria in places like Longtown, Brampton, Kirkoswald, Lazonby and Maryport the stones are red, pink or brown, as they are to the south-east of St Bees. In the Fylde, Lancashire, stone cottages, usually whitewashed, can still be found here and there, as they can in Staffordshire, as well as in some of the mellow villages of northern Salop. Although New Red Sandstone covers much of the Midlands and West, little is found in cottages, for timber in this area was plentiful well into the seventeenth century, and except in some areas stone was rarely used for domestic buildings. Along the Welsh border, in Hereford and Worcester and in particular in the hills of southern Salop, cottages built of one of the oldest sandstones, belonging to the Ordovician series, can be found. The villages of Holdgate, Newcastle, Llanvair Waterdine and Cardington, a village built of large stones reminiscent of a Dartmoor village, are all typical of the many built with this stone in the area.

Two building stones not previously mentioned, but which played an important part in cottage architecture, are chalk and flint. The use of chalk, one of the youngest of the limestones used for building, although used in churches and other early buildings, was mainly confined to humbler buildings. The chalk is found in the southern and eastern parts of the country; the North and South Downs, the downs of Berkshire, Dorset, Hampshire and Wiltshire, the Chilterns, the Gogmagogs, and the Lincolnshire and Yorkshire Wolds are all of chalk, as well as a large part of Suffolk and western Norfolk. One of the whitest of our building stones, it often contains tinges of other colours, caused either by muddy impurities or other minerals. The most striking example of this is around Hunstanton, Norfolk, where below the white chalk is an older layer of red chalk. Cottages in and around Old Hunstanton sometimes incorporate both white and red chalk as well as a brown carstone, brick and local flint.

Compared with other stones, chalk is soft, and one of its attractions was the ease with which it was quarried and cut into blocks, its only disadvantage being that some types did not weather well. This softness made it unsuitable for quoins, jambs and plinths, and so brick, or

93. Seventeenth-century stone cottages at Chipping, Lancashire.

sometimes a more durable stone, was introduced at these vulnerable points to provide greater protection. The ease with which chalk could be cut into blocks made it possible to be coursed and even to be given an ashlar appearance with fine joints, but often, as at Brancaster, Titchwell and the Burnhams – all in Norfolk, Flamborough, Humberside and elsewhere on the Yorkshire Wold – many cottages are built of chalk rubble. Because of its softness it was vulnerable to the damp and it was desirable to protect the chalk, often, when thatched, with generous over-hanging eaves, or a coat of limewash (as at Northwold), or plaster. Not all chalk needed this protection for often, as in parts of Humberside, and at Uffington, Oxfordshire, the stone was hard, but more often the chalk would, if not protected, soon crumble away.

Not all areas where chalk was found was it suitable for walling; in Kent, apart from some isolated areas at the foot of the North Downs as at

Boxley, the chalk was too porous, while in Surrey little is found. In Lincolnshire and South Humberside, although at one time chalk must have been widely used, today, except in isolated places as at Swaby, chalkstone cottages are rare. Cottages constructed of chalkstone — sometimes referred to as 'clunch', although this term really refers to the more marly type of chalk found in Cambridgeshire — are to be found mainly to the east of the limestone belt, the only area west of the belt being around Beer, in the eastern corner of Devon, where a shelly chalkstone was quarried and used extensively in many churches and cottages in East Devon and West Dorset. East of the limestone belt, the main counties where chalk cottages are to be seen are Dorset; Wiltshire, where the village of Compton Bassett has many delightful cottages; Hampshire; West Sussex, in villages like East and South Harting, Elsted, and Treyford; Berkshire; the southern part of Oxfordshire around Uffington, where nearly the entire village is built of chalk; Bedfordshire, around Totternhoe; Cambridgeshire, in villages like Burwell and Swaffham Prior; western Norfolk, where it is often used in conjunction with flint and carstone; and many parts of the Yorkshire Wold, where it was commonly used on humbler dwellings like those at Speeton. Apart from isolated examples, as at Uffington and Burwell, which have a few seventeenth- or early eighteenth-century houses, most of the smaller chalk buildings date from the late eighteenth and early nineteenth centuries. At Burwell, cottages constructed with a brick front wall and side and rear walls of rubble chalkstone continued to be built well into the nineteenth century.

The use of flint as a building material has been known from the Early Iron Age; the Romans made extensive use of it, while during the Saxon and Norman periods flint was a building material of paramount importance. Its use continued throughout the Middle Ages, but it was not until much later — in East Anglia about the time of Elizabeth I, when wood began to grow scarce — that it became the usual material for cottages and farm buildings.

Flints are irregular-shaped nodules of silica and, although extremely hard and virtually indestructible, are brittle and can be fractured in any direction. They are found in the upper layers of the Chalk formation and when dug are practically black, usually with a white 'rind' over their surface, varying considerably in size, some being as large as 12 inches. Flints, being easy to split, could be either snapped across or polled, or alternatively knapped — large flints snapped across and the split surfaces dressed to give faces approximately 4 inches square. Both polled and knapped walling was reserved for the more pretentious buildings; for cottages the flints were undressed, built either uncoursed or, when small flints were used, roughly coursed. Because of the nature of the material, a great deal of mortar was required and so the strength of the wall depended upon the type of mortar used. It was essential that the external

94. Stone cottages at Downham, Lancashire, typical of many
found in the villages of the North.

face of each flint was completely ringed with mortar and since only clay
or, later, lime mortar was used, both of which dried slowly, the excessive
amount of mortar required restricted each rise to no more than a foot
or two at any one time before it was necessary to be left to dry out. As
the flint used was generally small and round, the wall always had a ten-
dency to bulge out and to overcome this, brick, or where available
stone, was introduced to provide greater rigidity. This was achieved by
two methods; first the quoins, jambs, eaves and verges were built of
brick or stone, not only for greater strength but also the nature of the
material made it impracticable to build square corners; and secondly by
the introduction of lacing courses. These lacing courses (*See* 95C) comprised a continuous course of bricks or stone extending the full width of
the wall every 3 to 6 feet. In Norfolk, to further strengthen the walls,
cottages were sometimes constructed with a brick internal lining into
which the lacing courses were bonded. Where the flints were small and
regular in size the wall was often coursed and to strengthen these walls

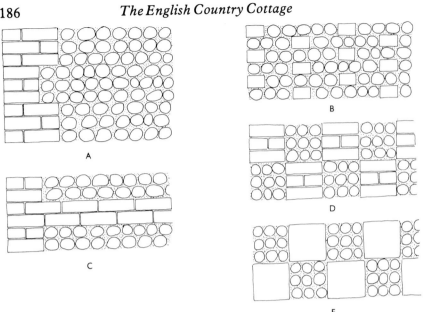

95. Decorative flintwork: A. brick dressing; B. bonders producing chequer; C. lacing course; D. brick and flint chequer; E. stone and flint chequer.

brick bonders were introduced, replacing every fourth, sixth or eighth flint to give a chequered appearance (*See* 95B). Examples of this form of construction can be found in North Norfolk, particularly along the coast at places like Blakeney and further inland at Edgefield.

Flint cottages are to be found throughout the chalk belt, from Norfolk in the north to Dorset in the south and across to Sussex and Kent in the east. Norfolk has a high proportion of these cottages, particularly along the North Norfolk coast between Stiffkey in the west and Sheringham in the east, where round sea-washed beach pebbles were extensively used. In fact, in such villages at Cley-next-the-sea, Blakeney, Weybourne and Salthouse and further inland at Langham, Binham, Wiveton and Baconsthorpe, all the older buildings are constructed of these pebbles. Sometimes, to good effect, these cottages are white- or colour-washed and, on occasions, the ones along the coast are even tarred, usually on the sea-ward side, as protection against the weather. Further along the coast, at Brancaster, large irregular flint nodules from 9 to 12 inches across can be seen with the joints 'galleted'. Along the Suffolk coast, north of Aldeburgh, sea-washed pebbles, like those on the North Norfolk coast, were used. The other principal area for flint cottages in East Anglia is in Breckland, in villages like Eriswell, Wangford, Lackford and Icklingham, where the flints are richer, with a darker lustre than

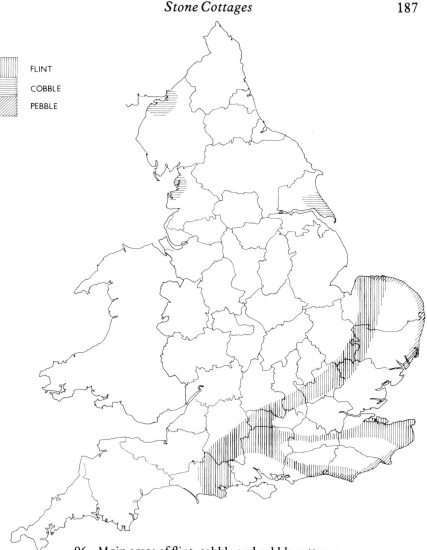

96. Main areas of flint, cobble and pebble cottages.

almost anywhere else. Further south in Suffolk, flint cottages, sometimes built with fragments of brick and conglomerate stone all jumbled together, appear here and there among the plastered cottages. Apart from this area of Suffolk, flint cottages are to be found in the western half of Essex, Hertfordshire, the southern and eastern parts of Oxfordshire, Buckinghamshire, Bedfordshire and Cambridgeshire. Nowhere in these counties, however, are they found in anything like the profusion as on the North Norfolk coast and Breckland areas.

Of the southern counties Sussex has perhaps the most cottages built of flint. They are found on the Downs in villages like Compton, East Marden, East Dean, Cocking and Amberley, along the coastal plain in such villages as Aldingbourne, Eartham, Felpham, Patching and Rustington, with an occasional incursion north into the Weald in the villages of Ashurst and Washington where the Downs meet the Weald. In and around Brighton there are cottages of sea-washed beach pebbles like those in Norfolk. Kent too has many flint cottages and those at Downe are typical of the flint cottages found scattered all over the chalk uplands of the North Downs, spreading eastward to the Isle of Thanet. Like Kent, flint was employed extensively for cottages in Surrey from the ridge of the North Downs northwards, in such villages as Chelsham, Farleigh and Wanborough. In rural Hampshire as well as Berkshire, flint is easily the favourite building material. In Hampshire these cottages are intermingled with ones of brick and half-timber, like those in the villages of Catherington, Droxford and Hambledon. Often brick is found in conjunction with flint, not, as elsewhere, simply as dressings to quoins and jambs, but in alternate bands with the flint. Further west in Dorset and Wiltshire flint is still abundant on the Downs and intervening villages. Typical is the village of Hilton, Dorset. In both counties the best effects were obtained when flint was employed with local stone, either in alternating bands or chequers. Bands are more common in Dorset and to the eastern side of the county in the villages of Tarrant Hinton and Winterborne Stickland, cottages with bands of flint alternating with brick can be seen, but this practice is less common than in Hampshire. With such a variety of building materials it was only to be expected that in Wiltshire combinations were thought out which are not only durable but decorative. Flint with plain brick dressing, flint and brick bands, flint and stone bands, as in the Avon Valley north of Salisbury, were all used, but it is the chequered flint and stone cottages, like those at Winterbourne Stoke, Tilshead and Wylye, which are perhaps the most attractive. When used in bands or chequers the flints are usually polled to expose their dark inside.

A material similar to flint, found not in chalk but in many different rocks, is chert. Although of silica like flint, it differs in that flint is always black or dark grey beneath its 'rind', whereas chert is usually brown. Although found along the northern extremities of the Weald, it can be best seen where the counties of Devon, Somerset and Dorset meet in the villages of Colyton, Shute Barton and Awliscombe.

Similar to flint in the way they are used in buildings but not from the geological standpoint, are pebbles and cobbles. Derived from a great variety of rocks, the distinction between the two is one purely of size — pebbles being usually less than 3 inches diameter and cobbles varying greatly in size up to a foot or sometimes more across. These pebbles and cobbles are fragments of broken rock which have been transported either

97. Old whitewashed stone cottages at West Kirby, Merseyside.

by glacial ice or water and have in the process been rounded. They are therefore found in fields, in river-beds and, in Cumbria between Millom and St Bees, along the beach, where they are known as 'cobble-ducks'. Cobbles are found in Lancashire (from Blackpool northward), the Cumbrian coast and in the Lake District. Usually laid unbroken and random, they were generally used in the construction of field walls, barns and some of the humbler cottages in these areas. In North Humberside in the alluvial plain of Holderness, cobbles, either collected from the boulder clay or washed out of the boulder clay and gathered from the beach (known as 'boulder stones'), were at one time extensively used for cottages as well as other buildings including churches. These stones were sometimes a foot long and 5 to 6 inches thick, and could therefore produce only clumsy, irregular-looking walls which required a great deal of

98. Cottage, Low Tilberthwaite, Cumbria, with one of the few remaining spinning galleries in the Lake District.

mortar with broken pieces of brick sometimes forced into the gaps. Cottages and farm buildings constructed of these cobbles can be found in many villages near Spurn Head, particularly Skeffling and Easington, and northwards along the coast.

As previously mentioned, stone cottages were often rendered – generally roughcast or pebble-dashed – or whitewashed. Both processes were employed not so much for their decorative qualities but to provide additional protection against the weather. The traditional consistency of roughcast comprised an aggregate containing sand, gravel or stone chippings mixed with slaked lime and water. An undercoat of lime and sand was applied to the wall surface and while still wet the roughcast was thrown on, either by hand or trowel from a wooden board known as a 'hawk'. Roughcasting is found on cottages throughout the country in areas where walls are roughly constructed, such as in the South-west and the Lake District, or in areas where the stone is soft, like those of Cambridgeshire, Buckinghamshire and Bedfordshire. Pebble-dash is similar to roughcast but, instead of a mixture of gravel and lime, small pebbles without the addition of lime are thrown onto the wall. Because both were cheap and efficient they have been widely used throughout the country. In all parts of the country where cottages were built of

99. Cottages, Birk Howe, Little Langdale, Cumbria.

rubblestone, whitewash was the traditional surface treatment which was both cheap and easily applied. The lime was slaked and applied thickly to the wall, filling in cracks and holes and keeping the cottage in good repair. The process would be repeated every year or two, so some cottages, especially in the North and West, often have a crust of whitewash more than a quarter of an inch thick. This whitewash, particularly if the tone of the stone is of a dark nature, often adds a welcome touch of

100. Flint and pantiled cottages, Cley-next-the-Sea, Norfolk.

brightness to the cottages and charm to the landscape.

The character of all stone cottages not only reflected the materials with which they were built, but also the temperament of the people, their way of life and the aspect of the land. Of all cottages, the stone ones perhaps harmonize better than any other with the surrounding landscape. Invariably built of local stone, many seem to be extensions of the landscape, much in accord with the surroundings in which they are placed. William Wordsworth, writing of the Lakeland cottage, expresses what is true of so many stone cottages in other areas:

These humble dwellings remind the spectator of a production of nature and may rather be said to have grown than to have been created; to have risen, by an instinct of their own, out of the naked rock – so little is there in them of formality, such is their wildness and beauty.

101. Nineteenth-century brick cottages at Warter, Humberside.

The bleak, exposed nature of the Peak District, Cumbria, the Yorkshire Dales, the Lancashire slope of the Pennines, Cornwall and Dartmoor; the harsh climate; the isolation; the nature of the stone available (granite, gritstone and slate – all almost impossible to dress) all contributed to the rugged simple styles, somewhat forbidding upon first acquaintance, but which blend happily with their respective surroundings, yet would look out of place in most parts of the South. The Cotswolds cottage, with its refinements so suited to its own district, would look out of place in almost any other part of the country, particularly in the North. Even in the western part of the Midlands, always rich in timber, with its rich arable lands and pastures, the New Red Sandstone adds interest to the landscape, blending as it does with the colour of the soil. This is the great value of using local stone, for it is this harmony with the landscape that adds so much to their character, whether they are the granite cottages of Dartmoor, the flint cottages of North Norfolk, the chalk cottages of the Downs, the limestone cottages of the Cotswolds and limestone belt, the gritstone cottages of the Peak District, the slate and granite cottages of Cumbria, or the sandstone cottages of the Yorkshire Dales and Moors – all are akin to their environment. It was not until Victorian times, with the easy transportation of stone, brick and slates, that the vernacular tradition was unhappily broken in all but a few isolated areas.

Brick Cottages

If a survey was made today of the cottages of England the great majority of them would be constructed of brick, and of these most would have been built since 1800. Although bricks have been used from Roman times, it was not until the thirteenth century that the first English bricks were made. Unlike the Roman bricks, which were cut to size out of a slab of clay and were more like tiles than bricks, English bricks were made in moulds. The earliest examples of these bricks are in East Anglia, particularly around Colchester where the outbuildings at Little Coggeshall Abbey, dating from about 1190, and the rectangular chapel of about 1225, although principally of flint, have brick dressings which though badly weathered are clearly part of the original structures. At Little Wenham, Suffolk, there is a small fortified house, built about 1275, constructed of various materials, including a large proportion of brick of various colours. It was probably the influence of Flemish immigrants settling along the East coast which encouraged the practice of building in brick.

It was not, however, until the fifteenth century that brick gradually became more popular, and then only in the East and South-east. Up to this time the word 'brick' had not entered the English vocabulary, being known before this as 'waltyles'. It was Hampton Court Palace, erected by Cardinal Wolsey and Henry VIII, that made brick a fashionable material. After this, other grand houses – like Sutton Place, Surrey; Layer Marney Towers and Lees Priory, both in Essex – were constructed. The use of brick continued to flourish and in the sixteenth century during the reign of Elizabeth I many notable brick houses – Melford Hall and Kentwell Hall, both in Suffolk; Charlecote Park, Warwickshire; Sissinghurst Castle and Cobham Hall, both in Kent; Moyns Park, Essex; Doddington Hall, Lincolnshire; Breccle Hall, Norfolk; and Burton Constable, Humberside – were built.

With such an increase in the use of brick it was not long before it came into use on smaller domestic buildings, but then only in the construction of chimneys, often built into timber-framed buildings of an earlier date. These bricks were made from suitable earth found locally, dug during the winter, and left so that the frost could break it up. In the spring, it was wetted and trodden out by foot, on hay or straw strewn on the ground to prevent sticking, until all pebbles and other foreign bodies had been removed, placed into wooden moulds, left to dry for a month before finally being fired, probably for about a week. As the clay was often dug

102. Main areas of distribution of brick cottages.

adjacent to the building, an improvised kiln known as a 'clamp' was used.
These were large stacks of dried bricks daubed on the outside with clay.
Brushwood was often the only fuel and consequently, as the control of
the kiln temperature was difficult, bricks of irregular shape and different
colours were produced. The size of these bricks also varied greatly in different areas and although some attempt was made to standardize the
dimensions – in 1590 it was laid down that bricks should be 10 by 5 by $2\frac{1}{2}$
inches – little was achieved. The average size of bricks at this time was
about 8 by 4 by 2 inches.

Slowly the use of brick gained momentum, partly because whilst the price of wood was rising the price of bricks was falling, and partly because of the risk of fire. Following the Great Fire of London, legislation was introduced making brick or stone walls compulsory in the capital. London was not the only town so devastated, for many towns and villages in the seventeenth and eighteenth centuries were similarly destroyed. Some were rebuilt in stone but many, including those where stone quarries were not too far away, among them Blandford, Tiverton, Wareham and Northampton, were rebuilt largely if not wholly in brick. At the end of the seventeenth century a machine known as a 'pugmill' – which resembled a giant mincer – was invented. Powered by a horse, this machine removed the necessity for men to tread out the earth. As the horse walked round and round, the coarse mixture was fed in at the top, emerging at the bottom as smooth 'dough' free from all pebbles and other impurities. The clay was then pressed into wooden moulds and left for at least two weeks before firing. The fuel was sometimes wood, but the introduction of coal-fired kilns, at the beginning of the eighteenth century, led the way to even cheaper bricks.

Although brick had gained popularity among the merchants and professional classes of London and the Home Counties even before the Great Fire, it was not until the last quarter of the seventeenth century that, thanks to the falling price, it reached the cottage-dweller, and then only in places like the Fens, Breckland and other areas where materials, such as timber and stone, were not available.

The use of brick flourished until the latter part of the eighteenth century when it suffered a setback. In 1784 a brick tax was imposed at the duty of two shillings and sixpence per thousand; it was increased in 1794 to four shillings per thousand and again in 1803 to five shillings per thousand. This resulted at first in a temporary increase in the size of bricks – a height of 3 inches and in the Midlands and North as much as $3\frac{1}{4}$ inches became common, both aesthetically disastrous – since at first they were taxed by number and not size. This was met by the imposition of a double duty on all bricks measuring over 150 cubic inches and, later, in some country areas where no other suitable building material was available, the revival of timber framework, particularly for cottages, clad with weatherboarding or tiles. In all areas where no suitable building stone was available, brick replaced timber as the principal building material, invading but not overwhelming the vernacular tradition as it did later. Small brickworks, dotted about throughout the counties of the East, South-east and Midlands, produced bricks with their own local characteristics which harmonized with their localities.

In 1850 the tax was abolished and this coincided with the vastly improved methods of manufacture, which resulted in a great saving in both time and labour. Grinding machines replaced the old pugmill,

103. Brick and cruck cottages, Rothley, Leicestershire.

enabling the clays of the North and the North Midlands, previously considered unsuitable, to be used; mechanical pressing into metal moulds and wire cutting replaced the old hand processes, and kilns no longer burned intermittently but continuously. This resulted not only in a considerable fall in the cost of production but it was also possible, for the first time, to make bricks of exactly the same size, colour, and texture. Many of the old brickworks, producing bricks from local clays, could no longer compete. Bricks were not only restricted to former brick areas, for these mass-produced bricks were sent by rail and canal to all parts of the country where they were cheaper than local products, and so in nearly all villages a break was made with their time-honoured local materials. Only areas too remote, undeveloped, or rich in local stone, like Cornwall, the Lake District, and the Cotswolds, remained unaffected. Elsewhere, particularly in the North which had up to this time few brick buildings, industrialization brought about the use of harsh red machine-pressed bricks of disagreeably large proportions – a thickness of 3 inches is common. In the colliery villages of Lancashire, Yorkshire, County Durham and Northumberland, as well as the manufacturing towns of the North and Midlands, the overriding factor was cheapness, which resulted not only in the use of those incongruous materials – brick and Welsh slate – but the spread of rows of featureless terraced cottages into the countryside.

One of the most pleasing features of English bricks was their colour and texture, derived from the local condition under which they were made. The colour was mainly determined by the constitution of the clay and the materials contained within it, which acted as a staining agent. As with stone, the most important of these was iron, which is contained in the vast majority of brick clays, producing red bricks of infinitely different shades. Each geological formation has clay which when burnt produces bricks of the same colour. Thus, the marls of the Triassic system of the Midlands and West produced, in pre-industrial days, the deepest reds. Later, when the shales of the Coal Measure of the northern counties were used, these produced an even redder brick. The most beautiful red bricks are to be found to the south and east of the limestone belt, of which the clays of the Weald have often been said to be our best, as can be seen from the numerous red-brick cottages and farmhouses in the area built in the eighteenth and early nineteenth centuries. Equally attractive are bricks made from some of the Eocene clays found in the Thames Valley and around Southampton waters.

Another impurity in clay is lime, producing the so-called 'white' bricks which are, in fact, usually a dusty-looking yellow. The main source of these bricks is the bluish clay of the Gault, the main belt of which runs from Cambridge, along the foot of the Chilterns and Berkshire Downs, into Wiltshire. Although 'white' bricks are found intermittently along its length, it is at its northern end where most are to be found. A belt of Gault also encircles, apart from its south-eastern corner, the Weald and the area north of Maidstone also produced these white bricks. The Gault belt was not the only clay from which white bricks were obtained, for some of the Pleistocene clays of Suffolk, like those at Woolpit, also produced white bricks, known as 'Suffolk whites', which can be seen throughout the southern half of the county. In southern Oxfordshire, Berkshire and parts of Hampshire, grey bricks, also due to the presence of lime, can be found from Thame to Hungerford. Often, as at Cuxham, near Watlington, cottages can be found constructed of two bricks – red at the sides and grey to the front, or grey and red in alternate courses. Brown bricks, of various shades, are to be found in many areas, such as parts of Lincolnshire, most of Humberside, in Nottinghamshire along the lower Trent Valley, and in Yorkshire in the Vale of York and northwards in that relatively flat land which separates the moors on the east from the dales and fells of the west. All these brown bricks contain lime and a little iron.

Not only did the clay used affect the colour of the brick but also the process of firing. Changes in colour could be obtained by increasing the heat and so those in the kiln exposed to the greatest heat would emerge the darkest. So white bricks would be turned brown and red bricks would be turned into various shades of purple.[1] The fuel used also had

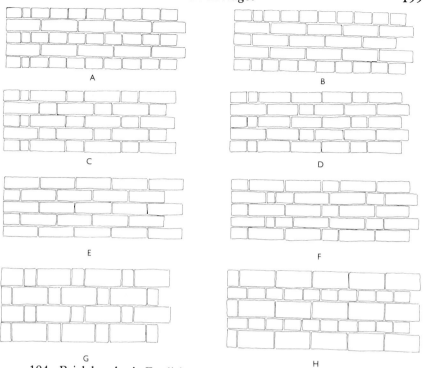

104. Brick bonds: A. English; B. English garden wall; C. Flemish;
D. Flemish garden wall; E. stretcher; F. Monk or Yorkshire; G. rat-
trap; H. Dearne's.

some effect on the colour of the bricks. Flared headers, used in diaper
work, were obtained by burning furze, the ends of the bricks so placed
that they came in contact with the flames. When coal-fired kilns were
introduced, these flared headers could be obtained by placing the bricks
close to the fire holes within the kiln, the bricks emerging darker than the
rest.

All brickwork needs to be bonded – that is, to arrange the bricks in
such a way as to obtain the maximum strength and at the same time giving the building a pleasing and interesting appearance. Much of the early
brickwork was built in a haphazard way without any particular pattern
or bond, and the charm of old brickwork is due as much to this mingling
of headers and stretchers as to the colour of the material. In early brickwork when a bond was used it was always English – alternate courses of
headers and stretchers (*See* 104A). This bond remained in general use
throughout the fifteenth and sixteenth centuries, but in the seventeenth
century it was gradually replaced by Flemish bond – alternate headers
and stretchers in the same course (*See* 104C). Although called Flemish
bond it is seldom to be found in Flanders. Less strong than English bond,

because there are more straight joints, it is more pleasing to the eye and also more economical for it used fewer facing bricks. From the end of the seventeenth century Flemish bond has remained the bond most used in all walls of 9 inches wide and over. Stretcher bond (*See* 104E), widely used today in cavity walls, comprise rows of stretchers, the only headers being at quoins. Not used in structural walls, it is commonly found in brick-nogging to timber-framed buildings or as cladding to cob or clay-lump walls. Many other bonds are encountered on cottages. English garden wall bond (*See* 104B) a variation of English bond, in which there are three or five courses of stretchers to one of headers, is one of the most popular of all bonds, especially in the North and Midlands. The bond has many of the advantages of English bond but is cheaper. Similarly, there are variations of Flemish bond, among the most common being Monk or Yorkshire bond (*See* 104F) where there are two stretchers instead of one between each header, a bond found more often in Yorkshire, Humberside, Lincolnshire, and parts of East Anglia. Flemish garden wall bond (*See* 104D), in which there are three stretchers between each header in place of the single stretcher of Flemish bond, is another bond commonly encountered, especially in the South where it is known as Sussex bond. In all these bonds there is a saving in facing bricks and because of the irregular size of bricks it is possible to produce a wall of more uniform thickness, the differences in each brick being more readily accommodated in the joints in the width of the wall. Another bond, found only in cottages or farm buildings, is rat-trap bond (*See* 104G), sometimes known as Chinese bond. Similar to Flemish bond in that there are alternate headers and stretchers in the same course, rat-trap bond differs in that the bricks are laid on their edge instead of their bed. A variation of rat-trap bond is rat-trap Sussex bond, in which three stretchers are used between each header. The result of both these bonds is that a cavity is formed within the wall with a saving on the number of bricks used. These bonds have a disagreeable appearance, but are to be found on many cottages constructed in the nineteenth century. Another form of hollow wall sometimes to be found on humble buildings is Dearne's bond (*See* 104H). This is a variation of English bond, in which there are alternate courses of headers and stretchers, but with the stretcher courses laid on edge, the headers acting as ties and the bricks laid on edge having a 3-inch cavity between.

Jointing and pointing of brickwork can also enhance its overall appearance. Because of the irregularities of early bricks wide joints were essential, which results in a pleasing visual effect with the continually varying width of joint – seldom less than half an inch – over the face of the wall. In the seventeenth century bricks became more regular in size, producing an overall reduction in width of mortar joints. When cut and rubbed bricks were introduced in Georgian times (although seldom to be found on cottages), even thinner joints were required. All these joints were pointed with a simple weathered or struck joint, but in Georgian times 'tuck' pointing was introduced giving the illusion of a fine joint to ordinary brickwork. This was achieved by raking out the joints and re-pointing, flush with the wall face, with coloured mortar to match the colour of the bricks. Subsequently the joints were scored with grooves, never more than a quarter of an inch wide and sometimes as little as an eighth of an inch, into which were pressed flat narrow strips of chalk-lime putty and afterwards trimmed. The process was laborious and expensive and was consequently generally restricted to larger houses, although occasionally it is to be found on cottages.

Not all brickwork is plain, and from Tudor times the use of patterns, either with the use of different coloured bricks on the surface of the wall, or by raised decorations, have been a feature of English brickwork. Originating in northern France in the second quarter of the fifteenth century, the art of producing coloured patterns on the face of the wall soon spread to this country; Tattershall and Herstmonceux Castles are amongst the earliest examples of this. By Tudor times this patterning had become fashionable and by the reign of Henry VIII few large brick buildings were erected in the southern and eastern counties without patterned brickwork being incorporated. Even for smaller houses the builder often had a choice of colours, for not all bricks burnt equally and since patterns were made nearly always of headers it was simple to select those bricks with burnt ends. Easily the favourite pattern in Tudor times was a diaper of diamonds (*See* 105A). This vogue for diamond pattern largely ceased after Henry VIII but regained popularity in Georgian times. With the introduction of Flemish bond an all-over chequer pattern (*See* 105B) could be achieved and became fashionable, and throughout the Georgian period was the most common form of patterning. It was not restricted, as in Tudor times, to larger houses, and became a popular pattern on cottages, particularly in the villages of the Weald of Kent and Sussex where almost all the cottages of the eighteenth century are built with the front wall of a simple chequer of red and blue bricks. In other parts of the country, for example East Anglia, decorative use of bricks is less common. In Victorian times, although diapering remained popular, on cottages a brick of a different colour was introduced at quoins, jambs and for arches. Often band courses (usually two or three courses) were incorporated at first-floor level and sometimes at the eaves. In East Anglia white bricks were often used for these dressings and bands contrasting with the red of the general brickwork. In southern Cambridgeshire, parts of Suffolk and Bedfordshire red bricks were used with the drab yellow bricks of those areas, while in southern Oxfordshire and Berkshire grey and red bricks are similarly used.

Moulded bricks and terracotta can be found here and there on smaller houses, but raised decorations on cottages were confined to string courses, known as platbands, obtained by the use of two or three courses of ordinary bricks projecting from the face of the wall usually at first-floor level. Beneath the eaves oversailing courses were used breaking the

105. Brick patterns: A. diapered; B. chequered.

transition from wall to roof. The simplest were dentilations: plain, a course of headers with every other one projecting (*See* 106A); and 'dog-tooth', obtained by laying the bricks diagonally to form a serrated edge (*See* 106B). In addition a plain course of bricks, projecting beyond the face of the dentilation or dog-tooth was used. Of the two the first was most commonly used, but both can be seen on many cottages built in the eighteenth and nineteenth centuries.

On the eastern side of the country hipped roofs are less common and

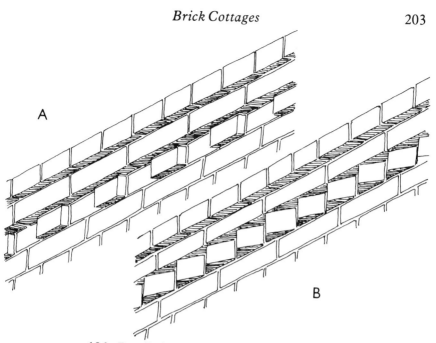

A

B

106. Dentilations: A. plain; B. dog-tooth.

most gables are carried up above the level of the roof to prevent wind getting under the thatch or tiles and lifting them off. Although Dutch and crow-step gables were used on larger buildings, on humbler dwellings it was more difficult to provide a straight gable which was both cheap and reliable. Often they were finished by adding a brick or, where available, a stone coping, but as these were not bonded to the wall they were vulnerable. On many cottages another Dutch device known as 'tumbling in', was commonly employed (*See* 107). The bricks would be laid diagonally and at right angles to the slope of the roof to form a series of triangular wedges, thus producing a straight gable securely built into the remainder of the wall. The earliest example dates from 1656 on the outbuildings to Westerfield Hall, Suffolk, and it remained popular in all the eastern counties from Kent to North Yorkshire and as far inland as parts of Cambridgeshire until the latter part of the eighteenth century. In some parts, for example in the villages around the Wash where it can be seen in small cottages as a single triangular wedge at the base of the gable, it remained in favour as late as the early part of the nineteenth century. In Norfolk it can also be seen on cottages built of flint, while in Humberside, at Waddingham, Kirton-in-Lindsey, and other villages at the northern end of the limestone belt, it was used on stone cottages. Introduced to overcome a practical problem, it had the added advantage of providing a decorative finish to the gables of many small cottages.

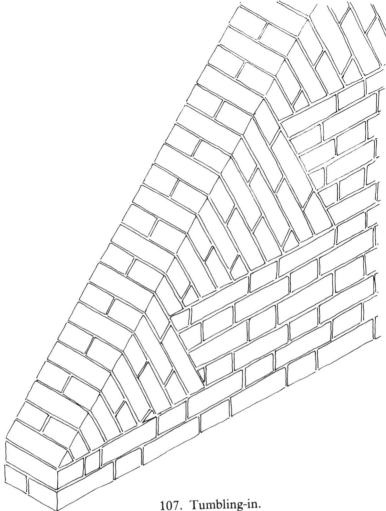

107. Tumbling-in.

Most of the brick cottages built in the eighteenth and nineteenth centuries had walls 9 inches thick, or in many cases only $4\frac{1}{2}$ inches thick,[2] and, as many of the bricks were of a porous nature, inevitably dampness penetrated the wall. As early as 1805 William Atkinson[3] recommended that "in constructing walls for cottages or other edifices in brick a great saving might be made on materials without sacrificing much in regard to strength by leaving the walls hollow". He recommended two skins with a 6-inch cavity between, tied together with brick ties. In 1821 Thomas Dearne[4] recommended a similar form of construction but with only a 2-inch cavity between the skins, the two being tied together with headers with a 2-inch closure on the inner skin. John Loudon advocated almost exactly the same form of construction some years later as did H. Roberts in 1850.[5] It is impossible to say how popular these cavity walls were, but as all were tied together with absorbent brick, moisture was still liable to penetrate to the inner skin. It was not until the latter part of the nine-teenth century that cavity walls of two skins tied together with wrought-iron cramps began to be recommended, but it was not until this century that it was widely used.

Like mud and rubble stone walls, some brick walls have always received some form of surface treatment either rendering – plaster, pebble-dash or roughcast – or simply whitewash or colour-wash. On brick cottages whitewash or colour-wash was frequently used and, although not so commonly used as in Scotland, Ireland and Wales, the old tradition is still preserved in some parts of this country, particularly in East Anglia, Cambridgeshire, Lincolnshire and Essex. In these places many cottages are to be found painted to give the same overall appear-ance as their older, plastered counterparts. It is this desire for unity that is so important to the visual effect of so many villages. The traditional covering was limewash and for an old building with no damp-proof course it is still the best, being porous and allowing the rising dampness to dry out. Today, modern whitewashes, distempers and stone paints are generally used, but on damp walls the dampness cannot escape and so the covering is liable to blister and flake. Rendering on brick cottages is more prevalent, particularly on those built during the early part of the nine-teenth century when it was often used to hide the poor quality brickwork.

Roofs

For many centuries the size of a cottage was governed by the limitations of the roof construction, for the roof span was restricted by the length of available timber. So the simplest roof was one that covered a narrow rectangular plan, and the many picturesque and irregular-shaped cottages of today are the results of additions to the original buildings. One common extension to cottages, as with other domestic buildings, was the use of the 'catslide' extension of the main roof over an outshut at the side or rear.

108. Cottage with 'catslide', Steyning, Sussex.

The choice of roof covering also affected the shape of the roof for each material had its appropriate pitch, its weight affecting its construction, the shape of the roof and whether it was one and a half storeys – with dormers – or two storeys. Thatch, plain tiles and limestone stone-slates of the Cotswolds could all easily incorporate hips, dormers and valleys, whereas slate, sandstone stone-slates of the North, and pantiles were more appropriate to simple gabled roofs without dormers and valleys.

The basic shapes of roofs fall into two groups: the hipped family, where the roof slopes in from all sides; or the gable family, where the opposite end walls continue up above the eaves. Within each family there are several variations. Another type of roof, the mansard, occurred at the end of the eighteenth century and enjoyed popularity at the lower end of the social scale, providing a cheap and effective way of creating a room in the roof with sufficient headroom to be used as a normal first-floor room. Found in the eastern counties, especially in Lincolnshire and Cambridgeshire in and around the Fens, the roof has two pitches on each side of the ridge, the lower one much steeper than the upper one, with the lower one often incorporating a dormer.

CONSTRUCTION

Roofs are either single-framed, consisting only of rafters often with various bracing members, or double-framed, consisting of purlins, which either spans from wall to wall without intermediate supports or are supported along their length by trusses and rafters. The early roofs were double-framed and the pre-Reformation roof was commonly a crown-post with a central purlin in which there was no ridge-piece, the close-set rafters being halved and pegged at their intersection. At intervals of about 10 feet, a crown-post, complete with struts, rose from the centre of a cambered tie-beam to support the longitudinal purlin, which in turn supported the collars and rafters. There were numerous minor variations to this precise arrangement – the shape and number of struts, as well as the shape and ornamentation of the crown-post.

The crown-post roof was predominantly southern and in the North another type of roof, the king-post, was used. Here a king-post, rising from a tie-beam or collar, supported a ridge-piece with, in addition, side purlins, supported by struts off the tie-beam, running between and housed into the principal rafters to support the common rafters. Like the crown-post roof there were many variations to this general arrangement. The use of side purlins and a ridge-piece made the king-post roof similar to that of the cruck roof, previously described.

In the sixteenth century the crown-post gave way to another double-framed roof, the queen-post. This roof consisted of a series of framed trusses each comprising a pair of principal rafters connected by a tie-beam from which rose a pair of uprights, known as 'queen-posts', equidistant from the tie-beams centre and supporting the collar at or near its ends. Sometimes from each queen-post were two struts, one supporting the rafter and the other the collar. Between each truss ran the purlins supporting the common rafters in a similar way to the king-post roof. Both crown-post and king-post and the various roofs in these families are seldom to be found on humbler buildings, but queen-post roofs, although

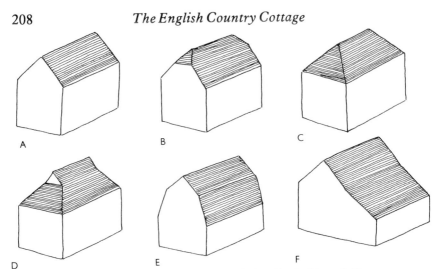

109. Roof shapes: A. gabled; B. half-hipped; C. hipped; D. gambrel; E. mansard; F. catslide extension on gabled roof.

ambitious and undoubtedly expensive, were not by any means confined to important buildings and are to be found occasionally in small farmhouses and cottages. The use of windbraces, a common feature on early roofs to counteract longitudinal movement, was generally abandoned towards the end of the sixteenth century.

From the beginning of the seventeenth century onwards, especially in cottages, simpler roofs were constructed and as the roofs were no longer intended to be visible as the earlier roofs had, roof framing followed wall framing into the depths of inferiority. Simple collar-beam roofs with one purlin on each side but without posts and struts were used, the purlins being supported by a collar-beam.

Another form of roof was the collar-rafter roof. This roof was a single roof with no purlins, each pair of rafters separately triangulated with a collar jointed to the rafters. Both types of roof were particularly suitable for small buildings for the absence of a tie-beam did not restrict the headroom, the 'forest' of rafters, collars and bracings being used to support the ceiling plaster. So on cottages of one and a half storeys, with the introduction of dormer windows, it became possible to provide an upper floor relatively cheaply. A rough method of roofing barns and outbuildings by means of side purlins strutted from the tie-beam had been in use for some time and this form of construction was introduced into house construction. This rather crude method was sometimes refined by the introduction of a collar-beam forming a tie-beam truss. In all these roofs a ridge-piece is uncommon, the pairs of rafters being halved and pegged at the apex. The low-pitched roofs of the North, carrying the heavy traditional stone-slates of the area, seldom had any trusses, the

110. Thatched and plastered cottage, with 'catslide', Ludgershall,
Buckinghamshire.

111. Whitewashed stone cottage, March Baldon, Oxfordshire.

cottages here were often almost square in plan and with such a depth and weight to carry, their use was impracticable. A more suitable method was found, the rafters being supported on purlins running from gable wall to gable wall, or gable wall to internal dividing wall.

On timber-framed buildings the rafters were housed over the wall-plate at the top of the wall, but on a wall of solid construction an independent timber wall-plate was introduced, bedded on top of the wall for the ends of the rafters to be fixed. When the roof was carried on a thick wall of stone each rafter was triangulated at the foot by short pieces of timber – a process known as 'ashlaring' – to form a flush internal face to the wall.

ROOF COVERINGS

The traditional roof-coverings for cottages comprise thatch, slates of split stone or slate, and burnt tiles. Concrete tiles and asbestos slates, sometimes to be found on cottages, are twentieth-century innovations and are both aesthetically objectionable.

THATCH

The old word 'thack' originally meant any kind of roof-covering and as the materials employed in early days were invariably reed, straw, heather or other vegetable products like flax, sedge and even broom, the word 'thatch' has acquired its now more limited connotation. Of all the roofing materials, thatch is the one most suited to cottages for no other becomes so rapidly an integral part of the countryside, being as happy in the Fens as in the downs of Hampshire, Wiltshire and Sussex. No other is as much at home on the cob cottages of Devon as it is on the stone cottages of the Cotswolds or the timber-framed cottages of Sussex and Hampshire or the plastered cottages of East Anglia. Because it was the lightest of all roofing materials, thatch was, on some buildings (where the walls were too weak to carry heavy loads such as those constructed of cob or clay-lump), the only material suitable.

Today thatch is essentially a rural material, but this was not always so. In medieval times most buildings, except for buildings of importance, thatch was the commonest type of roof-covering in almost all parts of the country, including most towns. There are many instances of fires in towns for which thatch was to blame and in many towns a coat of white-wash was applied to the thatch to give it protection against sparks. In 1212 a coat of lime plaster was made compulsory in London to reduce the risk of fire and at the same time a restriction was made on the use of the material on any new roof. Other towns followed suit, but outside the towns thatch remained popular in all parts of the country well into the Tudor period. Not until the time of the great rebuilding did thatch, on all but the poorest cottages give way in some parts of the country to more permanent materials. Although elsewhere it continued in use much longer, it was always regarded as a humble material available only for the poor, and this is confirmed by Palsgrave who, in 1530, wrote: ". . . I am but a poor man, sythe I can not tyle my house, I must be fayne to thacke it . . ." In Northumberland, in 1805, it was reported that thatch which "used to be universal covering" had nearly fallen into disuse for cottage roofs.[1] A few years before, in 1796, William Pitt put forward objections to thatch, which was still in use in Staffordshire[2] on some roofs deemed too weak to support tiles: these were; that it was liable to be torn off by storms, that it harboured vermin, robbed the land of manure, and caught fire easily. Even in the Lake District during the early part of the nineteenth century slates were only used by those who could afford them, thatching with rushes being far more common.[3] Yet in some areas it remained popular even for larger buildings, and in East Anglia, especially in Norfolk where between fifty and sixty still survive, many churches were thatched.

Reed, straw and heather are the three principal materials that have been used for thatching. Of these reed is the best and, although the initial expense is more, if well laid it will last at least sixty years and can in a few rare cases last as long as a hundred years. Found in the wet areas of England – fresh and salt-water marshes, margins of estuaries, rivers and lakes – it is in the broads and marshes of Norfolk that it is mainly found. It is also found in limited quantities along some of the tidal rivers of Suffolk, along the River Blyth at Reydon Marshes and the River Alde at Snape, as well as some of the rivers of Essex. Today, with the decline of suitable straw, reeds have been cultivated in parts of Hampshire and Dorset. Straw was for many centuries and in most parts of the country the principal thatching material. Wheat, rye, as well as oats and barley, although these two were less suitable, were all used. Of these, rye-straw was the best, for it was the longest and strongest, able to withstand wind, sun, rain, frost and snow. Rye-straw, which has a life of about thirty years, was popular in Lancashire and elsewhere, wherever available locally, but is rare today. The most commonly used cultivated grass was and still is wheat and, although not so good as rye, it can, if the quality of the straw and workmanship is good, last almost as long. Known as 'long-straw', it often needs to be remade after fifteen years or so, the straw being rather short and attacked both by birds and weather. Long-straw thatching, found on many cottages of the corn-growing districts of the South Midlands, has its own distinctive appearance for the straw is applied lengthwise, giving a gentle moulded appearance. A speciality of the South-west is what is known as 'wheat-reed' thatch. Botanically it has no connection with true reed, but owes its name to the method of laying which is similar to true reed in that only the ends of the straw are exposed, producing a longer lasting and much neater roof. A straw of about

112. Cruck cottage, Styal, Cheshire.

113. Thatched cottages, Ickwell Green, Bedfordshire.

3 feet long is used which should not be beaten or bruised, and today this is obtained by a device known as a 'comber' being fitted to the threshing drum to strip the ears. The straw emerges tied in bundles and ready for use. Roofs thatched with combed wheat-reed (which, with its smooth finish, resembles true reed in appearance) can last fifty years. Although at one time confined almost entirely to Devon and Dorset, because of the difficulty of obtaining long straw, wheat-reed thatch has, like true reed, spread into other areas. In the heaths and moorland regions where no corn was grown, heather was a useful alternative. It was widely used in Sussex and Devon, particularly around Dartmoor, as well as parts of the North, in Yorkshire, Durham and Northumberland. The heather was cut in the autumn when in bloom and laid out to dry with its roots uppermost. With shears it was possible to obtain a smooth finish and, although seldom used today, was cheaper than straw and was in wet areas less likely to rot. One disadvantage of heather is perhaps the dark colour, almost black, which it turns as it dries out. Sedge, a grass-like water plant which, unlike true grass, has no joints, is another material used for thatching. Found and used extensively in the Fens it can still be seen on cottages in some Cambridgeshire villages like Fordham, Wicken and Stretham. Sedge is still in demand for ridging, especially in Norfolk. Other materials used for thatching were flax, commonly used in Derbyshire, ferns and rushes. In Lancashire at the end of the eighteenth century fern was regarded as the best covering, being naturally dry and not likely to ferment like straw.[4] In Cumbria up to the beginning of the nineteenth century, rushes were a common thatching material and in Ravenstonedale the people were not allowed to cut them for thatching before twelve o'clock on the first Tuesday after St Bartholomew's Day.[5]

Of all these materials, straw made from cultivated grass was most commonly used. In medieval times the usual practice was to cut off only the ears of the wheat, the stalks remaining in the fields until the first frost when they could be broken off and stored until needed. In those days the thatcher started, as he does now, at the eaves, but over each layer was added a layer of wet clay beaten into the straw, a custom which remained in use for cottages until well into the seventeenth century,[6] giving a somewhat untidy appearance. Later it became customary to remove the ears of corn after it had been cut, the ears being threshed separately and the unthreshed straw tied into bundles. Fitzherbert in 1534 wrote:

In Sommersetshire about Zelcestre and Martok they doo shere theyr wheate very lowe, and all the wheate strawe, that they pourpose to make thacke of, they do not thresshe it, but cutte of the eares and bynde it in sheves, and call it rede, and therwith they thacke theyr houses.[7]

114. Seventeenth-century mud-and-stud and thatched cottage at
Thimbleby, Lincolnshire.

115. Cottages, Linton, Cambridgeshire.

In 1807 Thomas Rudge found a similar process being used in the Berkeley and the 'Lower Vale' of Gloucestershire.[8] Here the unthreshed straw was cleaned of weeds and short straw by an iron-toothed comb fixed in a wall. Such straw, which was then tied in sheaves, was called 'helm'. Another, and less satisfactory method was composed of stubble, the stalks about a foot long left by the reaper, which was cut and mixed with threshed straw. Henry Best, in 1641 wrote that the stubble was so short that he was glad to mix haver (oat) straw with it in the proportion of two parts of stubble to one part of haver. Thomas Rudge also found this type of thatch in Gloucestershire, around Gloucester and the 'Upper Vale', in 1807.

Before thatching the straw was, and still is, soaked, making it more pliable and as Henry Best remarked ". . . wette strawe coucheth better and beddes closer". After this the straw must be prepared, a process called 'yealming', where the straw is drawn (that is, tidied), laid out straight and gathered in bundles to form yealms. This was originally achieved by various methods; in Gloucestershire, as previously mentioned, this was done by an iron-toothed comb, in Bedfordshire by drawing the straw under the foot, in Devon and Somerset the wheat-reed was sometimes prepared by a machine called a 'reed-maker', which combed out the short and bruised stalks, while in Dorset it was prepared by pulling it through a frame, a process known as 'reed-drawing'. Today, although straw still needs preparing, combed wheat-reed usually comes to the thatcher in bundles or 'nitches' and, apart from being tidied, butted on a spot board to even the ends, sprinkled with water and left to soak, is ready for thatching. Likewise, true reed is delivered in bunches and only needs grading into various lengths.

Basically there were four methods of applying thatch; sewing the thatch to the rafters, pinning it down by a system of rods, working the thatch into layers of turves or securing it by a series of weighted ropes passing over the surface. All these methods were used, either individually or in different combinations, giving a remarkable variation. Today the second is the most commonly used, although it is sometimes used in combination with the first. The third method, formerly employed extensively in the North, was probably at one time more widely used.[9] Various methods were used in securing the thatch to the turves. In one method a small quantity of straw was pulled out from one end of the yealm and wound round the top of it, making what was known as a 'staple'. With a thatching iron, an instrument with a slight fork at the end, the staple was pushed through the turves with the twisted head of wound straw keeping it in position. Although this method of thatching was still employed in the North in this century, it is unlikely to be found today. The fourth method, which was the most primitive, was confined entirely to the Celtic fringe and is now unlikely to be found in England.

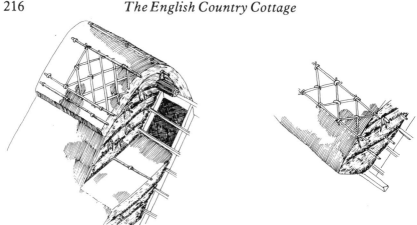

116. Long-straw thatching.

With long-straw, once the yealms have been carried up to the roof, work begins at the eaves and the roof is completed in sections, some thatchers staggering the courses across the roof, others working in sections, about 30 inches wide, up the roof. A double layer of yealms are laid at the eaves and these are either tied to the roofing battens with tarred twine, or swayed down by a horizontal rod or sway held by hooks driven into the rafter. Straw bands were once used for tying the yealms and before that the wrung vines of the blackberry. The sways are of hazel, although these are being replaced by some thatchers with lengths of mild tempered steel. The hooks, which secure the sways, are these days also of iron, but were originally pointed sticks, generally of hazel, split, twisted and bent in the shape of a hairpin and driven into the thatch. Their name differed greatly in various parts of the country; in East Anglia they were known as 'broaches'; in the West and South as 'spars'; in Devon and Cornwall as 'spears'; in Surrey, the Isle of Wight, Dorset and parts of Cornwall as 'sparrows'; in Northamptonshire, Warwickshire, Norfolk and Yorkshire as 'pricks' or 'prickers'; and in Derbyshire, Salop, Hereford and Worcester as 'buckles'. Today they are generally called spars. This widespread use of spars probably indicates that thatch was not formerly laid on battens as it is today but on some other material into which these spars could be driven. In Northumberland and Yorkshire turves are known to have been used, and elsewhere it was probably a foundation of brushwood or wattle. In some cases the sways were either tied or sewn to the rafters or battens. Subsequent courses are laid, overlapping the previous one by two thirds, these too being either tied or more commonly swayed down. When the ridge is reached yealms are placed longitudinally along it, tied together to provide a firm foundation for the cap. This cap is formed by placing the final yealm over the ridge, bending it down on either side of the roof and securing it by means of split hazel or willow rods, known as 'liggers', fixed with hazel spars. A top ligger is generally laid along the ridge and three more on either side. The construction of the ridges were formerly as varied as that of the thatching. Mortar was commonly used, remaining in general use in the North until the beginning of this century.[10] Another method was to lay turves over the ridge. Today a ridge cap is sometimes employed on straw thatch, forming an additional thickness of thatch along the apex of the roof. Liggers are also fixed at the eaves and verges, these being, together with the ridge, the most vulnerable to be damaged by wind. The verges

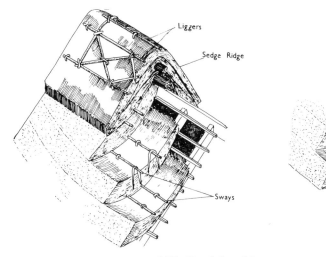

Liggers

Sedge Ridge

Sways

117. Reed thatching.

are then cut with a long-handled knife and trimmed with shears. Finally, the main roof and eaves are combed and trimmed. A long-straw roof needs protection from the birds; this was once achieved by an application of lime, applied annually, or clay, but today wire netting is generally used. Even so, it seldom lasts for more than twenty years and will probably need re-ridging and patching every ten years or so.

Unlike long-straw, reed is laid so that only the sharp butt-ends of the stalk are exposed. These ends shed the water from tip to tip on its way down the roof and have the added advantage of discouraging the attention of birds. Work begins at the eaves and proceeds in the usual manner from right to left. The first layer is generally tied to the roof batten and each bundle is gently butted upwards into place, first by hand and then with a small flat wooden mallet, called a 'leggatt'. The next course is laid well down over the first and swayed low down with a hazel or steel sway and iron hooks in a similar way as long-straw thatch. Subsequent courses are similarly laid, each completely covering the sway securing the lower courses, the reed, curving out from the rafters to its lower end to expose the butt-ends, being continually dressed with the leggatt to keep them in alignment up the roof. This procedure continues up to the ridge where the last course projects above the roof and is cut off level with the ridge. As reeds are brittle and stiff and cannot be bent a ridge-cap of a more pliable material, usually sedge, is used. A foundation for the ridge is formed with a roll of reeds, about 4 inches in diameter, placed along the full length of the ridge on which the ridge-cap is fixed. First a layer of sedge is laid over the ridge to form a skirt, pushed tightly together and held down with hazel spars driven into the reed. A narrower roll is then prepared and fastened through the skirt into the first roll, over which yealms of sedge are bent. The cap is secured by hazel liggers and spars in the same way as the straw ridge. A sedge ridge, being less durable than reed will probably need replacing about every twenty years.

In appearance, combed wheat-reed closely resembles that of reed, so much so that it is often indistinguishable at first glance, yet in construction they differ. The eaves and verges of a combed wheat-reed roof are laid with 'wadds', extra large bundles of reed, butted and tied firmly together and laced to the roofing battens with cord. To align and tighten the wadds in the cord the butts are dressed with a leggatt. The remaining courses are laid on a back-filling of reed scattered over the battens. Half a nitch is then butted on the roof, held with one arm and dressed into position before being temporarily secured with a reed sway and dressed again with the leggatt. When sufficient reed is in place it is permanently secured with a sway and iron hook, or by stitching. At the ridge a tightly packed roll of reeds, about 4 inches in diameter, is fixed along the length of the ridge. The top courses which oversail the ridge are not cut off but are twisted and folded back, the twisted ends being forced against each other and secured with a reed sway sparred into the ridge roll. Reed is again spread over and secured to the roll, on which a further, smaller roll is sparred to the first. Another layer of reed is spread, forming part of the ridge-cap. The small ends of these reeds are folded under and are so placed that their ends are just above the top of the second roll, meeting those on the other side. A third, smaller roll is fixed along the ridge and a ligger is started. The ridge course is formed by bending more reed in half, positioning it under the ridge ligger which is fixed as the ridge is completed. Hazel side liggers, three to each side, are fixed in the usual way. A good ridge will be very narrow on the top and have a depth of thatch of some 18 inches. The roof is finally dressed with the leggatt and lightly trimmed as much as is necessary with the shearing hook.

118. Thatched cottages near Somersby, Lincolnshire.

Basically these are the methods of fixing the three materials most commonly employed in thatching today, yet so varied is the craft in detail, both locally and individually, that they can be little more than a generalization.

No other material is capable of such variation in design, with every thatcher adding his own individual style and distinctive touches, often handed down from generation to generation, to regional or local characteristics. It is in the treatment of dormers, gables and ridges that the thatcher can best express his talents. Dormers with their own pointed gable and decorative ridge are to be found in East Anglia, as well as in some other areas, particularly where reed is used. Perhaps more attractive are the dormers embraced in a continuous and pronounced sweep of the roof. In some cases the thatch is taken down between the upper-floor windows to produce a dormer which is in effect set in a flat wall. In the neighbourhood of Ampthill, Bedfordshire, the thatch around the dormers is cut with almost complete semi-circles. In Hampshire and the Isle of Wight the thatch is sometimes brought down between the windows to provide a small canopy over the front door. Notable examples of this are at Godshill and Beaulieu. The ridge, perhaps more than any other part of the roof, is where the thatcher can evolve his individual style. Ridge-caps, with their lower edges decorated with scallops and zigzags, are frequently used, further decorated with liggers pegged to the surface of the ridge, commonly arranged in two parallel lines with smaller rods, called 'slats', arranged in a lattice pattern between them. Where there is no

119. Cottages, Godshill, Isle of Wight.

ridge-cap, a decorative surface treatment of liggers and slats is usually provided, as it is at the gable, eaves and over dormers.

A recent survey estimated that some 50,000 thatched buildings in England still survive, and considering the widespread replacement by Welsh slates, tiles, and corrugated iron it gives some idea of the former widespread use of the material. Suffolk has more thatched buildings than any other county, but to see thatch at its best one must go to Norfolk where many cottages, thatched in Norfolk reed, survive. Further west, in Essex, Cambridgeshire and Lincolnshire, thatched cottages, although rarer than at one time, are a familiar sight. Even further west, in Bedfordshire, Buckinghamshire, Hertfordshire and parts of Oxfordshire outside the limestone belt, there are a substantial amount. Along the belt itself and to the west of the limestone belt there are still many to be found. In Leicestershire, Warwickshire, Hereford and Worcester and Gloucestershire, straw thatch was once the traditional roofing material and is still to be found on many cottages when it can be obtained. Today in this area, as elsewhere, those who can afford it rethatch with Norfolk reed or wheat-reed from the South-west. In Kent, Surrey and East Sussex, because of the quality of local tiles, thatch is not often found, but from West

120. Cottages at Castleton, Derbyshire, with sandstone slab
roof.

Sussex westwards to Devon including the Isle of Wight thatch is abundant and is the second major area in the country. In Cornwall, on the south coast away from the force of the Atlantic gales, thatch can be found in and around the villages of Coverack, Crantock, Ruan Minor and Veryan. Elsewhere in the country thatch is rare, but can be found here and there.

During the first half of this century, when the craft of thatching was in decline, thatch was replaced by more durable materials such as slates, tiles and corrugated iron. Even today in Norfolk, Suffolk and elsewhere there are a distressing number of steeply pitched roofs covered with corrugated iron, often painted red, fixed over old thatch. This practice of leaving the thatch on and covering with another material was widespread and not only corrugated iron was used but, strangely enough, other materials such as pantiles. In recent years the number of thatchers has stabilized and, although it cannot be described as flourishing, the craft is in a healthier state than for many years. Despite the expense there is a desire to preserve the best in the countryside and its crafts. Coupled with this is the fact that the ownership of many thatched cottages has passed from the indigenous inhabitants, who could not afford to replace it, to the more affluent ones who can.

STONE-SLATES

Stone-slates – an unfortunate term, for geologically they have, of course, nothing to do with slate – are to be found in many areas, including the Cotswolds, Oxfordshire, Northamptonshire, Leicestershire, Dorset, Somerset, parts of Sussex and Surrey, the Welsh border counties of Hereford and Worcester, Salop, Cheshire and most parts of the North from Derbyshire to Northumberland. They were at one time extensively used in these areas and preferred to tiles before, during the nineteenth century, being ousted in favour of the cheaper Welsh slates. In the year 1530 Palsgrave wrote, "I sclate a house with stone-slates: it is better to sclate a house than to tyle it". In 1813, Joseph Plymley[11] noted that there were some good quarries of stone-slate in the south-western district of Salop, but during the nineteenth century Welsh slate was the only material used, even replacing thatch. Plymley continues ". . . at the present price of straw the comparative expense of blue slates which are gotten from the neighbouring counties of Wales is not excessive". This was undoubtedly true in other areas close to the Welsh borders and later, with improved transportation, elsewhere in the country.

Limestone slates were basically thinner than those of sandstone and can be seen at their best along the limestone belt. In the Cotswolds some of the best stone-slates were quarried at the celebrated quarry at Stonesfield, Oxfordshire, but there were many smaller quarries, like those at Eyford and Slaughter, producing local stone-slates for their own districts. Because stone-slates were not flat a steep pitch was desirable and so in the Cotswolds the pitch is never less than forty-five degrees and is generally between fifty and fifty-five degrees and in some cases over sixty degrees. This steep pitch can clearly be seen at Arlington Row, Bibury, where the glorious undulating roof adds to the charm of these old cottages. The weight of a Cotswold roof is considerable – every 100 square feet weighs nearly a ton – and consequently a substantial roof structure is required. The steeply-pitched golden brown and honey yellow stone-

121. Stone cottages at Firwood Fold, near Bolton, Greater Manchester.

slated roof of the Cotswolds, encrusted with moss and lichen, adds the final touch to many Cotswold cottages. Further north, along the limestone belt in the north-eastern corner of Northamptonshire, stone-slates comparable with those of the Cotswolds were quarried at Collyweston. Not so pleasing in appearance as Cotswold stone-slates, they have a great advantage over them in that they are thinner, weighing no more than half of those of the Cotswolds. These are to be found on many cottages in the area and their use spread into the adjoining parts of Leicestershire, Lincolnshire, Cambridgeshire and Bedfordshire. Although the stone-slates of the Cotswolds and Collyweston are the finest of the limestone roofs there are many to be found all along the limestone belt from Dorset

122. Old cottage near Corfe Castle, Dorset, with an undulating
and sagging roof of Purbeck stone.

to Yorkshire. Some of the most charming are those of Purbeck stone and
many cottages still roofed in these slates are to be seen around Corfe
Castle. Very heavy and thick, weighing about $1\frac{1}{4}$ tons for every 100
square feet, they produce an unforgettable roof, sagging under their
immense weight, the thick bottom edge casting delightful shadows.

As a roofing material sandstone is more widely distributed and
although aesthetically less pleasing than limestone, is an equally appropriate roof for the austere cottages of the North as the timber-framed
buildings of the Welsh border counties. The sandstones are thick, heavy,
roofing slabs, sometimes called flagstones, which can be as much as 4 feet
wide and 3 inches thick and so heavy that two men can hardly lift them.
This immense weight has caused many roofs covered with them to col-
lapse. A lower pitch was often essential, and although Horsham slate
roofs, which weigh even more than a Purbeck one, have a pitch of about
forty-five degrees, in the North the pitch is never more than thirty
degrees and sometimes even less. Also used for flooring field walls and
chimney cappings, it was for roofs that Horsham stone was generally
thirty degrees and sometimes even less. Also used for flooring field walls
and chimney cappings, it was for roofs that Horsham stone was generally
used and is still fairly common in much of Sussex and Surrey, south of

the North Downs, and also, but to a lesser extent, in the adjoining part of Kent. Although many of the older roofs of the Welsh border counties have been replaced by red tiles and Welsh slates, many sandstone roofs still exist. In Hereford and Worcester they come from the Old Red Sandstone and can still be seen on many cottages like those at Pembridge. In Salop too, sandstone roofs can be found, but here the sandstone comes from the Ordovician rocks. In Cheshire the roofing slates are of gritstone and, although a sombre grey and very heavy, they are still to be found here and there on timber-framed cottages and are an attractive feature on many of them. From Derbyshire northwards the sandstone slates come from the Carboniferous series and were for centuries the traditional roofing material. These 'flagstones' are large, thick (often in excess of an inch), roughly finished, dark in colour (usually dark brown or dark grey), and laid to a low pitch and, although they cannot compare visually with the limestone roofs of the Cotswolds and Northamptonshire, their rugged, broad surface, blends not only with the simple rugged buildings of these areas but also with harsh moorland landscape in which some of the most pleasing are still to be seen. During the last hundred years or so, like many other areas, cheaper materials – tiles and Welsh slates – have unfortunately replaced many of the Carboniferous sandstone roofs and each year, inevitably, the number increases. However, many still exist. In the Peak District there are still plenty of cottages roofed with these slates, as there are in Lancashire, North and West Yorkshire and in Northumberland.

Both limestone and sandstone stone-slates were laid in a similar manner. Each stone-slate was not fixed with nails but with an oak peg hooked over the battens. In the North, particularly in the Lake District, sheep's bone pegs were sometimes used. Today copper nails are used, for these are cheaper than oak pegs and equally as good. Slate-stones were formerly bedded on vegetable materials, such as hay and straw, which had the advantage of covering the joists and preventing the penetration of rain and snow. In many districts moss was used – not ordinary moss but bogmoss, found on the moors of Yorkshire and the like. The mossing of roofs was a specialist trade; in Yorkshire and Derbyshire men known as 'mossers' obtained their living by forcing moss up under the slates with the aid of a heavy square-ended trowel, known as a 'mossing iron', to keep out draughts and snow. As the moss decayed it was replaced with new. The slates were laid in diminishing courses with the largest at the eaves and smallest at the ridge; in the North, slabs up to 4 feet wide were sometimes used at the eaves with comparatively small slabs at the ridge, while with limestone slates the graduation was less marked and because they were smaller swept and laced valleys could be easily obtained.

Ridges were sometimes of freestone, either sawn out of the stone as in the Cotswolds, or worked by hand out of the solid to form a special V-

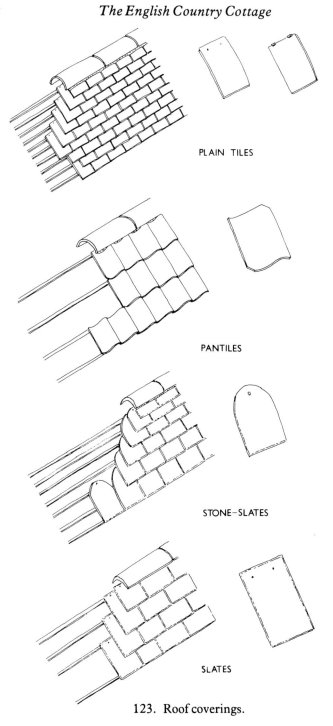

PLAIN TILES

PANTILES

STONE-SLATES

SLATES

123. Roof coverings.

shape as in the Pennines. Sometimes simply a cement mortar fillet was used, but is a poor substitute. Formerly it seems that, in some areas at least, ridges were not provided. In 1813 Joseph Plymley thought that the stone-slate roofs of Salop would be firmer if the ridges were covered with 'crests' of stone instead of turf or no crests at all.[12]

SLATE

In England slate is to be found in parts of Cornwall, Devon, Leicestershire and the Lake District, but unfortunately the majority of slate seen in this country is the blue-grey slate from Wales, the least attractive of all the slates. The use of slate was, because of its weight and difficulty in transportation, restricted to the vicinity of the quarries, but the improvement in distribution during the second half of the eighteenth century led to its increased use. It was not, however, until during the second half of the nineteenth century, with the improvement in rail transport, that the use of Welsh slate, on all types of buildings in both towns and country districts alike, became widespread. Welsh slate could not only be split into slabs of uniform thickness and size, but was also considerably thinner than other roofing materials, consequently the roof weighed less than one-fifth that of a limestone or sandstone roof, enabling the roof timbers to be substantially smaller and the roof considerably cheaper. Also the pitch of the roof could be as low as twenty-two degrees which produced a further saving. With such aforesaid savings over other roofing materials it is easy to see why it was so popular in Victorian times, especially as in 1831 the tax on slate was lifted, while on tiles it remained. In the Victorian period thousands of small brick cottages roofed with Welsh slates were built throughout the country, breaking the time-honoured tradition of using local materials. In the Welsh Marches, as well as many other parts of the country, Welsh slates became the universal roofing material during the nineteenth century, replacing the former indigenous and more attractive thatch and stone-slate.

In Cornwall most of the roofs are of local slate – a fine-grain, compact slate which is not too heavy. Dark grey in colour, the most common are small slates known as 'peggies', a name derived from the method of hanging them with oak pegs over battens. The slates of Devon are richly textured and very attractive, but have not the strength of the best Cornish slate and have not been quarried to any great extent for over a hundred years. In some places in the South-west, to give added protection against the Atlantic gales, the slates are laid in cement and the whole roof covered with a cement slurry. Another form of protective treatment often used, especially in the fishing villages, was a mixture of red lead and tar. The slates of Devon and Cornwall are always in random widths, nicely graduated with the largest at the eaves and the smallest at the ridge, and sometimes torched on the underside.

124. Seventeenth-century timber-framed cottages with stone slate roofs at Pembridge, Hereford and Worcester, formerly a group of six almshouses built by Bryan Duppa in 1661.

125. Old stone cottages, Boscastle, Cornwall, with the slate roof covered with a cement slurry.

In parts of the South-west, particularly in North-west Devon and North Cornwall, 'rag slates' were preferred. These are slates trimmed only on the parts that show, the ragged edge being concealed beneath the slate above. They are larger, thicker and rougher than peggies, often needing additional trimming on site and are usually nailed directly to the rafter and not fixed to battens. 'Scantles' were also used, which are similar to rags but are smaller and thinner.

The other great slate area is the Lake District, where all the older buildings and the majority of new buildings are all roofed with slate. Here there is considerable variation in both colour – greys, greens and blues are all to be seen – and texture – some very rough, others much smoother. In common with the sandstone roofs of the North, the pitch of these slate roofs is shallow, between thirty and thirty-five degrees, and even a quite modest roof can weigh up to ten tons. Like other stone and slate roofs, except Welsh slate, the courses are always graded and in the Lake District can vary as much as 24 inches at the eaves to as little as 6 inches at the ridge. Slate was also quarried at Swithland, to the north of Leicester, and was commonly used in that area, before replaced in the nineteenth century by Welsh slate. Still to be seen in some of the villages in the area, their variable size and colour give their roofs a distinction which the later Welsh slates can never achieve.

Originally all slates were, like stone-slates, bedded on straw, hay or moss, and fixed with oak pegs fitted into holes in the slates and hooked over battens. Later iron nails were used, but these rusted and today they are usually substituted with nails of copper, galvanized iron or other non-ferrous metal. Most slated roofs are gabled with few valleys, for these required substantial lead gutters which were always vulnerable. Hips and ridges were originally covered with pieces of freestone – usually sandstone – shaped and bedded in mortar. Later, purpose-made ridge and hip tiles were made of clay, sometimes matching the slate but often red. Ridges and hips were also covered with lead, dressed over a lead roll and fixed with lead tacks. In the Lake District a slate, known as a 'wrestler', was evolved to alleviate the use of ridge pieces which interlocked at the ridge. Cut with a slot about 2 inches below the top edge, they interlocked into a slate similarly cut on the other side of the roof slope, and were bedded in mortar to prevent rattling. Seldom to be seen today the method was probably devised to make the best use of local material in an area where there was no suitable stone to work into ridges.

PLAIN TILES

The manufacture of clay plain tiles for use as a roof-covering or for tile-hanging followed the development of brick-making, for they were usually made at brickworks, often fired with bricks within the same kiln. Like bricks, the use of plain tiles was confined to the eastern and south-

126. Timber-framed and pantiled cottage at Husthwaite, North Yorkshire.

eastern parts of England and likewise were favoured in many towns outside the stone-producing areas as a fire-resistant material. Early roof tiles varied greatly both in size and manufacture and in 1477 not only was the size of the tile standardized for the first time as $10\frac{1}{2}$ by $6\frac{1}{4}$ by $\frac{5}{8}$ inches but the precise method of preparing the clay was also laid down. Whether the statute had much influence is doubtful, for in Kent they continued to measure 9 inches by 6 inches and in Sussex the width was often $6\frac{3}{4}$ inches wide, while in Leicestershire plain tiles have always measured 11 by 7 inches. In 1725 the sizes laid down in 1477 were re-affirmed.

Plain tiles are double-lap tiles, that is to say that there is a double thickness of tile over the entire roof, each tile overlapping two others, leaving only about 4 inches exposed. Like slates, plain tiles are laid in regular courses, not overlapping their neighbours in the same course. Like slates and stone-slates, tiles were formerly bedded on hay, straw and moss, a process which continued in some parts until the beginning

127. Stone and pantiled cottages at Hutton-le-Hole, North York-shire.

of this century. One such area was Surrey, where the practice of bedding roofing tiles on clean straw was still followed for poorer quality work.[13] To completely weatherproof the roof the tiles would usually be torched – pointed in lime hair mortar on the underside. Today, all roofs, except thatch, have bitumen felt fixed to the rafters beneath the tile battens. The tiles were usually laid at a pitch of forty-five degrees or more, with a pitch of between fifty and sixty degrees being visually the most pleasing. Early plain tiles were fixed to riven oak laths by means of small pegs, generally of oak but sometimes of hazel, willow or elder – which was "supposed to make the most durable pins of all"[14] – driven through the tiles and hooked over the laths. Later, in the nineteenth century, nibs were provided on each tile to hook over softwood battens, and in addition every fifth course, or in windy and exposed positions or when the pitch is above fifty degrees every third course, the tiles were nailed. Hips and valleys were not difficult to form and in this the tiler followed the tradition of the stone slater. Valleys could be laced and swept, but these required

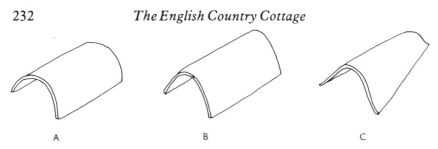

128. Ridge and hip tiles: A. half-round; B. saddle; C. bonnet.

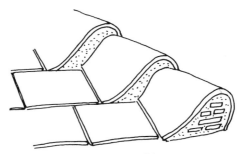

129. Bonnet-hip.

time and skill and therefore seldom are found on cottages. Lead or pur-pose-made valley tiles were more commonly used. Hips also required special tiles and both saddle back (*See* 128B) and bonnet tiles (*See* 128C) bedded in mortar give the roof great charm. Also half-round tiles (*see* 128A) sometimes known as hog-backs, were used. Both saddle-back and half-round tiles were really made for ridges and these were bedded in mortar, often tilted slightly upwards at the ends with the ends filled in with mortar and small pieces of tile. In Victorian times serrated or other forms of fancy ridge-tiles, often made of terracotta, were commonly used.

Early tiles were hand-made with an exaggerated camber in both their length and breadth and this, coupled with the slight variation on both size and shape, gives an aesthetic appearance, with its shades of light and shadow that few Victorian or modern roofs of machine-made plain tiles can match. These undulations may not always be entirely due to the ir-regularity in the tiles, but also to the sagging of battens and rafters or the settlement of the walls. Some older roofs in Kent, Sussex and Essex are carried almost to the ground by the extension of the main roof, known as a 'catslide'. The effect is remarkable. Towards the eaves of some tiled roofs there is a change in the pitch. This was achieved by the addition of sprockets – small pieces of shaped wood attached to the rafters near their feet – and the result is not only pleasing but also practical, for on steeply pitched roofs it provides a check on the flow of rainwater which might otherwise overshoot the gutter.

Like bricks, the colour of clay tiles depends upon the clays used. In Cambridgeshire, the Gault, which produces dull yellow bricks, yields tiles of a similar colour, and elsewhere in the county, in villages like Elsworth and Eltisley, and in the neighbouring part of Suffolk, around Mildenhall, roofs of variegated colours – yellows, brown, pinks, greys and some reds – arranged in a haphazard fashion, can be seen. The vast majority are, like bricks, various shades of red, with those from Kent, Sussex and Surrey some of the finest, having displaced thatch a long time ago. Essex, and the southern part of Suffolk, in places like Kersey, Boxford and Lavenham, also have excellent plain tiles, as does Hertfordshire and parts of Bedfordshire and Buckinghamshire. In the North Midlands and the North the tiles, being products from the carbonaceous clay, are less attractive. On the hills of the North these tiles look completely out of place, but this has not restricted their widespread use.

PANTILES

Although resembling the plain tile in material and manufacture, the pantile differs from them in size, shape and appearance. The size of a pantile was fixed during the reign of George I as not less than $13\frac{1}{2}$ by $9\frac{1}{2}$ by $\frac{1}{2}$ inches, and these dimensions have been maintained ever since. Pantiles are single lap tiles, each tile lapping the one underneath, but in addition they also overlap the one at the side by a sideways lap where the bent-down edge overlaps the turn-up edge of the adjacent tile. They could be laid to a low pitch of thirty-five degrees, or even slightly less, provided some precautions were taken to prevent snow or rain penetration. This was achieved by torching, sometimes with clay or, as in Norfolk, a layer of reed and clay, or with lime hair mortar. Because it was a single-lap tile requiring a gentler pitch, a pantiled roof was light, requiring a relatively light structure and producing an economical roof. The size and shape of a pantile made it more suitable for simple roofs, both hips and valleys being difficult to form and dormers awkward to incorporate. The range of colours, like that of plain tiles, usually consists of various shades of red, although in Norfolk almost black tiles, often glazed, are sometimes found, as at Little Walsingham.

The first pantiles were imported from Holland during the seventeenth century, and were later supplemented, at the beginning of the eighteenth century, with the first English pantiles. Because they originated in Holland the oldest are found in those places which engaged in trade with that country, but their use soon spread over all the Eastern counties from London northwards. Pantiles are, therefore, to be found in Essex, Suffolk and Norfolk, especially the northern part where most of the older

130. Brick, flint, chalk and pantiled millers' cottages, Burnham Overy, Norfolk.

131. Stone and pantiled cottages at Belmesthorpe, Leicestershire.

buildings have them. In Cambridgeshire too there are plenty, as there are in Lincolnshire, Humberside and North Yorkshire, where many cliff villages like Staithes and Robin Hood's Bay are roofed almost entirely of pantiles, while away from the coast they can be found in most of the villages in the eastern half of North Yorkshire. William Marshall, in 1788, noticed that "north of Grantham they are becoming the almost universal covering",[15] and four years later John Tuke also stated that pantiles were taking the place of thatch in North Yorkshire.[16] Further inland, pantiles are to be found in Leicestershire, in the villages to the north-east of Melton Mowbray, as well as much of Nottinghamshire. Many of the villages in all these areas, especially those in Norfolk, Lincolnshire and Humberside, owe much to the effect of light on pantile roofs. In the western half of the country, except for Somerset and in particular Bridgwater which was one of the main areas of production in the country, pantiles are rare, as they are in the South-east where there was a plentiful supply of excellent plain tiles.

Chimneys and Fireplaces

The medieval house, whether a manor house or a simple cottage, never had a fireplace or chimney-stack. In all cases the fire was placed centrally in the hall on a stone, if one was obtainable, with the smoke escaping the best it could through the roof and windows. Of the poor widow's cottage in Chaucer's *The Nun's Priest's Tale* we are told "Ful sooty was hir bour and eek hire halle". In the larger more substantial house with a lofty hall, smoke gablets – openings at the junction of the ridge and hips – were provided to assist in the extraction of smoke, while in the cottage an aperture in the roof or louvred opening was all that was provided. Bishop Hall, in 1610, found little difference between the cottages of Chaucer's time and his own where the opening was formed of "a headlesse barrel" and the cottage was thick with soot, "a whole inch thick, shining like a black-moor's brows".

Brick or stone chimneys were exceptional until the fifteenth century. In an ordinance of London compiled in 1419 it was "... ordered that henceforth no chimney shall be made except it be of stone, tiles, or brick and not of plaster or wood under pain of being pulled down". Although the use of brick and stone for the construction of chimneys became necessary in towns, in rural areas, according to William Harrison, the open hearth continued to be usual until the end of the sixteenth century and this is verified by the number of houses during that century which had a brick chimney inserted in them. Yet it seems likely that even in the South-east and East Anglia, always the most advanced parts of the country, the average cottager would have to content himself with a hood constructed of substantial oak posts and beams with the spaces filled in with wattle and daub and plastered inside to withstand the heat, with a flue constructed of wattle similarly covered with daub but seldom plastered. The wattle extended through the roof and when thatch was used this would be taken round and up the face to form a thatched chimney. The use of this type of chimney was widespread and continued in use in some of the more primitive areas of the North until the last century. In Northumberland, some hundred and twenty years ago, in the oldest cottages "a few sticks were twisted together and plastered with clay for a chimney"[1] and in the year 1808, according to T. Batchelor, cottages in the north-eastern part of Bedfordshire were timber-framed with wattle and daub infilling, with their chimneys composed of the same material.[2] Even in the more sophisticated South-east, in parts of Surrey and Sussex, shafts constructed of wattle and daub were still in use until the

132. Cottage, Ashton Bawdley, Salop.

last century when they were described as "hard as brick".[3] Remains of this primitive type of flue have been found in recent years during renovations of old buildings. By the beginning of the seventeenth century, however, the use of brick or stone for chimneys became universal and many villages brought out regulations to govern the construction of chimneys. At Clare, Suffolk, in 1621, a decision was made by the head-boroughs that every chimney should in future be built of brick and stand $4\frac{1}{2}$ feet above the roof; but nearly a century later, in 1719, people were being fined for their clay chimneys.

With such an increase in fireplaces, Charles ll introduced, in 1662, the Hearth Tax, which was voted to the crown forever. With the exception of small cottages, all houses were charged at the rate of two shillings for every hearth, fire or stove, and the tax yielded some £200,000 per year. It was one of the most unpopular taxes ever levied and was a great burden on the small-house owner. The tax was finally repealed, after it had been in existence for over twenty-five years, when William III realized that it "was very grievous to the people".

These stacks were at first built as an external projection on an outside wall, and in timber-framed buildings that position interfered less with the construction than any other. In the sixteenth century this arrangement gave way to a stack constructed in the centre of the house between the hall and parlour, known as an 'axial stack'. This new design, which started in the south-eastern counties, spread throughout the Midlands as

133. Cottage, Neen Sollars, Salop.

134. Colour-washed stone cottages, Bossington, Somerset.

far as the Welsh border by the eighteenth century. Not only new cottages and small farmhouses were built with this new arrangement but many existing timber-framed ones were cut and adapted to accommodate a new axial stack. Although many smaller houses frequently had one fireplace, that in the hall-kitchen, one advantage with the axial stack was that the parlour too could be heated by back-to-back fireplaces or even, in the larger houses, the chambers above could all share one stack.

Not all stacks of this period were axial. In parts of Hereford and Worcester, as well as the adjoining parts of Salop and Gloucestershire, stacks, constructed of local stone and built outside the gable wall, continued to be popular in timber-framed houses (*See* 132 and 133). Likewise, in the stone areas, like the Cotswolds, the axial stack never gained popularity and in the simple single or two-ground-floor-roomed cottage the fireplace was placed inside the gable wall. In the South-west, during the sixteenth century, the stack on the front wall serving both the hall and chamber above it became fashionable. It can be found all over Devon, especially in East Devon, and between Exmoor and the north coast of Somerset, as well as in Cornwall (*See* 134 and 135). One of the best examples on a smaller house are the almshouses at Cheriton Fitzpaine, Devon, built in the second half of the seventeenth century. Where a gable fireplace was used, an oven was also provided, either at the side of the fireplace or more commonly behind it, protruding outside the gable wall, often under an attractive pyramidal or lean-to roof. These became popular in the seventeenth century with the desire for fresh bread, and can be seen in many seventeenth-century cottages in the South-west, the Cotswolds and the West. Another innovation in Devon was the smoking chamber, used for smoking bacon, which consisted of a chamber adjacent to the fireplace with an opening at low level and a corbelled flue at the top joining the main flue.

In the eighteenth century the axial stack, which had been almost universally adopted, gave way to large gable-end chimney-stacks. This was brought about by the desire to have better access to the chamber above, and with the axial stack taking up much of the centre of the cottage this was impossible. To overcome this the stacks were moved to the gable ends and the interior division altered to three rooms; the central one, the hall, being unheated and containing only the staircase. With these gable stacks it became easier to incorporate an oven which, like those of the stone areas, generally projected from the external wall behind the fireplace. With the coming of semi-detached and terraced cottages the fireplaces were generally built in the party wall, back-to-back, both using the same stack.

Chimney-stacks were made of brick or stone, according to the local material available. Brick was considered best, being more fire resistant and adaptable, and in many stone areas was preferred to the local material. Unlike the massive brick multi-flue stacks of larger buildings which, in Tudor times especially though to a lesser degree in Elizabethan and Jacobean times, received the attention of craftsman's art, the brick chimney-shaft above the ridge on humbler buildings with only one fireplace was rarely decorated or moulded in any way. Usually it was square in section and plain except for one or two projecting courses around the top and a drip course where the thatch met the shaft to protect the joists. On most cottages this simple form of decoration is most pleasing.

In the Cotswolds, dressed stone, although liable to be affected by the heat, was often used, and provided excellent opportunities for decoration, sometimes in the form of a moulded cornice and often incorporating a moulded water-tabling to protect the joint between stack and roof. Rubble stone, although frequently found on cottages, was less suitable because of the difficulty in bonding, especially at the corners when the stone was small. To overcome this, circular stacks were built, like those in parts of the Lake District and in the South-west.

The only flaw on most chimneys is the conglomeration of chimney-pots and cowls which, apart from television aerials, do more to destroy the skyline than any other single thing. A comparatively modern innovation, they were seldom to be found on cottages until Victorian times. Before this time the draught was improved by a number of simple

135. Cottage, Bicknoller, Somerset.

devices. In the stone districts, slabs of stone inclined together to form an inverted V-shape over the top of the shaft were often used and are still to be seen on many cottages of the North, particularly in the Lake District. Another method, to be seen in many places throughout the country, was to raise a single slab supported on each corner by stone or brick piers. In the Cotswolds, as in other stone areas, it was a common practice to use four pieces of thin, wedge-shaped stone slabs or slates set at converging angles, with the top either pointed or in the form of a truncated pyramid. Although clay chimney-pots first gained popularity in England during the reign of George III, it was not until about 1850 that there was a large-scale introduction of them, probably due to the widespread use of the Victorian grate over that of the basket and hob used by the Georgians. Thousands of pots were added to existing stacks, often out of keeping with the original design. One type, known as 'tall boys', was up to 7 feet long and sometimes used to overcome the problem of lofty single stacks.

The early fireplaces were large for they were intended to burn logs and brushwood and therefore required a large hearth, and in consequence the flues were much larger than those constructed later when coal was used. Also, in cottages with only one fireplace (that in the hall-kitchen), they were also used for hearth cooking. In cottages the fireplace was usually spanned by a stout oak lintel, often cambered, for it had to support the weight of the stack above. The back of the lintel was splayed to encourage a draught up the chimney and, although in more ambitious houses it was sometimes moulded, it was usually plain except for a chamfer on the lower edge. In some stone areas, like the Cotswolds, the lintel was occasionally of stone. The jambs, whether brick or stone, were usually plain, but on occasions were chamfered or rounded. Some of the fireplaces were so large that an inglenook was provided. In the statesmen's houses and cottages of the Lake District the hearth occupied from a half to a third of the room, with space large enough for chairs beside the fire, and sometimes with a separate fire window to light it. In Victorian times many large fireplaces were bricked up and smaller fireplaces inserted. In the kitchen the large fireplace and the back oven was replaced by the cast-iron range.

Wood and coal were not the only fuel used by cottagers. Furze and brake were collected from the common wastes, and must have been the fuel commonly used both for cooking and warmth by a large number of villagers all over the country. Where wood was scarce, 'dythes' or dried cow-dung was commonly used. Both in Buckinghamshire and Northamptonshire the dung was collected from the fields, mixed with short straw, kneaded into lumps, daubed on the walls of buildings and, when dry, used as fuel. At Naseby, Northamptonshire, in 1792, the vicar complained that the cottages, instead of being drawn over with lime plaster and lined out to appear like stonework, were covered each year with cow-dung spread on the walls to dry and then used as fuel.[4] Edward Laurence, in 1727, mentioned Yorkshire and Lincolnshire as counties where dung was frequently used as fuel and suggested that a restrictive covenant should be inserted in all leases preventing this.[5] In 1750 the inhabitants of Portland used cakes made up of cow-dung mixed with straw and dried against the walls of their houses as fuel, a practice still used there some fifty years later.[6] A similar method of drying the material was used in Leicestershire in 1755.[7] At the end of the eighteenth century this practice was also in use in some parts of Cornwall; Edward Daniel Clarke[8] remarked that on their tour there an old woman followed their horses with a basket, hoping to increase her supplies. Peat was also commonly used which was thought to be a particularly healthy fuel.

Floors, Ceilings and Stairs

Early ground floors, even in the homes of the nobility, were usually of earth, trodden or beaten hard, and strewn with rushes or straw. To overcome the problem of dust and wear the clay was mixed with ox-blood and ashes which hardened sufficiently to be polished. Although in Elizabeth's reign the more important houses were being paved with plaster of Paris or stone flags to imitate the marble paving of the Continent, plain earth floors continued to be the general floor for humbler dwellings until the seventeenth and eighteenth centuries when, in clay districts, bricks and, in stone areas, stone flags began to be used. Henry Best[1] of Elmswell, Humberside, a farmer in the seventeenth century, described his method of laying earth floors. The earth was dug, raked until "indifferent small" and water added until it was the consistency of mortar. It was then allowed to lie for two weeks until the water had settled and the earth began to harden, when it was beaten smooth with broad, flat pieces of wood.

The *Dictionarium Rusticum*, first published in 1704, states that earth floors should be made from loamy clay with one-third new soft horse-dung, made from grass, mixed with a small quantity of coal ashes. Before being laid, this material was tempered, rested for ten days, tempered again and rested for a further three days.

In areas where lime and gypsum were available these too were used. J. Lawrence in *The Modern Land Steward*, published in 1806, states that these floors should be made one-third lime, one-third coal ashes and one-third loamy clay and horse-dung tempered to a "tough and glewy" consistency. This mixture was then spread on the earth and compacted by treading and beating with a rammer. In Gloucestershire, at the beginning of the nineteenth century, 'grip floors' were fashionable; these were composed of lime and ashes, laid in a moist state to a thickness of 4 to 5 inches, and rammed with a heavy wooden slab until it acquired a hard and smooth surface.[2] In 1788, William Marshall[3] found cottage floors in Yorkshire constructed of lime and sand mixed together to form a mortar similar to that used for bricklaying, but made "stronger and softer". In Devon a local material called lime ashe, the waste from the bottom of the lime kiln, was sometimes used for these plastered floors. No matter what type of floor at the best all these solid floors were cold and damp. Although boarded ground floors became fashionable in the larger houses from the beginning of the eighteenth century, for humbler dwellings this was unusual before the nineteenth century and even then

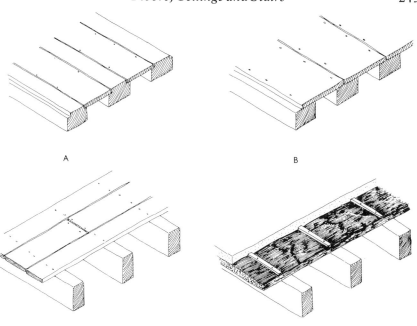

136. Flooring: A. joist and boarded; B. close-boarded with boards fixed parallel to joists; C. close-boarded with boards fixed across joists; D. plaster on a layer of reed or straw.

being restricted to the parlour while retaining their solid floors in all rooms in constant use. These boarded floors afforded greater comfort, being warmer and drier than solid floors.

The open hall, a ground-floor room open to the roof, was the principal room of the early dwellings, whether a manor house or a simple cottage, and remained so in some cottages in backward areas until the nineteenth century. From the fifteenth century, however, it became customary to insert an intermediate floor over all or part of the house. These upper floors were constructed in a variety of ways; the boarded floor being superior. In the days of close joists the boards and joists ran parallel, the boards fitting into rebates in the joists with the joists forming a considerable part of the floor (*See* 136A). Another method and a stronger one, was the close-boarded floor (*See* 136B). The boards were still laid parallel to the joists, but, instead of being rebated into the joists, were laid over them, being either pegged or, when it could be afforded, nailed to them. From the end of the sixteenth century, when joists were set wider apart, it became common practice to lay the floor-boards across the joists and not parallel to them in order to distribute the weight over several joists. This type of floor enabled boards of varying widths to be used for the first time, an important consideration when the supply of timber began to decline. Few, if any, boards would span the room, the carpenter's aim being simply to fill the area and produce the soundest floor he could with the boards available, disregarding where the joists came. Oak, as always, was the carpenter's first choice for boards, but in the seventeenth century elm competed with it and from the beginning of the eighteenth century softwood came into general use.

Early boards were either riven or pit-sawn. The earliest method, and one commonly practised, was riving or cleaving with a riving-iron, sometimes known as a 'thrower', which was driven into the timber with a hardwood club, called a 'beetle'. The trunks were quartered and then split parallel with the medullary rays, producing feathered or slightly wedge-shaped planks. When laid, but before being fixed, the boards were reduced to the same thickness by means of an adze worked across the grain. The method was wasteful, producing short boards – the length depended on the quality of the timber, the straighter the grain the longer the boards – some being only a few feet in length and rarely of any substantial width. The best pit-sawn boards were also obtained by quartering the trunk and cutting obliquely across the medullary rays. This too was wasteful, particularly when the boards were laid parallel to the joists, and were of a similar width. The most economic method, with very little waste, was to cut the log into planks without first quartering it. This method produced planks of varying width with a proportion of wide boards, a common feature of many old floors. The boards did, however, tend to twist and so needed to be securely fixed. Pit-sawn boards were longer than riven ones but shorter than those produced later by machinery. Many old oak-boarded floors still survive, but many have been replaced by softwood.

There is clear evidence that floor-boards were not always fixed, often being inserted by the tenant and, like the glass of windows, were not infrequently included in an inventory along with the furniture. The reason is not clear for, although it has been suggested that if both joists and floor-boards were loose it would be easier to remove part of the floor in order to get in bulky goods, in many instances the joists and main beam were fixed, with only the boards being described as "loose and moveable". Joists laid on the main ceiling beam and not jointed to it have been occasionally observed by archaeologists, and it may be that the fixed boarded floor evolved from a fixed main beam with loose joists and boards on it. Clearly, many chambered floors in cottages developed from a simple loft, where the cottager, perhaps using the tie-beam of the roof truss as his ceiling beam, would loosely board over all or part of the roof-space to provide himself with additional accommodation or storage space. One such cottage is the 'croglofft' of Wales and Ireland. This had a single room open to a low roof with, at the end opposite the hearth, a cubicle partitioned off, and above this a low open loft reached by a ladder. This arrangement was probably similar to many primitive cottages in this country. In this and many other cottages the principal bedroom remained on the ground floor, the upper storey being a cramped ill-lit loft. It was not until later, by raising the eaves or by the insertion of dormer windows, that it eventually became a bedroom, perhaps with a permanent floor provided.

Not all upper floors were boarded, and where lime or gypsum was readily available, in place of boards, a well-tempered plaster was often employed (*See* 136D). In the East Midlands from the sixteenth to the nineteenth century it was in common use for every class of house, from an Elizabethan mansion to the smallest cottage. In this area – Lincolnshire, Nottinghamshire and part of Leicestershire – gypsum was used, while in the Cotswolds lime was the main ingredient. Whether gypsum or lime was used, the mixture was similar to that described for ground floors, although in addition burnt brick was sometimes mixed in as an aggregate. These plaster floors required the usual ceiling beams and joists, across which a layer of reed or straw was laid and secured by a batten on which a layer of plaster, 2 or 3 inches thick, was spread. The plaster was trowelled smooth and allowed to dry slowly to prevent cracking. In the Cotswolds the reed or straw was replaced with wattle, fixed between the joists, and packed with clay before the plaster finish was applied,[4] while in Derbyshire sawn laths were used. In all cases the underside between the joists would be plastered. Although eventually these floors would sag and crack, they were solid, as well as producing a more even finish, and there was a considerable saving in timber, which in some areas was becoming expensive by the seventeenth century.

There is also evidence that upper floors were made of earth, which may seem unusual today but perhaps it was natural to make them of the same material as the ground floor. Constructed in a similar way to plastered floors – laid on a layer of straw or reeds over the joists – earth floors provided a cheap alternative to both boarded and plastered ones, and were probably used in those areas away from the sources of lime and gypsum and where timber was scarce. One such area where these upper floors were known to have been used was the eastern half of Lincolnshire.

In the early house the main beam and joists were left exposed and the floor upon these consisted the ceiling of the roof below. In the larger, more important houses these beams and joists were richly moulded and carved, but on the majority of ordinary dwellings they were generally plain, except for the main beam which was sometimes chamfered. The spaces between the joists were plastered and whitened, improving the lighting of the room as well as making the timbers more conspicuous. In some areas, particularly in East Anglia, this was achieved by placing a

layer of reeds about an inch thick on the joists prior to fixing the floor-
boards. The underside of these reeds, like the floors of the Midlands,
were subsequently plastered. In many of the smaller houses, however,
this did not occur until the eighteenth century, the underside of the floor-
boards being the only ceiling. Consequently the warmth from the downstairs fire escaped upwards through the cracks in the floor-boards.

From the beginning of the eighteenth century, with the decline in the
quality of timber[5] and the desire to improve the comfort of the buildings,
many cottages for the first time had ceilings 'underdrawn' with plaster,
often with the main beam exposed. With the availability of sawn laths
and the improvement in the quality of plaster this process afforded little
difficulty. Like plastered walls and partitions, these ceilings were sometimes filled with chaff. In South Yorkshire and in some parts of the Midlands thick-stemmed reed-grass was fixed to the underside of the joists in
place of laths, being secured to the joists with battens. Similarly the
upper floor, often in the case of cottages constructed partly in the roof-
space, could be ceiled. In East Anglia these upper rooms were sometimes
plastered between the rafters directly on the underside of the thatch, a
process known as 'sparkling'.

When cottages first began to be chambered over, the upper floor was
reached by means of a simple ladder or the slightly more elaborate com-
panion way – a steep straight flight with the steps which were solid triangular timbers housed to the string, so that the foot was placed beneath
the slope of the step above – passing through a framed opening in the
joists or, in some cases, a trap-door. The ladder was most commonly
employed and remained in use in some areas, like South Yorkshire, until
the last century.[6]

Later, when fireplaces became common in the sixteenth and seventeenth centuries, it became the practice to place the stair against the
stack. In the eastern half of the country, with the axial stack in the centre
of the cottage, the stair was placed between the free standing stack and
the rear wall away from the entrance, although in the smaller cottage in
Essex and East Anglia the stair was sometimes built between the entrance and the stack. In this case the flight was occasionally straight, but
more often all these were spiral or newel stairs turning through a
hundred and eighty degrees between ground and first floor, with the
steps housed into a central newel. In both cases these steps would be solid,
for the framed stair with separate strings, treads and risers, did not
come into general use until well into the seventeenth century and in cottages much later. In the West Midlands, as in Staffordshire and further
north in Cheshire, the axial stack with the stair adjacent was a common
occurrence, but in Hereford and Worcester, as well as the cottages on the
limestone belt, like those in the Cotswolds and Somerset, the stack was
usually on the gable wall, although here again, like the cottages of the

eastern counties, the stair was placed alongside the stack. In the statesmen's house of the Lake District the stair was at the back, either a newel stair in its own projection or sometimes, in the smaller houses, a ladder within the main building. A similar arrangement can be found in some of the cottages in Devon where the stair is housed at the rear in its own stone or cob enclosure. In some stone districts, like Devon and the Cotswolds, these newel stairs often had steps of stone. In the eighteenth century these stairs, particularly those adjacent to fireplaces, were cased in and became, in fact, 'staircases' set in a cupboard with a small wooden door at the bottom. This was often the only cupboard that the cottage possessed with the limited floor-space available, but the fashion of using chests for storage made up for this deficiency. In the eighteenth century, with the growing desire for framed stairs, the axial stack was abandoned in favour of a stack on the gable wall, and with this the newel stair was replaced in favour of a straight flight, usually situated in the hall which became no more than an entrance lobby between the two heated downstairs rooms and opposite the main entrance. In some smaller cottages a quarter- or half-turn stair was provided within one of the downstairs rooms.

Doors and Windows

In the small medieval cottage often the only opening was the door, providing not only access to the cottage but also the only source of light. Probably the opening was covered with ox-hide or coarse fabric which could be pulled up like a blind, a custom which persisted in the north of Scotland until the eighteenth century. At a mud house at Great Hatfield, Mappleton, Humberside, the original window, and also the door, were of harden, a kind of coarse sack cloth, which "could be lifted up like a curtain, and there was no inner door".[1] Light doors made of timber and wattle were also used. The doors of the Yorkshire charcoal-burners' huts and those of the bark-peelers' huts of Cumbria were all made of wattle and it is known that more permanent buildings in Cumbria were also made of similar material.[2] Thomas Rudge, in 1807, states that in the Cotswolds doors were "little more than strong hurdles, made of split ash, or willow, with little workmanship or skill".[3] That the doors of the early dwellings were flimsy is evident from Chaucer's *Canterbury Tales*, in which the miller breaks doors by simply butting them with his head. These early doors were loose, without any hinge or handle, being pulled over the opening once the person was inside.

The earliest true door was the battened one, consisting of vertical boards secured at the back by horizontal battens. Diagonal braces between the battens were often added to prevent the door sagging for, being made out of oak, they were extremely heavy. The doors were comparatively easy and inexpensive to make, the boards being simply butt-jointed and fastened to the batten by wooden pegs. In the fourteenth century the battened doors belonged to churches and halls and by the time it had filtered down to the cottage it had often become obsolete, except in doors of no significance, in the more important buildings. The battened door remained in general use in cottages (although of much lighter construction than the earlier doors) until the eighteenth century when, with the introduction of the panelled door, it was considered too inferior for the front entrance of many cottages, and was relegated to back doors and outhouses. In many districts, however, it is still possible to find on old cottages a softwood front door of the battened type, now known as framed and braced doors, covered with tongued and grooved boarding. The heck-door, a door divided horizontally in two to enable the upper part to be opened to admit light and air while the lower half remained closed, was a form of battened door at one time widely used. Although rarely seen today as a front entrance door, it can still be found as a kitchen door in many cottages and small farmhouses. A transitional door, battened and also panelled, was used in the late seventeenth and early eighteenth centuries and can still occasionally be seen. The inner side consisted of vertical boards with battens, while the outer side simulated the panelled door with applied mitred mouldings. By the eighteenth century, although many Renaissance features in the design of front entrance doors were being used on many smaller houses, the cottage remained unassuming in character, being restricted to a simple panelled door, often not even moulded, set in a frame. Internal doors followed the development of the external doors. In the sixteenth century the few internal openings that existed were probably hung with coarse fabric, with the battened door not being in general use until much later, while the panelled doors were seldom used, and then only perhaps in the parlour.

Early doors had no frames, the actual doors being hung directly to the opening whether timber or stone. Although strap and hook hinges had been used since medieval times and continued to be used throughout the Tudor and early Stuart period, they did not come into use on humbler dwellings until the sixteenth century. The earlier entrance doors were commonly hung on 'harr-hinges' set in a simple arrangement of posts, lintel and sill. The vertical board on the hanging side of the door was increased in thickness – the harr-tree – and it projected at top and bottom, these ends being shaped to form dowels to fit and rotate in holes in the lintel and sill. This primitive form of hanging doors was still found in parts of the North and West this century, although in the South and East it became obsolete many years ago. Ironwork was first confined to the strap-hinge, coming into popular use in the seventeenth century in all but the humblest cottage. Other fittings, however, continued to be made of wood until the eighteenth century and the introduction of cheaper iron. The age-old wooden bar (known by various names as a 'stang', 'slot' or 'spar') placed across the door was the most common lock and continued to be used in many cottages this century and probably still is in many country areas. One end of the bar was fitted into a wooden staple, while the other end was fitted into an L-shaped catch, both secured to the door-frame. Bolts were made by shortening the bar and attaching it to the opening side of the door by means of two wooden staples, and made to slide, when the door was closed, into another staple fixed to the frame (*See* 138). A development of the spar was the 'sneck', a simple wooden latch that could be opened from the outside (*See* 137). A short wooden bar was hinged to the door at one end, with the unfixed end sliding up and down in an oversized staple on the door and dropping into a catch on the frame. The latch could be opened from the outside by a string which passed through a hole in the door and was secured to the latch. Dr Whitaker,[4] writing at the beginning of the nineteenth century about Samlesbury Hall, a house built in 1532, states that "... the inner doors are

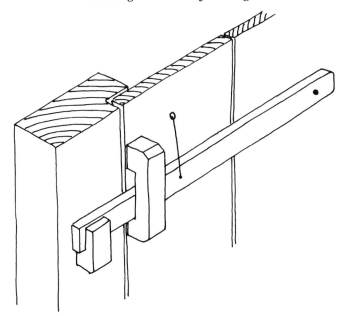

137. Wooden latch.

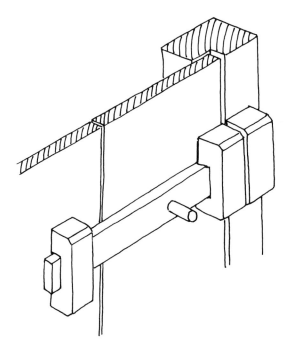

138. Wooden bolt.

without panel or lock, and have always been opened, like those of modern cottages, with latch and string". So the method of opening new cottage doors in that part of the country was the one which had been used in important buildings three hundred years before. Later a spoon-shaped peg was fitted under the latch which, when pressed down, raised the latch – a forerunner of the familiar iron thumb-latch. To secure the latch and prevent the latch being raised, a piece of wood, called a 'snib', was inserted in the staple. Although these latches can still be found on internal doors, from the eighteenth century, with the rapid increase in the supply of cheap iron, wooden fasteners were replaced by iron ones.

The early medieval cottage probably had few if any windows. These openings, 'wind-holes' as they were known, had a dual purpose of letting in light as well as of letting out smoke. Where they were provided they were kept to a minimum for they were a source of draught and damp. These early windows were simply holes, not protected in any way, and such holes survived into the nineteenth century. Dr Guest describes in his *Origines Celticae* a pair of cottages in Berkshire built 'on crucks' which were lighted by a hole in the gable, which evidently served to let out smoke as well. Early windows were unglazed, even in superior houses, for glass was expensive, and although glass was made in the thirteenth century at Chiddingfold, Surrey, as well as in Staffordshire, Salop and Cheshire it was of indifferent quality and most glass was imported from the Continent. Glass remained a luxury until the sixteenth century and up to 1579, when the practice became banned by law, glazed lattices were treated as furniture, being taken down and stored safely when the owner was away or carried from one house to another and temporarily installed in the openings.

So up to the end of the sixteenth century and, in many labourers' cottages as late as the early part of the eighteenth century, most windows were unglazed. In place of glass, oiled paper or the horn of cattle, obtained by peeling or shaving thin slices from the horns, as well as lattices of wood, wickerwork and even reeds were all employed, but oiled cloth, preferably linen, stiffened by a wood lattice arranged in a diamond pattern and fitted to each opening was most commonly used. William Horman,[5] writing in 1519, states that instead of glass "Paper or linen clothe straked across with lozenges make fenestrals". William Harrison, in 1577, informs us that in

> . . . old time our country houses, instead of glass, did use much lattice, made either of wicker or fine rifts of oak in checkwise. Some of the better sort did make panels of horn instead of glass, but as horn in windows is now quite laid down, so our lattices are also grown into less use, because glass is come to be so plentiful and within a very little so good cheap, if not better than any other . . .

This reference to glass relates more to the houses of merchants and yeomen farmers than to humbler dwellings. The husbandman would not have expected glazed windows until the seventeenth century while the labourer, especially in the West, probably had to wait longer, even into the eighteenth century, for glass in his humble cottage. Then he might get nothing better than lattices tied with wire to the vertical bars of wooden-mullioned windows or to the horizontal bars of stone mullioned windows, so that they could not open. So in many cottages the unglazed windows covered with oiled cloth remained in common use until the seventeenth century, and in remote areas until the eighteenth century.

Although in Tudor times windows in the larger houses had some form of tracery in the heads, the windows in cottages were plain, usually rectangular, often situated at high level beneath the ceiling or just below the eaves. These windows, made of oak, were divided by plain mullions, square in section, set diagonally and, in the case of a timber-framed cottage, set in the bressummer or wall-plate at the top and a sill at the bottom. Often each light was sub-divided with a smaller intermediate vertical bar, also set diagonally. Examples of this type of unglazed window still survive, although they are usually blocked up. However, as the early lattices required no structural preparation, other than the provision of vertical bars to which they could be tied, it is difficult to decide if such a window was originally glazed or not. Where the window was covered with oiled cloth a slightly different arrangement occurred. The window was fully framed, as for an unglazed window, but the mullions were not set diagonally. Externally, around each light, was a rebate to which the cloth, probably stiffened with the diamond-patterned lattice, was fitted. Internally the cloth was supported by a smaller intermediate vertical rail similar to that of the unglazed window. Such windows can still be found on some cottages of the sixteenth and early seventeenth centuries.[6]

Internal wooden shutters, formed of vertical boards and horizontal battens, were often used on these windows, providing security and protection from draughts and bad weather. These shutters were hinged at either the top, bottom or sides and either inside or outside the building. Those fixed at the top were lifted up when light was required, those internally being secured by a hook to a ceiling beam and those externally being kept up by means of a pole; more commonly they were fixed on the outside, hung at the bottom, and lowered when light was required. These boarded shutters continued in use, for purposes of security, long after the adoption of glazed windows. Although hinged shutters were used, on cottages it appears that sliding ones were most commonly employed obviating the use of iron strap hinges. These shutters were made to slide horizontally in grooves — in the case of a timber-framed cottage they would be either attached to or forming part of the bressummer or wall-plate and the sill – and extending beyond the window so the shutter could fully open. Depending on the width of the window one or two shutters were used.

All the early glass was blown in cylinders or muffs, which when split along their length gradually opened up and flattened as they cooled. The glass produced was frequently rough, speckled, with a greenish tint, which was cut up into small panes, known as 'quarries'. In the sixteenth century these quarries were diamond shape, but later rectangular panes, a little larger in size, were preferred. Each quarry was placed into lead cames – small grooved bars – which in turn were jointed together to form one large lattice, known as a 'leaded light'. When these leaded lights were fixed, as most were for very few, even in the larger houses, opened to provide ventilation, they were stiffened by horizontal saddle bars set inside the glazing and fixed into holes in the mullions or jambs. To these bars the lattice was secured either with lead tapes or, later, with wire.

Throughout the seventeenth century the mullioned window, whether built of stone or timber, remained in favour and in cottages continued to be until the middle of the eighteenth century. The long horizontal runs of narrow mullioned lights were replaced by ones square in shape divided into two or three lights by mullions. A transome was also occasionally introduced, so placed that the light above the transome was smaller than the one below. Leaded lights remained the general form of glazing these windows until the eighteenth century, when, with the improved quality of glass and influx of imported softwood, glazing bars of wood, being cheaper than lead cames, came into general use and gradually filtered their way into cottages. These early glazing bars were unmoulded and clumsier than later ones. During this period, in many cases for the first time and then often only a simple small pane in a window of fixed glazing, some form of ventilation by opening lights became normal, either in the form of side hung casements in wood or wrought iron or horizontal sliding sashes. This later form, the so-called Yorkshire sliding sash (*See* 139), with one light fixed and the other sliding, was first introduced at the beginning of the eighteenth century, remaining in common use until the early part of the nineteenth century. They were particularly suited to cottages and other rural buildings with low ceilings and small squat windows, providing a cheap alternative to the fashionable vertical sliding sash. It can still be seen on numerous cottages throughout the country, being equally popular on ones constructed of brick, stone, timber or mud.

Towards the end of the seventeenth century the vertical sliding sash window made of wood was first introduced, but it was not perhaps until the latter half of the next century that it found its way into many cottages, often replacing, for the first time, the small unglazed windows of the century before. Examples of unglazed windows with the lights

139. Yorkshire sliding sash.

blocked up with later sashes added alongside can still be seen. At first the upper sash was fixed with the lower sash sliding in grooves, being held by a hook or wedge. It was not until the end of the eighteenth century that the counterbalanced double sash replaced this system. The panes remained small for although the quality of the glass improved, the size obtainable remained small. The size of the glazing bars was reduced in section until, by the beginning of the nineteenth century, were no wider than half an inch and were, except in the poorest dwelling, moulded.

Cylinder glass, because it was cheaper, continued to be used in cottage windows until the middle of the eighteenth century when it was largely replaced by crown glass, a superior and clearer glass. This glass, which was used in Normandy as early as the fourteenth century and in this country from the seventeenth century, was also blown, not into muffs but by the use of a glass-blower's pontil (a hollow iron rod) into a disc, called a 'table'. The molten material on the end of the pontil was spun round and round with the palms of the hands, and by flattening out the bubble on the end with a wooden bat the glass-blower could produce a disc varying in diameter from 3 feet to 4 feet 6 inches. The disc was always thicker towards the centre, culminating in the 'bull's eye' in the middle where the glass had been attached to the pontil. The bull's eye was normally discarded, but, being the cheapest, it was used, particularly in the eighteenth century, and can still be seen in cottage windows. Crown glass of the eighteenth and early nineteenth centuries, with its wavy surface, can still be seen in many sash windows. Crown glass remained the main type of glass produced until about 1840 when, for the first time, cheap but good quality sheet glass was manufactured. The excise duty on glass, first imposed in 1746, was finally abolished in 1845, making the glass even cheaper. For the first time large panes could be manufactured, leading to the omission of the glazing bars, so that lights in one single pane, or occasionally divided by a single bar down its centre, became common. Unfortunately many earlier windows were also altered to accommodate these larger panes, which is aesthetically displeasing. Likewise, these large panes were suitable for the durable iron casements, preferred in many stone areas, which during the nineteenth century often replaced wood, especially in cottages.

Like so many other improvements in housing over the centuries, windows were subjected to taxation. First introduced in 1696, the Window Tax was levied according to the number of openings on all houses worth over £5 a year; it was increased on six separate occasions between 1747 and 1808, before being reduced in 1825 and eventually repealed in 1851. The effect of this unpopular tax was to put a restraint on building and to avoid excessive payment many people blocked up some of their windows. Blocked windows can still be seen in many cottages, but it would be a mistake to attribute all these to the Window Tax.

The formation of the opening for both doors and windows varied with the material in which they were formed. In the timber-framed cottage there was no difficulty in forming an opening; the timber lintel and sill being simply framed to adjacent studs with, if necessary, additional studs being incorporated next to the windows to form the jambs. In most cottages constructed with inferior stone a timber lintel was also frequently used, only in areas where stones were capable of spanning an opening, like the granite cottages of the South-west or the granite and slate cottages of the Lake District, were stone lintels used. Where the stone could be dressed, as in parts of the limestone belt like the Cotswolds, the cottages occasionally incorporated moulded heads, jambs, sills and mullions, often with a dripstone above, like the cottages at Great Tew. In some areas, like the Lake District, slates were inserted above the windows to form dripstones, as the cottages at Little Langdale, Cumbria. Where the cottages were of flint, and sometimes chalk, brick arches with brick jambs were used. On cob or clay-lump cottages too, timber lintels were commonly employed. Although occasionally on the poorest brick cottage timber lintels are found the vast majority are formed of brick arches, usually a slightly cambered soldier arch. In Georgian times the rubbed arch became fashionable and was extensively used, but seldom on many cottages.

Notes

PART ONE

The Medieval Cot
1 M. Beresford and J. G. Hurst, *Deserted Medieval Villages* (1971) pp. 104–107
2 D. Wills, *Estate Book of Henry de Bray of Harleston* (Camden Society, 1916) pp. 49–51
3 Hunter, South Yorkshire, *The Deanery of Doncaster*, i p. 370
4 *Archaeologia Aeliana*, xxii (1900)
5 T. H. Turner, *Domestic Architecture in England* i (1853) p. 282

The Birth of the English Cottage
1 I. S. Leadam (Ed), *Domesday of Inclosures* (1897)
2 V. C. H., *Sussex* ii p. 193
3 R. Carew, *Survey of Cornwall* (1602) p. 66
4 C. Fiennes, *Journey* Ed. C. Morris (1947) p. 51
5 R. Reyce, *Breviary of Suffolk* (1618), p. 51
6 Lt. Hammond, *Short Survey of 26 Counties* (ed. 1904), pp. 42–43
7 C. Fiennes, *op. cit*, pp. 196 and 202
8 *Bishop Hall's Satires*, Book v. satire i
9 W. Howitt, *The Rural Life of England* (1838)

The Agrarian Revolution
1 P. Kalm, *Kalm's Account of his Visit to England on his way to America in 1748* (1892)
2 N. Kent, *Hints to Gentlemen of Landed Property* (1775) p. 261
3 N. Kent, *Agricultural Survey of Norfolk* (1796) p. 163
4 A. Young, *Political Arithmetic* (1774) p. 102
5 R. Warner, *Tour through the Northern Counties* (1812)
6 W. Mavor, *General View of the Agriculture of Berkshire* (1808)
7 S. Shaw, *A Tour of the West of England in 1788* (1789)
8 M. Batey, *Nuneham Courtenay* reprinted from *Oxoniensia* xxxiii (1968) pp. 108–24
9 U. Price, *Essay on the Picturesque* (1794)
10 J. C. Loudon, *Encyclopaedia of Cottage, Farm and Villa Architecture and Furniture* (1836)
11 R. Beatson, *On Farm Buildings in General. Communications to the Board of Agriculture* (1797), i, p. 206
12 T. Davis, *Address to the Landholders of the Kingdom* ... (1975)
13 J. Miller, *The Country Gentlemen's Architect* (1787) plates 1 and 2
14 J. Plaw, *Rural Architecture* (1794)
15 Most of the following information unless noted is analysed from these reports
16 C. P. Moritz, *Journey of a German in England in 1782*
17 W. Marshall, *Rural Economy of the Southern Counties* (1798), i, pp. 30–31
18 H. Misson, *Memoirs and Observation in his Travels over England* (1719)
19 W. Ellis, *Chiltern and Vale Farming Explained* (1733)
20 P. Kalm, *op. cit* pp. 181–2, 201
21 L. Simond, *Journal of a Tour and Residence in Great Britain by a French Traveller* (1815) pp. 181, 189
22 Rev. W. Gilpin, *Remarks on Forest Scenery* (1791), ii, pp. 39, 45
23 G. White, *Natural History of Selbourne* (1789)

24 E. J. Climenson (Ed), *Passages from the Diary of Mrs Philip Lybbe Powys* (1899) p. 206
25 W. G. Maton, *Observations of the Western Counties, 1794 and 1796* (1797)
26 Dr Pococke, *Travels through England* (Camden Soc. New Series xliv)
27 W. Marshall, *Rural Economy of Gloucestershire* (1789), i, pp. 30–37: ii p. 16
28 Rev. E. Butcher, *An Excursion from Sidmouth to Chester . . . in 1803* (1805) p. 152
29 W. Stukeley, *Itinerarium Curiosum* (2nd Edition) ii, pp. 57–58
30 W. Hutchinson, *View of Northumberland, Anno 1776* (1778)
31 J. Houseman, *Topographical Description of Cumberland, etc.* (1800)

'Peace and Plenty'

1 Lord Ernle, *The Land and its People* (1925)
2 T. Postans, *A letter to Sir Thomas Baring, Bt., M.P.* (1831)
3 M. Garnier, *The Annals of the British Peasantry* (1895)
4 Lord Ernle, *English Farming Past and Present* (1932)
5 R. Elsam, *Hints for Improving the Conditions of the Peasantry* (1816)
6 W. Howitt, *The Rural Life of England* (1838)

The Housing of the Victorian Rural Poor

1 A. Somerville, *The Whistler at the Plough* (1852) pp. 402–4
2 J. Caird, *English Agriculture in 1850–51* (1852, new ed. 1968)
3 Lord Ernle, *English Farming Past and Present* (1932)
4 H. Rider Haggard, *Rural England* (1906)
5 Dr J. Simon, *Seventh Report of the Medical Officer of the Privy Council* (1864) p. 11
6 J. Caird, *op. cit*
7 J. L. Green, *English Country Cottages* (1900)

Housing for All

1 H. Rider Haggard, *Rural England* (1906)
2 For plans of these and other cottages see L. Weaver, *Book of Cottages* (1919)

PART TWO

Timber-framed Cottages

1 W. G. Hoskins, *Provincial England* (1963) p. 104 states that domestically Leicester was all half-timbered before the introduction of brick during the last quarter of the seventeenth century
2 J. C. Cox, *Royal Forests of England* (1905)
3 W. G. Hoskins, *The Making of the English Landscape* (1955)
4 L. F. Salzman, *Building in England down to 1540* (1967) p. 202
5 Quoted in C. F. Innocent, *The Development of English Building Construction* (1916)
6 J. Moxon, *Mechanick Exercises* (1677–79) p. 136
7 O. Cook and E. Smith, *English Cottages and Farmhouses* (1954)
8 C. F. Innocent, *op. cit*
9 *Bishop Hatfield's Survey* (Surtees Soc. 1856) p. 32
10 R. Reyce, *Breviary of Suffolk* (1618) p. 50
11 *Northamptonshire Rec. Soc.* ix p. 151
12 Quoted in C. F. Innocent, *op. cit*
13 J. Parkinson and E. A. Ould, *Old Cottages and Farmhouses and other Half-Timber Buildings in Shropshire, Herefordshire and Cheshire* (1904) p. 3
14 More than half of those included in Parkinson's and Ould's book have now been demolished
15 The Royal Commission on Historical Monuments, *North-East Cambridgeshire* (1972) p. xxix

16 C. F. Innocent, *op. cit*
17 Quoted in C. F. Innocent, *op. cit* p. 142
18 M. Wood, *The English Medieval House* (1965) p. 225
19 E. Mercer, *English Vernacular Houses* (1975) p. 137
20 J. Gage, *History and Antiquities of Hengrave in Suffolk* (1822) p. 44
21 H. Forrester, *The Timber-Framed Houses of Essex* (1959) p. 37
22 John Cordeaux, *Notes and Queries* 5th Series, iii p. 487
23 Rev. E. Butcher, *An Excursion from Sidmouth to Chester . . . 1803* (1805) p. 19

Mud Cottages
1 M. Beresford and J. G. Hurst, *Deserted Medieval Villages* (1971) p. 91
2 W. B. Stonehouse, *History of the Isle of Axholme* (1839) p. 233
3 *Transactions of the Leicestershire Archaeological Society* (1925–27) p. 233
4 L. F. Salzman, *Building in England down to 1540* (1952) pp. 88 and 187
5 M. Beresford and J. G. Hurst *op. cit*, p. 91
6 C. Fiennes, *Journey*, ed. C. Morris (1947) p. 202
7 A. Pringle, *General View of the Agriculture of Westmorland* (1794) p. 84
8 Rev. J. Mastin, *History and Antiquities of Naseby* (1792) p. 7
9 William Pitt, *General View of the Agriculture of Leicester* (1809) p. 26
10 W. Stevenson, *General View of the Agriculture of Dorset* (1812) p. 85
11 C. F. Innocent, *The Development of English Building Construction* (1916) p. 135
12 R. W. Brunskill, "The Clay Houses of Cumberland", in *Transactions of the Ancient Monuments Society*, New Series, Vol. 10 (1962) pp. 57–80
13 M. V. J. Seaborne *Northamptonshire Past and Present* (1964) pp. 215 and 217
14 W. Stevenson *op. cit*, p. 85
15 S. O. Addy, *The Evolution of the English Home* p. 40
16 W. Stevenson, *op. cit*, p. 86
17 Charles Vancouver, *General View of the Agriculture of Hampshire* p. 67
18 C. E. Clayton, "Cottage Architecture", in *Memorials of Old Sussex* p. 291

Stone Cottages
1 M. Beresford and J. G. Hurst, *Deserted Medieval Villages* (1971) pp. 93–94
2 C. Fiennes, *Journey* Ed. C. Morris (1947) pp. 196 and 202
3 W. Marshall, *Rural Economy of Yorkshire* (1788)
4 W. Marshall, *op. cit* i p. 101

Brick Cottages
1 Dr N. Davey, *A History of Building Materials* (1961) p. 65
2 Select Committee on Building Regulations, 1842. *Minutes of Evidence*, 1392
3 W. Atkinson, *Views of Picturesque Cottages with Plans* (1805) pp. 15–16
4 T. Dearne *Hints on an Improved Method in Building* (1821)
5 H. Roberts, *The Dwellings of the Labouring Classes* (1850) pp. 24–25

Roofs
1 J. Bailey and G. Culley, *General View of the Agriculture of the County of Northumberland* (1805) p. 27
2 W. Pitt, *General View of the Agriculture of the County of Stafford* (1796) pp. 21–22
3 F. W. Garnett, *Westmorland Agriculture, 1800–1900* (1912)
4 J. Holt, *General View of the Agriculture of the County of Lancaster* (1795) p. 16
5 F. Garnett, *loc. cit*
6 H. Aldrich, *Element of Civil Architecture* 3rd Edition (1824) p. 86
7 J. Fitzherbert, *Book of Husbandry* (1534) chap. XXVII
8 T. Rudge, *General View of the Agriculture of the County of Gloucester* (1807) p. 46–47
9 O. Cook and E. Smith, *English Cottages and Farmhouses* (1954) p. 24 Illust. 40
10 C. F. Innocent, *The Development of English Building Construction* (1916) p. 209

11 J. Plymley, *General View of the Agriculture of the County of Shropshire* (1813) p. 106
12 J. Plymley, *ibid.*, p. 106
13 W. G. Davie and W. Curtis Green, *Old Cottages and Farmhouses in Surrey* (1908) p. 28
14 R. Nevill, *Old Cottages and Domestic Architecture in South West Surrey*, (1889) p. 33
15 W. Marshall, *Rural Economy of Yorkshire* i (1788) p. 100
16 J. Tuke, *General View of the Agriculture of the North Riding of Yorkshire* (1800) p. 35

Chimneys and Fireplaces

1 T. H. Turner and J. H. Parker, *Domestic Architecture in England* II (1853) p. 200
2 *General View of the Agriculture of the County of Bedford* (1808) p. 21
3 R. Nevill, *Old Cottage and Domestic Architecture in South-west Surrey* (1891) p. 19
4 Rev. J. Mastin, *History and Antiquities of Naseby* (1792) p. 7
5 *The Duty of a Steward to his Lord* (1727)
6 Dr. Pococke, *Travels through England* (Camden Soc. New series xliv) p. 288
7 Resta Patching *Four topographical letters written in July, 1755* (1757) p. 6
8 Edward Daniel Clarke, *Tour through the South of England . . . 1791* (1793) p. 116

Floors, Ceilings and Stairs

1 Henry Best's Farming Book (Surtees Soc., 1857)
2 Thomas Rudge, *General View of the Agriculture of the County of Gloucestershire* (1807) pp. 45–46
3 W. Marshall, *Rural Economy of Yorkshire* (1788) p. 135
4 W. G. Davie and E. G. Dawber *Old Cottages, Farmhouses and other Stone Buildings in the Cotswold District* (1905) p. 15
5 *Ibid* p. 16 describes the joists used for old cottages as '. . . generally of unsquared joists of timber, often with the bark left on . . .'
6 C. F. Innocent *The Development of English Building Construction* (1916) p. 168

Doors and Windows

1 S. O. Addy, *Evolution of the English House* (1898)
2 C. F. Innocent, *The Development of English Building Construction* (1916) p. 224
3 T. Rudge, *General View of the Agriculture of the County of Gloucester* (1807) p. 100
4 Dr. Whitaker, *History of Whalley* (1818) ii p. 500
5 W. Horman, *Vulgaria* p. 242
6 Harry Forrester, *Timber-framed Houses of Essex* (1959) p. 53 states that one survives on a cottage in Church Street, Great Coggeshall, Essex

Bibliography

Addy, S. O. *The Evolution of the English House* (1898)

Barley, M. W. *The English Farmhouse and Cottage* (Routledge & Kegan Paul, 1961) *The House and Home* (Vista Books, 1963)

Batsford, H. and Fry, C. *The English Cottage* (Batsford, 1938)

Brunskill, R. W. *Illustrated Handbook of Vernacular Architecture* (Faber & Faber, 1970)

Burnett, John *Plenty and Work: a Social History of Diet in England from 1815 to the present day* (Nelson, 1966)

Chambers, J. D. and Mingay, G. E. *The Agricultural Revolution, 1750–1880* (Batsford, 1966)

Clifton-Taylor, Alec *The Pattern of English Building* (Faber & Faber, 1972)

Cook, Olive and Smith, Edwin *English Cottages and Farmhouses* (Thames & Hudson, 1954)

Darley, Gillian *Villages of Vision* (Architectural Press, 1975)

Davie, W. G. and Curtis Green, W. *Old Cottages and Farmhouses in Surrey* (Batsford, 1908)

Davie, W. G. and Dawber, E. G. *Old Cottages and Farmhouses in Kent and Surrey* (Batsford, 1906) *Old Cottages, Farmhouses and other Buildings in the Cotswold District* (Batsford, 1905)

Dunbabin, J. P. D. *Rural Discontent in Nineteenth-Century Britain* (Faber & Faber, 1979)

Forrester, Harry *The Timber-Framed Houses of Essex: A Short Review of their Types and Details, fourteenth to eighteenth Centuries* (Tindal Press, 1959)

Fussell, G. E. *The English Rural Labourer* (Batchworth, 1949)

Graham, P. Anderson *The Rural Exodus: the Problem of the Village and Town* (Methuen, 1892)

Heath, F. G. *British Rural Life and Labour* (P. S. King, 1911)

Innocent, C. F. *The Development of English Building Construction* (Cambridge University Press, 1916)

Martin, E. W. *Country Life in England* (Macdonald, 1966)

Mercer, Eric *English Vernacular Houses* (H.M.S.O., 1975)

Minchington, W. E. (Ed) *Essays in Agrarian History* (David and Charles, 1968)

Mingay, G. E. *Rural Life in Victorian England* (Heinemann, 1977)

Nevill, Ralph *Old Cottages and Domestic Architecture in South-West Surrey* (Billing & Son, Guildford, 1889)

Oliver, Basil, *Old Houses and Village Buildings in East Anglia* (Batsford, 1912) *The Cottages of England: A Review of their types and features from the sixteenth to eighteenth centuries* (Batsford, 1929)

Parkinson, J. and Ould, E. A. *Old Cottages and Farmhouses in Shropshire, Herefordshire and Cheshire* (Batsford, 1904)

Rowntree, B. Seebohm and May, Kendall *How the Labourer Lives: a Study of the Rural Labour Problem* (Nelson, 1913)

Samuel, Raphael *Village Life and Labour* (Routledge & Kegan Paul, 1975)

Savage, W. G. *Rural Housing* (T. Fisher Unwin, 1915)

Sisson, Marshall *Country Cottages* (Methuen, 1949)

Trevelyan, G. M. *English Social History* (Penguin, 1971)

Warren, C. Henry *English Cottages and Farmhouses* (Collins, 1948)

West, Trudy *The Timber-frame House in England* (David & Charles, 1971)

Woodforde, John *The Truth about Cottages* (Routledge & Kegan Paul, 1979)

Place Index

Page numbers in *italics* refer to illustrations

General Index

Page numbers in *italics* refer to illustrations